China's Art of Revolution

China's Art of Revolution

The Mobilization of Discontent, 1927 and 1928

Marcia R. Ristaino

Duke University Press   Durham 1987

© 1987 Duke University Press
All rights reserved
Printed in the United States of America on
acid-free paper ∞
Library of Congress Cataloging-in-Publication Data
appear on the last printed page of this book.

To my Mother and Father

The philosophers have only *interpreted* the world in various ways, the point is, to *change* it.—*Karl Marx*

You can't break eggs without making an omelette—
That's what they tell the eggs.—*Randall Jarrell*

Contents

Preface

This book concerns a creative interlude in the history of modern China. It considers the years 1927 and 1928, when Communism, as it was introduced by representatives of the Communist International, entered a crisis period. In the struggle to survive the conservative backlash against their members and organizations, Chinese Communist revolutionaries understood the need to adjust and innovate upon basic Marxist-Leninist principles and concepts in order to produce a workable system that would ensure their movement's survival. Their contributions marked the emergence of a Communist strategy of revolution in China.

Forced out of the cities, the Communists operated in the vast and backward countryside. In this milieu they adopted an approach that emphasized qualities of flexibility and resilience to bridge the enormous gap between their own experience and orientation and that of the Chinese rural population. The task required relating to and accommodating key aspects of indigenous traditions, as well as the skill to restate these traditions in ways that incorporated modern concepts of organization, discipline, and social behavior. To bring about revolutionary change in the countryside, the Communists had to integrate their modern, and hitherto abstract, social and political concepts and tools with existing local customs and conditions. By so doing, they provided the essential political framework within which social change could occur. Where accomplished, their work produced an awakened and mobilized following committed and capable of carrying out Communist revolutionary goals and programs.

My interest in this transitional period arose in part from earlier work for the master's degree, when I examined the painstaking efforts of the seventeenth-century Jesuit Father Joachim Bouvet to introduce the principles and teachings of the Christian religion to a court dominated by neo-Confucianism. Working within a tradition established by Matteo Ricci, emphasizing cultural tolerance and accommodation, Bouvet became concerned with introducing concepts of the Western sciences and mathematics to court mandarins and the Chinese emperor. His teachings in these subjects became the medium through which eventually Bouvet intended to introduce the religious contents of Christianity. In essence, the Jesuits viewed science and mathematics, based on rational principles, as neutral enough in content to serve as a bridge for linking two disparate cultural traditions.

Similarly, Communist leaders dealing with entrenched peasant traditions also had to build psychological bridges to gain understanding and acceptance, and then support, for their foreign-originated Communist concepts and programs. To function effectively in the countryside, Communist leaders had to forge vigorous connections with local life. Those most successful were the ones who could accommodate indigenous traditions and beliefs while introducing new concepts and methods that demonstratively alleviated existent widespread poverty and social injustices.

The intention of this work is to trace the steps, through the important events of these two years, that led the Communists to the formulation of their strategy of revolution. Their successes and failures will be shown to have sharpened their awareness of what was needed to survive and succeed, and led them to further organizational innovations and ideological insights.

Of course, the Communist strategy of revolution acquired further depth and sophistication in later years. It acquired the added and essential dimension of a full-scale social revolution. But it was first formulated during this earlier crisis period, and an organizational basis for it was set that would prepare the ground for later development. A thoroughgoing Chinese social revolution required a political organization and framework for its realization. It is the Communists' understanding of this premise that the following work documents.

I have many individuals to thank for supporting and preparing me for this undertaking. Professor Danny W. Y. Kwok directed my master's work at the East-West Center in Hawaii and was a source of inspiration and support through his teaching and friendship. In the Washington,

D.C., area (and beyond), so many are indebted to the mentorship of Father Joseph Sebes, S.J., of Georgetown University. I had the pleasure of working with him in consultations on my master's work and by his directing my Ph.D. dissertation.

I am very grateful for the support and professional relationships with my colleagues at the Library of Congress. Robert Worden had the patience and forbearance to read an early draft version of this book. It was my good fortune that Leo Orleans introduced me to Duke University Press and encouraged my work as I progressed.

Professor Arif Dirlik gave invaluable service by reading, and offering suggestions, on the completed manuscript. Of course, any errors or omissions are entirely my own responsibility. Special thanks are owed to Richard Rowson of Duke Press for being uncommonly generous with professional advice and encouragement throughout every phase of the book's development.

It is impossible to extend sufficient gratitude to the family members and friends who provided the emotional support that made the inevitable difficulties and strains of producing a first book easier to manage. To name one is to risk omitting others. However, it is with much gratitude that I recognize the extraordinary patience and consideration shown to me by my husband Dick and daughter Elizabeth. They encountered many hours of my absence and seclusion in the researching and writing of this book. Their help and support made it possible.

I am grateful to Susan Cha for assistance in checking some translations of Chinese language materials. Also, I want to recognize the professionalism with which Karen Flanders accomplished the word processing of the manuscript.

M. Ristaino
October 30, 1986

South China

Chapter 1. Introduction

Art in general consists of the truths of science arranged in the most convenient order for practice, instead of the order which is most convenient for thought.—John Stuart Mill

The period from the summer of 1927 until the summer of 1928 represents a watershed in the development of Chinese Communism. The First United Front, an alliance between the Kuomintang (KMT) and the Chinese Communist Party (CCP), had ended by mid-1927, compelling the Chinese Communists to confront the issues and problems of an independent existence. Following political direction from the Communist International (Comintern), the Party adopted major policy changes, the most sweeping of which was replacing its commitment to operating as a "bloc within" the bourgeois KMT with commitment to pursuing agrarian revolution and the method of armed struggle. The Party's goal became the establishment of soviets of workers', peasants', and soldiers' deputies in preparation for seizing power in China.

In the latter half of 1927 the CCP staged a number of unsuccessful armed uprisings against major urban centers. In the wake of these defeats the Party began to regroup, strengthen battered Communist organizations, and develop new organizational forms better suited to the existing conditions.

Underlying this process, and central to this book, was the emerging understanding evident during this period of the transforming role of the principle of democratic centralism, Lenin's organizational thesis aimed at accommodating the policymaking levels of a Communist Party to its working-level cadres. According to the tenets of democratic centralism, Communist cadres were to become fully conversant with the established points of a comprehensive political program, formu-

lated at the Party's senior level with Comintern guidance. This program set forth the Party's main social issues and goals and defined
their encumbering social and political relationships in Marxist terms.
At the same time, Party cadres were to be obedient to the Leninist
imperative that they function as faithful and accurate spokesmen for
the Party's authoritative political program.

In addition, the earliest Communist practice of the mass line was
initiated in China during the period under study. According to the
mass line, Party cadres were to convey their own heightened social
consciousness, spelled out in the Party's political program, to their
urban and rural constituencies. They were to evoke in each group a
similar understanding of the basic issues and unify a commitment to
bringing about organized social change in conformity with the general
goals stated in the Party's political program.

We will see that beginning in early 1928 the Chinese Communists
developed new operational strategies and tactics designed to enhance
or protect their tenuous position, then largely limited to rural base
areas. Under pressure to survive, and practicing revolution according
to the terms of democratic centralism and the mass line, Party leaders
produced a fairly complex and comprehensive conception of rural-
based revolution that emphasized the employment of skilled and disciplined leadership cadres, the tailoring of Communist policies and
programs to suit actual local conditions and constituencies, and the
strategic necessity for revolutionaries to extend Communist power
and influence mainly in protected rural areas. While continuing to
coordinate rural activities with any ongoing urban activity, Party cadres were to avoid direct attacks on urban centers until such a time that
a strong and pervasive position of Communist strength existed in the
countryside surrounding the urban target. This approach embodied
the famous strategic formula, usually associated with Mao Zedong, of
using the countryside as a base for seizing urban political centers.

From 1927 to 1928 the Communists fashioned what can be viewed as
their art of revolution. They developed a body of knowledge and general principles based on study and observations of actual conditions
and their own participation in ongoing events. Most important, they
began to channel that knowledge and experience through the mecha-
nism of democratic centralism and to develop the mass line. This
approach began to bring the CCP into a close and responsive interac-

tion with its own constituencies, thereby narrowing the gap between Marxist revolutionary principles and the practice of revolution in China.

This book proposes that, to the extent that Party cadres were successful in mastering the art of revolution, Marxism-Leninism became nationalized or its concepts restated in meaningful indigenous terms. To achieve this end, Party activists had to accommodate the Communist revolutionary program with real local conditions. They had to provide the new and foreign concepts with a nurturing link to long-standing Chinese cultural patterns and traditions. This intricate process, when carried out successfully, allowed the ensuing social movement to become transformed into a vital and genuine social revolution.

The developments of this period did not of course occur in a vacuum. Previous experiences with revolution provided intellectual antecedents to developments in 1927. The Party's relationship to its constituencies before 1927 set the stage for the changes that took place after mid-1927. In addition, the nature and development of the First United Front acted to inhibit and delay the Communists' development of their art of revolution until after the alliance collapsed. These factors provided a context that must be examined to bring into relief the significance of the changes beginning in 1927.

Intellectual Antecedents

Nineteenth-century Chinese reformers were concerned with preserving the essence of the Chinese traditional system while recommending measures to reconstitute its powers for coping with immediate and overwhelming social and economic problems. They were succeeded by others of a more revolutionary cast, who viewed the traditional culture as the primary source of China's plight, and thus saw the reform measures as hopelessly flawed. Shunting aside the piecemeal approach of their reformist predecessors, this group, which provided participants in the May 4th and New Culture movements, launched a full-scale attack against the traditional system based in Confucianism. They also initiated an eclectic search among other traditions and thought systems for a replacement.

Their motivations were not far removed from those of their reformist predecessors. However, as Maurice Meisner has shown, their comprehension of the meaning of China had evolved from a cultural perspective to a political one, which viewed China as a nation confronted by external oppressors.[1] While they published their scathing attacks on traditional Confucian values, their goal was to "save China" and find a "way out" of the downward spiral of events. Their conception of what was actually involved in "saving China" was clarified by the issues and events surrounding the May 4th Movement, which was precipitated by the Versailles Treaty that awarded the German interests in the Shandong peninsula to Japan rather than returning them to China. Chinese intellectuals were both disillusioned and outraged by the Western decision. The experience made them more receptive to radical nationalism.

Besides territorial threats, the generation of the 1920s agonized over the endemic internal scourges of warlordism, famine, floods, banditry, and economic stagnation, all exacerbated by the absence of effective government control. They sought feverishly for a means to reconstitute China as a viable political, social, and economic entity. For many, the answers seemed to be most forthcoming in the few available tracts on Marxism-Leninism.

Arif Dirlik, in *Revolution and History*, explains that the legacy of New Culture thought was to liberate those wanting to change China from the constraints of tradition and imbue them with a scientific outlook.[2] To reformers, Marxism had particular appeal because it took as its starting point the study of society and social processes, and approached the subject in precise scientific terms.

In fact, Marxism, with its Leninist interpretation, came to hold mythopoeic appeal to many of the May 4th generation as a compact theoretical and ideological system for interpreting the modern world. For them, Lenin's "Theses on Imperialism" bridged the more circumscribed and Europe-centered Marxism and the new conditions in the colonial and semi-colonial regions under imperialism. Lenin's analytical framework provided an explanation and even an optimistic approach to the overwhelming problems and chaotic conditions existing in countries such as China.

Lenin in his analysis pointed to the escalating friction between the imperialist powers competing for gain, spheres of influence, and colonies in the underdeveloped world. Capitalism's expansion into a global network created tensions that increased the potential for war among imperialist powers. Further, imperialists' acquisitive actions had the

effect of engendering revolutionary movements, spawned on nationalistic sentiments and directed against the imperialist powers in the
outlying regions.

Lenin identified two potential revolutionary factors that he claimed
could erode the foundations of capitalism in the European heartland.
They included the revolutionary potential of incipient nationalist movements directed against the imperialist forces, and the unique opportunities for revolutionary action afforded by the intense and destructive
rivalries among imperialist powers racing to secure further concessions.
Lenin claimed that these two factors made global capitalism most
vulnerable at its outer reaches, and this gave countries like China a
potential revolutionary role to play in the world socialist movement.[3]

The strategy Lenin offered for overthrowing capitalism at its periph-
ery was to organize national liberation movements to be carried out
under a broadened class alliance, which included participation from
the national bourgeoisie and the peasantry, the first as a temporary
partner and the second as a supporting ally to the proletariat. Binding
the alliance and charting its direction was to be a disciplined, vanguard Communist Party.

Lenin established a link between promoting nationalist movements
and serving the ends of socialist revolution. He explained that a special
feature of semicolonial countries like China, operating under the economic distortions caused by imperialism, was that the national bourgeoisie still had a recognized revolutionary role to play. They too were
oppressed under the conditions of imperialism, and to the extent that
they were, the proletariat could collaborate provisionally with them.[4]

Chinese intellectuals were very impressed with the nationalistic
implications of Lenin's extension of Marxism and by its efficaciousness
for explaining the problems of Chinese society. They were certainly
affected by the success of the Russian Bolsheviks, under Lenin's
leadership, at carrying out their own revolution in a backward country
and in the face of concerted opposition from the great powers. But
because they tended to view Marxism-Leninism mainly from Lenin's
perspective, as a philosophy for social action that might serve specific
ends, intellectuals of the 1920s paid more attention to its practical
teachings and scientific social analysis than to the theoretical foundations of Marxism.

Many of the intellectual characteristics prevalent during this period are represented in one of its major spokesmen and the Chinese Communist Party's first general secretary, Chen Duxiu. Lee Feigon, in his recent biography, adds to our understanding of Chen by presenting his strong connections to his Chinese context and traditional roots. Chen was interested primarily in preserving the "national essence."[5] Although he was disturbed by the divisiveness of Marxian concepts of class struggle, Chen was attracted to the tools of Western social analysis, namely Marxist scientific socialism, because of its potential for charting a direct and rapid path to restoring unity, sovereignty, and prosperity to the Chinese people. Also, Lenin's theory of imperialism seemed to allow for superseding class struggle with the national struggle of impoverished nations against rich and powerful ones.

Chen became a committed Marxist, but with little understanding of what Marxism entailed.[6] As was true of other Chinese Marxists in his company, he was most impressed with the nationalistic aspects of Leninism. But Chen was far less cognizant of the full import of Lenin's major contributions concerning the transforming role to be played in the Chinese revolution by the proletariat led by a disciplined Communist Party. Rather, Chen saw the Chinese proletariat and its embodiment in the CCP as an elite group that through exemplary behavior and sincere dedication to social change meant to inspire in its constituencies an equally sincere commitment to social change and development. As Dirlik has argued regarding Chinese Marxist intellectuals, and Chen was certainly one, it was not until 1927 when the revolutionary movement failed that they began to appreciate the full significance of Marxist sociology as a total theory of society.[7] A similar observation can be made concerning Marxist political activists. It took the pressures of defeat and possible extinction for CCP leaders to begin to grasp the full extent of Lenin's contributions for making revolution in China, including the indispensable political tools of strong Party leadership and an independent CCP organization. This book will show that after 1927 the new Party leadership really began to comprehend Leninist organizational theories and concepts. When these were applied with their own development of the mass line, the two systems together provided the long-sought-after means to regenerate China by effecting cultural, economic, and political change.

The Urban and Rural Context

Massive urban-based movements like the May 4th Movement and the May 30th Movement demonstrated the explosiveness of public issues linked to imperialism, inflation, and militarism. The Party gained crucial experience and succeeded remarkably in channeling these public sentiments by organizing labor unions and staging worker demonstrations and strikes. In July 1921 a Labor Secretariat was established in Shanghai under Zhang Guotao's leadership. In 1922 Communist labor leaders joined with KMT activists to launch the famous Hong Kong Seaman's Strike, lasting from January 12 until May 5 and including more than 100,000 participants. It brought Hong Kong trade to a standstill and forced significant concessions from the British.

The scope and significance of these organizational activities were broadened during the course of the May 30th Movement. This event centered on the intolerable working conditions and harsh treatment of Chinese at foreign-owned factories. The powerful expression of public nationalistic feeling over these issues deeply impressed social activists in both the CCP and the KMT. It provided a rich environment for them to develop their skills and experience at observing participants' responses, identifying the key issues, negotiating a political platform around those issues, and building a labor union, student union, or other urban body, organized to achieve the specific goals in the political platform.

The Party's success at mastering these skills was evidenced by the CCP's leadership of the Hong Kong–Guangdong Strike and Anti-British Boycott beginning in June 1925. Its activities were sustained over a year and contributed to the rise in CCP membership from a thousand in January to over ten thousand during the summer of 1926.

Communist organizers further developed their repertoire in the course of the extensive social mobilization that accompanied the Northern Expedition beginning on July 9, 1926. Party organizers established worker organizations and initiated strikes in the cities along the campaign route. Their rural counterparts set up peasant organizations and initiated rent-reduction movements and land seizures. In the meantime Party organizational work in the large cities continued to develop. For example, in Wuhan over three hundred trade unions carried out numerous strikes, seriously disrupting the economy of this key industrial city. In the early weeks of 1927 the British forces were driven permanently from their concessions in nearby Hankou and Jiujiang. In late February, as the National Revolutionary Army advanced toward Shanghai, Communist organizational strength was such that they could marshal 350,000 strikers in the streets. When the Army arrived in late March Shanghai was in the hands of half a million striking workers.[8]

Citing these and other figures Harold R. Isaacs, in his *Tragedy of the Chinese Revolution*, argued that by early 1927 the CCP had an adequate basis of mass support for seizing the initiative from the KMT to lead a successful democratic revolution in China. He correctly placed blame for the Party's failure to rise to the occasion on Comintern policies, which in effect shackled the CCP. What his analysis overlooked, however, is that while the Party did indeed have impressive organized support, most of the country, namely rural China, remained locked in anti-revolutionary rural traditions and was completely outside any revolutionary framework. In other words, no political organization, including the CCP, could lead and sustain a genuine revolution in China until a means was found to transform China's vast and backward countryside.

The problem of engaging the rural population in constructive revolutionary change is addressed by Elizabeth Perry in *Rebels and Revolutionaries in North China, 1845–1945*. She attempts to see if certain traditions of rural rebellion supported the transition to revolutionary collective action. Her research is focused on the Huaibei region of North China, a region dominated by scarcity of resources. Under the harsh conditions of this region, rebel violence was motivated by the practical concern of securing a livelihood. Perry defines the collective response of the first group studied, the nineteenth-century Nian rebels, as predatory violence directed at plundering community resources. In contrast, the second group studied, the Red Spear Society active in Huaibei during the Republican Period, involved propertied elements. It responded to predations aimed at seizing community wealth by displaying what the author defines as a protective response. The unifying characteristic of both of these very different responses was their parochial nature. They were behavioral adaptations to the ecological exigencies of a region plagued by endemic scarcity. The group motivation was toward survival, not social change.

In approaching the larger subject of revolution, Perry concludes that in Huaibei there is no "positive relationship between a history of rural insurrection and the success of modern revolution."[9] This is because traditional rebel behavior, as evidenced in Huaibei, was motivated entirely by parochial concerns. She argues that "we do not detect in these undertakings an effort to alter the basic economic or political structures themselves."[10] In fact, in the particular case of the Red Spears, their insular outlook strongly negated Communist organizational efforts to transform them into a revolutionary force in the late 1920s.

As this book will show, the Chinese Communists after mid-1927 also originated concepts and strategies designed to promote their physical survival. They formulated the mass line system, which was basically the adaptation of Marxism-Leninism to practical Chinese conditions. Party leaders drew upon solutions similar to those employed by traditional rebel leaders to deal with the prevailing environmental threats and harsh conditions. Added to these methods, however, were the knowledge, skills, and experiences derived from their exposure to scientific socialism and their participation in revolutionary activities. Let us look briefly at the principal aspects of this important development, which will be dealt with at length in this study.

As the presiding authority, the Comintern provided the theoretical analysis for the Chinese revolution as being in the bourgeois-democratic stage, and provided what it considered to be the appropriate basic or internal political program for the CCP. The contents of this program included reconstituting the Party as an active political force, carrying out the agrarian revolution, and establishing soviets eventually to seize power throughout the country. The task Party leaders faced was somehow to harmonize the relationship between what Moscow theorized and directed, and what actually could be put into practice under existing conditions in China. Driven out of the cities and hunted down in White Terror campaigns, Party leaders also had to consider strategies and tactics to enable the Party and Party organizations to survive and build essential protection and support. These practical concerns were exacerbated by the necessity of adhering to the substance of the authoritative internal political program.

The central problem became the successful implementation of the Party's Marxist-Leninist political program in a rural context. In short, what would be the Party's strategy for adapting its political program to a rural setting? The solutions that emerged were based on extensive

trial-and-error experience and fashioned in the crucible of the dangerous conditions of the period. The initial and essential step was to
formulate a preliminary operational program designed to serve the
Party goals as stated in the Comintern/Party or internal political program but tailored specifically to accommodate the interests and conditions of each rural group encountered. This became in essence the
Party's mass political program, as distinct from the internal political
program described above.

The successful implementation of the mass political program sum-
moned a definite operating style by Party cadres. Initially, they had to
become thoroughly informed about conditions in their locality. Once
they possessed a solid understanding of local conditions and a good
Party organization, they needed to develop an outward approach to
the community that transmitted a clear responsiveness to community
needs. In other words, they had to fashion a close identity between
Communist goals and those of the local populace. Their objective at
this stage was to evoke a collective awareness of the key issues fueling
local discontent.

During the next stage Party cadres had to *restate* the recognized
local issues in the terms of the Party's mass political programs matched
to each particular social group. This was done to provide a new and
generalized framework for the otherwise parochial concerns and to
engender an awareness among participants of their potential for thinking and acting as a group to realize the common and well-defined
goals. Once this was accomplished, organizational means were applied
to direct the political response being generated. A common basis of
understanding then existed in terms of both the mass political program and mass organization for the horizontal linkage of one group to
another. Thus, for example, a peasant association in one area had a
common frame of reference with others elsewhere. The building blocks
existed for constructing a broadened and theoretically even national
mass political movement by connecting the horizontally defined mass
movements, at several levels, up through the vertical or centralized
Party organizational system.

The overriding principles guiding this process were inspiration,
education, and persuasion—not coercion. The volition of the masses
was recognized as the key to revolutionary change. The objective was
to build a solid base of mass support motivated by its own strong

internal awareness and convictions. Then, if well-organized, linked, and coordinated on a broad scale, and backed with strategic military support, the masses could comprise an overwhelming force against the established, well-armed, and better-supplied Nationalist forces. This, in essence, became the CCP's operational strategy for surmounting the KMT threat by 1928.

During these developments Party cadres were to serve as well-informed and experienced guides, mediators, and coordinators of activity. This included communicating continually the results of their local activities to higher Party levels, mainly so that Party mass political programs could be kept relevant to specific mass groups and actual conditions in the developing movement.

A dialectical relationship was inherent in this process. The Party's ability to stay in touch with its constituents and stimulate and guide their political development depended on the Party's continued flexibility and adaptation of policies to accommodate actual local conditions. Indeed, to the extent that the Party could evoke change successfully, it also had to change.

Finally, we must understand how the Party developed operational strategies and tactics to promote the growth or survival of the movement as it came to be embodied in rural soviets. The Party's adoption of the soviet organizational concept permitted the inclusion in one umbrella organization of several groups—peasants, workers, soldiers, youth, women, and so on—all under comprehensive Party direction. Further, soviets offered possibilities for sustaining collective action over a long period of time mainly because they included military forces.

But to maintain or develop the soviets, Party leaders again had to respond according to the ecological conditions of the Chinese movement. The Party, where it encountered warlord division or weak government control, aggressively pushed military mobilization to expand soviet territory. Under the reverse conditions of a unified and powerful opposition, military force was directed to protect the existing territorial limits. There are clear parallels here with traditional peasant rebel strategies that Perry labels as predatory and protective survival strategies. The Communists also applied guerrilla warfare tactics and established secure base areas between provincial administrative divisions, just as occurred in peasant rebellions.[11] As we will see, however, the crucial difference was that the Communists operated from a long-term strategy according to which they mobilized an organized following around a carefully developed political program. This program accurately reflected group interests and defined each group's essential role in bringing about social change.

A key point is that the Party's internal political program, which guided, directed, and disciplined its organization at all levels in accordance with the rules of democratic centralism, was much less subject to change than programs directed at engaging and mobilizing mass support. The internal political program was formulated at properly constituted national Party congresses and was subject to the direction of the Comintern.

The reason that the time period considered in this study is so crucial is that by mid-1927 the Party's new independent status, together with the emergency conditions of the period, forced the Party to focus a great deal of attention on developing policy for mobilizing a mass following, and it was in this realm that the Party, dealing firsthand and intimately with the Chinese environment, could begin to exercise considerable independence from the Comintern. Like the traditional peasant rebels, the CCP was compelled for survival reasons to develop strategies and tactics designed to accommodate practical Chinese conditions. But unlike rebel leaders, Party cadres also employed a heightened social and political consciousness and developed organizational skills, all of which emanated from their early, if basic, grasp of Marxism-Leninism.

Several key aspects of the Party's mass approach had already been applied by Peng Pai in the early and mid-1920s. Peng's rural organizational activities in Haifeng County in South China are the focus of Robert Marks's work, *Rural Revolution in South China*. Working in the Marxist tradition, Marks argues that the harmonious interaction and sense of peasant security provided by what he defines as the traditional "moral economy" were seriously disrupted by the intrusion of the capitalist market into the rural economy in Haifeng.[12] Further, the new social and economic relations coming out of the 1911 Revolution significantly strengthened the landlord class, providing them with military powers. Within this context of social instability, economic chaos, and peasant insecurity, Peng Pai set about organizing a peasant union in Haifeng in 1922.

Peng was remarkably successful as a peasant organizer because he entered fully into the world of the peasants. Using methods similar to those of a modern anthropologist, Peng carried out systematic surveys of rural socioeconomic conditions to discover the sources of rural problems. Further, he studied the local folk beliefs and customs and then, using these as source material, wrote plays and folk operas to illustrate in familiar human terms the roots of peasant discontent and social tensions. This approach permitted Peng to make an elemental connection with the peasants and fully articulate their grievances and aspirations.

Peng was so effective that a cult developed among the peasants, giving him superhuman powers in the eyes of his followers. Marks asserts that the Cult of Peng Pai became a form of social organization that led and inspired collective action.[13] The lessons of 1927–28 tell us something different. The Cult of Peng Pai is better understood as a kind of chiliastic response, evoked by Peng's very effective approach, that was arrested in its potential for developing into a progressive social organization. The collective action that accompanied the cult involved reckless spontaneous revolts, seemingly without clear purpose other than destruction and incapable of sustaining prolonged peasant allegiances and action.

The reasons for the arrested development of Peng's movement are at least threefold. First, the Party Central had not yet developed an authoritative mass political program to guide an active peasant movement. Second, as Marks indicates, the Party Central did not even include a formal peasant department until the beginning in July 1925 of the Northern Expedition.[14] Without a Party platform and Party-directed peasant organizational system, Peng, while individually effective, faced hopeless odds. Finally, and most damaging to the development of the peasant movement, the terms of the First United Front as they evolved eventually required the Communists to cooperate with the KMT in restraining peasant activity. This policy brought loud protests from Peng and members of the Guangdong Peasant Committee, but to no avail. The Comintern/Party internal political program dictated that the United Front be maintained in order to carry out a bourgeois-democratic revolution. Correspondingly, Peng Pai and other Party activists had to censor themselves to fulfill the demands of official policy.

As we will see, however, when the policy constraints of the United Front relationship dissolved and the Communists faced the pressures of independent survival, Peng's tested methods and practical field experience, like those of Mao Zedong, Fang Zhimin, and others, contributed immensely to the Party's development of an effective mass political program and strategy for developing a mass movement.

Historical Background

The Party leadership's failure to develop a rural program and give it organizational substance before mid-1927 reflects to some degree the preoccupation of urban intellectuals with Party activities in the cities. But this is only a partial explanation. The Party Central's behavior is best understood in terms of both the control that the Comintern exercised over the young Communist Party, and Moscow's authoritative formulation of the prevailing United Front policies.

In August 1922 Comintern representative G. Maring (pseudonym of H. Sneevliet), at a special CCP plenum, explained that during the national-bourgeois stage of the Chinese revolution, the Communists should form a "bloc within" the KMT by joining the KMT as individuals while retaining their CCP memberships. The arrangement conceded to KMT head Sun Yat-sen presiding authority over all members in the proposed United Front. Party members objected to turning over the leading role in a national revolution to the bourgeois KMT, arguing that the CCP, as the party of the proletariat, could not join the KMT, a bourgeois party, without seriously and perhaps fatally abjuring Marxist principles.

In response to this persuasive argument, Maring explained that the KMT was not a coherent political party but a coalition of parties, and thus the CCP could join as the party of the proletariat and use its inside position to transform the KMT into a revolutionary force.[15] In due course, but amid expressed fears to be proven correct that this arrangement meant a serious loss of independence and policy initiative for the CCP, the Party acquiesced and adopted the Comintern's United Front policy at its Third Congress in June 1923.

Nikolai Bukharin, Stalin's leading theorist of Soviet Marxism and Comintern head during 1926–29, provided a doctrinal argument for the First United Front.[16] Basing his interpretations on his and Lenin's ideas on imperialism, Bukharin described a clearly staged process by which backward countries might arrive at socialism. The initial stage consisted of a thriving national revolutionary movement propelled forward by the destructive force of peasant revolution and directed against foreign imperialists and feudal landlords. He defined this stage as bourgeois-democratic and, in applying it to China, identified the KMT as the appropriate party to lead the national revolutionary movement, consolidate a strong nationalist government, and thus prepare the way for the subsequent socialist revolution.

In Moscow's view, the KMT, under Sun Yat-sen's respected leadership, offered the greatest potential for realizing these ends. Clearly, the Bukharin-Stalin leadership team's support for the revolutionary leadership role of the KMT also served Soviet state interests. The Soviet leaders saw the consolidation of a strong nationalist government to the south of the Soviet Union as protection for the exposed eastern front during their own period of economic consolidation.[17] But being careful to state these interests in the context of the revolution, they argued that only after the bourgeois-democratic stage was completed, and a strong and allied nationalist government existed in China, could conditions reach a level of development appropriate to the stage of proletarian socialist revolution under CCP leadership.

Events in China worked against Bukharin's conception of a gradual process marked off in measured stages. Sun Yat-sen's death in March 1925 deprived the alliance of a unifying force. The broad social mobilization brought about by the May 30th Movement further polarized the KMT between those who saw organized social change as an integral part of the national revolution, and others responding to spokesmen like Dai Jitao. Dai argued that internal class harmony was essential to the successful evolution of the national revolution and warned that the CCP was using the KMT to develop its own organization and influence. He claimed that the energies needed to combat imperialism were being sapped by divisive social movements like May 30th.[18]

The Northern Expedition, by the scope and magnitude of its success, pulled the already weakened United Front apart. Communist and leftist organizers, backed by the military presence of the National Revolutionary Army, established peasant associations and labor unions and carried out strikes, rent-reduction movements, and land seizures. The accompanying violence and social upheaval both terrorized and infuriated local landlords and merchants, many of whom had sons serving as officers in the National Revolutionary Army.

Chiang Kai-shek, head of the Huangbu (Whampoa) Military Academy and commander of the Northern Expedition, had no plans for using the National Revolutionary Army as an instrument and guarantor of radical social change. His goal was to unify the country under his leadership, through use of good political organization backed with military power. The remarkable successes of the Northern Expedition positioned Chiang to turn his power to crush the volatile and disruptive mass movements.

Chiang struck on April 12, 1927, and devastated the Communist position in Shanghai almost completely.[19] Several thousand Communists were executed or killed, while those CCP members or cells that survived were forced underground or to other cities inland. The cumulative effect was that Chiang's coup and the bold attack on the Soviet Embassy in Peking quickly set in motion broad reaction against the erstwhile Communist allies.

On April 18, Chiang proclaimed the establishment of a new national government at Nanjing. Shortly thereafter, the Nanjing government sponsored a "party-purification movement" that spread throughout Zhejiang, Fujian, Guangdong, Anhui, Guangxi, and Sichuan provinces, destroying in its path the remaining major centers of Communist activity. In Hunan and Hubei provinces Communist-controlled peasant associations, with membership counts in the millions, were actively fomenting land seizures "from below."[20] The outlying areas surrounding Changsha became a focal point, and in reaction the conservative KMT garrison commander of Changsha, Xu Kexiang, moved to crush the local peasant and labor unions, killing scores of Communist agitators in the process.[21] Similar events followed in Hubei and Jiangxi provinces. By the end of May the conservative reaction in the provinces comprising the Wuhan base area had rejected agrarian revolution and its Communist organizers.

With events going poorly in China, the Bukharin-Stalin China policies drew the attention of a major domestic critic, Leon Trotsky. Trotsky had a very different conception of the Chinese revolution based on his theory of "permanent revolution." He argued that backward, precapitalist societies, operating within a world context of advanced capitalist countries converting to socialism, tended to "grow over" from national revolution to social revolution in a process that involved the telescoping of stages—the national revolutionary or bourgeois stage leading into the proletarian stage and culminating in world revolution.[22] Trotsky stressed that the weak bourgeois class was incapable of leading the country through the proletarian socialist revolution because of its inherently compromised position under imperialism. In backward countries the bourgeoisie was too closely linked to foreign capital and landed interests. Only the proletariat, supported by the peasantry and led by independent Party leadership, could assume the revolutionary role of bringing down the old order and establishing the new.

Applying his perspective to China, Trotsky argued that the CCP should ally in a bloc with leftist KMT elements, but that the Party's historic mission required it to function as separate and independent. The CCP must be "*an independent proletarian party* which fights under its own banner and never permits its policy and organization to be dissolved in the policy and organization of other classes."[23]

For Trotsky, the foundation of a bloc with the KMT involved the establishment of worker, peasant, and soldier soviets. The CCP could work closely with those elements of the KMT that supported the development of soviets formed to join and consolidate the revolutionary ambitions of these oppressed groups. Once soviets existed, Trotsky advocated a transitional system of "dual power" composed of a national revolutionary government on the one hand and the Party-led soviets on the other. Under this system, preparations could be made for the transition or "growing over" to the higher stage of the Democratic Dictatorship of the Proletariat, with essential support from more advanced countries like the USSR.[24] Thus in Trotsky's view national liberation and social revolution must occur simultaneously, not in sequential stages as Stalin argued.

Bukharin and Stalin reacted to Trotsky's blanket critique of their basic political program for China, and the disastrous course of events there, with arguments forced to bolster their well-known theoretical conception of the Chinese revolution, while they strained to deal with their increasingly untenable position vis-à-vis the KMT. The impact on the CCP was further concessions in the interests of upholding the doomed Bukharin-Stalin United Front policy.

In a tortuous defense of their position at the Executive Committee of the Communist International's (ECCI) Eighth Plenum in May 1927, Bukharin and Stalin explained that the national democratic stage of the Chinese revolution had included a coalition of four classes until the national bourgeoisie, under Chiang Kai-shek's leadership, deserted the revolution with the coup in April. The remaining bloc of three classes including the petite bourgeoisie, workers, and peasants still represented the revolutionary traditions. This coalition actually offered even better opportunities for building the KMT into a genuine revolutionary organization. Therefore, to exit from the KMT at this point, even to form a "bloc without," would mean turning over to the KMT sole leadership of the revolution and isolating the CCP. As for organizing soviets, to do so would be to jump over the current national democratic stage during which the KMT was the recognized appropriate leader. The KMT should not be opposed by the establishment of independent soviets appropriate only at the stage of proletarian revolution.[25]

Trotsky presented counterarguments in speeches to the plenum, but was refused official publication; Grigori Zinoviev, a former Comintern president, was barred even from attending. The authoritative Bukharin-Stalin position required the CCP to remain in the KMT and work at turning the Wuhan government into a revolutionary Dictatorship of the Workers and Peasants.[26] Trotsky and his supporters were effectively subdued by the outcome of the Eighth Plenum, but because of the bitterness of the conflict, Stalin and Bukharin subsequently became even more determined to prove the validity of their United Front policy in China.

The April coup and ensuing conservative reaction confronted the CCP with a serious dilemma: how to respond to the grave military reaction against the peasant movement, which the CCP supported, and yet continue to preserve the United Front with the increasingly conservative leaders of the Wuhan government and its powerful military followers? The Comintern leaders had chosen to settle for the latter and thus registered their disapproval of "peasant excesses," which they said should be controlled and checked. Essentially, this was Mikhail Borodin's position as the Comintern's principal representative in China. It was based on the assumption that the KMT Left still was loyal to the revolution and that the damages to the Left had been precipitated by excessive actions taken by the peasants and workers. The other key Comintern representative M. N. Roy, on the other hand, declared in response to the recent events that the KMT was no longer on the side of the revolution and had become a target for destruction.[27]

Roy queried Moscow for guidance, and Stalin responded with his famous telegram instructing the Communists to reorganize the KMT Left, filling its ranks with peasant and worker leaders who emerged in the agrarian revolution; to form a new army, again from incipient revolutionary elements; and to punish anti-Communist KMT officers by means of a "revolutionary tribunal headed by the prominent non-Communist Kuomintangists."[28] Roy must have assumed that to implement such policies the CCP needed powerful military and political backing, because he approached Wang Jingwei and showed him the telegram, much to the consternation of Borodin.

Wang found Stalin's conditions in violation of the 1923 Sun-Joffe agreements, which had recognized the KMT as the leader of the national revolution. It appeared to Wang that the Communists intended either to transform the KMT into a Communist party or destroy it as the governing party. Wang showed Stalin's telegram to the Nationalist generals, who subsequently joined him in initiating preparations for the expulsion of the Communists from the KMT and the further suppression of mass movements.

In June and July the Communists offered further concessions in order to save the alliance. An eleven-point resolution reviewed the state of the alliance and recognized the KMT as the source of leadership for the national revolution. The Party declared that members working in the Wuhan government did so as KMT members and not as Bolsheviks. Further, it allowed that "in order to reduce the difficulties of the political situation," Party members in KMT government positions might resign at any time. Subsequently the KMT ministers of labor and agriculture, both Communists, agreed to step down. The Party instructed worker and peasant mass organizations to be responsive to KMT regulations and controls. In effect, the CCP, as instructed by Moscow, acknowledged publicly its total subordination to the KMT and reaffirmed its continuing priority of maintaining the United Front even at the cost of checking the development of the labor and peasant movements. In contrast, Trotsky in an unpublished letter to the Trotsky Opposition (June 23, 1927) condemned this subservience and called for "immediate withdrawal from the Kuomintang!"[29]

By late June, as Trotsky had predicted, the Communists also had lost the costly battle to win a solid commitment of support from militarist Feng Yuxiang, a long-time recipient of Communist financial aid.[30] Feng dashed Communists' hopes for gaining his services as a powerful military ally by joining forces with Chiang Kai-shek.

This policy of compromise, supported in China by Borodin and condemned by Roy as a "policy of defeat," did not succeed in preserving the United Front relationship. On July 15 the KMT central authorities met in Wuhan to take definite steps toward the expulsion of the Communists from the KMT. Just the day before, the Comintern finally adopted the view that the Wuhan government "has already become a counterrevolutionary force."[31] However, still clinging to the threads of a tattered United Front policy, the Comintern instructed the Communists to resign from the Wuhan government but to remain loyal to the KMT Party, which it still described as a revolutionary mass organization contaminated only by reactionary leadership. Borodin had left Wuhan on July 13 for the resort city of Lushan where, together with Qu Qiubai, he planned the reorganization of the top Party leadership. Chen Duxiu, in a letter dated July 15, submitted his resignation as Party general secretary.

At this point the course of events in China had exhausted all possibilities for successfully adjusting Moscow's rigid conception of the Chinese revolution to support a workable course of action. Thus Comintern authorities began to search for a scapegoat to explain the string of calamities in China. They placed the blame squarely with the Chinese Communist leadership, mainly Chen Duxiu. The Comintern Executive Committee charged that the Chinese Communist leadership had neglected to develop the agrarian revolution, and under Chen's leadership had subordinated the Party's interests to those of the KMT (a condition demanded by both the Comintern and Sun Yat-sen as far back as 1923). In short, the CCP had failed to successfully implement Moscow's contradictory and doomed policy of maintaining the support of Left KMT leaders, most of whom were property owners, for policies that would have relieved them of their power and wealth. Chen's hesitation—not to mention Borodin's—to implement those policies forcefully was condemned as capitulation and, worse, an attempt to sabotage the decisions of the Comintern.[32]

Thus the CCP faced an uncertain future while leaderless and under the continuing direction of Bukharin and Stalin. Though Stalin naturally claimed prescience concerning the course of the Chinese revolution, he regarded China as just one actor on his world stage. Moscow continued to be ill-informed about the actual nature of events in China and to prescribe faulty policies accordingly. It soon became clear to the struggling CCP leaders that having a future really required taking matters into their own hands.

Chapter 2. The Nanchang Uprising

The Nanchang Uprising of August 1, 1927, was the first step taken by the CCP to challenge the KMT for independent leadership over revolutionary activity in China. What remained of the Party's political influence after events such as the April 12 coup continued to be seriously eroded by widespread conservative reaction. Party leaders were desperate for an opportunity to establish some credibility for the CCP as a still-viable and potent political and revolutionary force in the country.

After the breakup of the First United Front, the physical survival of the CCP was even more in doubt, as it was left fully exposed to attack from rightist opponents. Under these deteriorating conditions, Party leaders sought to regain some political initiative by seizing control of a major city from rightist forces. They acquired military backing for their uprising and thus combined military organizations for the first time under CCP leadership. Finally, in carrying out their plans, they defied Comintern orders shaped by Moscow's continued insistence on a CCP alliance with "revolutionary elements" in the KMT. For all these reasons the Nanchang Uprising, though ill-fated and traumatic, represents a major event in the Party's historical development. August 1 is celebrated today in China as the birthday of the Chinese Red Army.[1]

Circumstances Leading to Revolt

Nie Rongzhen in his *Memoirs* reported that in early June 1927, after Feng Yuxiang had withdrawn support for the Communists, Feng, Wang Jingwei, KMT General Tang Shengzhi, and other KMT leaders concluded the Zhengzhou Agreement in Zhengzhou, Henan. By the terms of this agreement, Feng Yuxiang occupied Henan Province, and Tang Shengzhi withdrew his troops to join Wang Jingwei in Wuhan. This set the stage for a congregation of powerful forces, eventually to include Chiang Kai-shek, to make a major drive against the Communists.[2]

In this context conditions in Jiangxi province, particularly in its capital Nanchang, were encouraging to the Communists, who were determined to take a stand by seizing a major city. Commander of the KMT Third Army and head of the Jiangxi government Zhu Peite had been a supporter of leftist activities in the province, as this seemed often to benefit his own political fortunes. Even when the First United Front became defunct, and the Communists were outlawed from government and KMT participation, Zhu hesitated to openly confront Communist cadres and organizations in Nanchang. The relative safety of conditions in Nanchang attracted CCP leaders, many of whom moved there during the later weeks in July.

In addition to personal safety, the overall disposition of military forces in Jiangxi provided the Communists with some unusual opportunities. The main contingent of Zhu Peite's forces was positioned to the south of Nanchang to guard against possible advances by Qian Dajun's forces in south Jiangxi. Nanchang and Jiujiang were under the protection of Zhang Fakui's Second Army—the famous "Ironsides" force.[3]

Zhang Fakui was a leftist of Cantonese descent whose mission was to protect Jiangxi province against Nanjing's KMT troops. As such, his armies offered some protection to the Communists, who intended to work underground in Jiangxi, from anti-Communist drives elsewhere. Zhang was sympathetic to the Communists, but he also was bound by his allegiance as one of the mainstays of Wang Jingwei's Wuhan government. After mid-July this meant supporting Wang's policy of so-called peaceful expulsion of the Communists.[4]

The breakup of the First United Front worked to divide armies with left-leaning commanders, because some units included Communist officers who recognized that their future was uncertain and even perilous. Such was the case with commanders of forces belonging to Zhang's Second Front Army stationed in Nanchang, Jiujiang, and the immediate vicinity.[5] These were the Fourth Army (25th Division), the Eleventh Army (the 10th, 11th, and 24th divisions) and the Twentieth Army (the 1st, 2nd, and 3rd divisions). The commander of the Eleventh Army's 24th Division was General Ye Ting, a Communist Party member.[6]

Nie Rongzhen was political commissar and Ye Jianying chief of staff of the 24th Division. He Long commanded the Twentieth Army, headquartered in Nanchang. General He had worked closely with the Communists since joining the Nationalist cause in 1925. Many of the troops in these commands belonged to the Communist Party or strongly supported it. The chief of public security in Nanchang was the Communist officer General Zhu De, the future commander in chief of the Red Army. Zhu also commanded a small training regiment. The extent of allegiance to leftist and Communist leaders has been estimated at 20,000–30,000 troops.[7]

With this potential for military backing, what of the Party's leadership and plans? A provisional or interim Political Bureau (Politburo), established at the July 13 Party meeting, ordered CCP representatives to withdraw from the Nationalist government. The five members of this Politburo included Zhang Guotao, Li Weihan, Li Lisan, Zhou Enlai, and Zhang Tailei.[8] Awaiting the Comintern's replacement for Borodin and having no official central leader after Chen Duxiu's resignation, Party Politburo members heatedly debated the future course of action for the Communists. Some, seeking a means to salvage Party influence and rebuild organizational strength, recommended a conservative approach that entailed eventually following the troops of Zhang Fakui back to their home base in Guangdong in order to begin again the Communist movement in an area where successful peasant movements were being organized. Others favored taking a more direct approach and called for an immediate armed uprising.

At meetings in Jiujiang (Jiangxi) beginning after July 19, Li Lisan, Tan Pingshan, and other key Party leaders expressed serious doubts about the reliability of General Zhang's continued support for the Communists, especially in light of reported KMT plans to meet in conference with Wang Jingwei at Lushan in order to discuss ways to purge the Communists from the Second Front Army.[9] One account reports that Wang Jingwei was concerned about the leftist tendencies of the Twentieth Army and the 24th Division, so he, Zhang Fakui, Sun Ke (Sun Yat-sen's son), and Zhu Peite met at Lushan to plan the destruction of these forces. As part of the plan, Zhang Fakui ordered He Long and Ye Ting to come to Lushan to attend the meeting and also to concentrate their troops at De'an. The idea was to lure these suspect troops into a location where they could easily be encircled and attacked by the Third Army.

Sensing the danger in these orders, He Long and Ye Ting met secretly aboard a boat and resolved not to go to Lushan nor to send their troops to De'an. Instead they decided to go with their troops at separate intervals to Nanchang. This decision brought them into open revolt against the Third Army and, in effect, left them little choice but to support the Communists at Nanchang.[10] To take advantage of these favorable military circumstances, Party leaders recommended the quick launching of an uprising at Nanchang, making good use of the fortuitous presence and support of Generals Ye Ting, He Long, and Zhu De.

Authorization for the revolt was sought from the Party Central at Hankou, along with guidance for a working organizational and political strategy for implementing the insurrection. Yun Daiying, Li Lisan, and Deng Zhongxia journeyed to Lushan to consult with Qu Qiubai, who was there meeting with Borodin concerning reorganization of the Party leadership. They discussed the dangerous circumstances and whether they should embark on staging an armed uprising.[11] Nie Rongzhen, a key military participant in the forthcoming uprising, has reported that he and Zhang Tailei also traveled to Lushan during this period to brief Borodin before his imminent return to the Soviet Union on the Nanchang developments and CCP plans. They hoped to receive guarantees of Soviet support and assistance for the uprising plans. Borodin, in his tentative status, offered no comment on the Nanchang plans.[12] Qu agreed to the uprising, and the Provisional Politburo authorized the formation of a Front Committee, under Zhou Enlai's leadership, to begin at once making military preparations in Nanchang. Regarding the requests for policy guidance and Soviet assistance, the Hankou Party Central found it necessary to consult the newly arrived representative from the Comintern, Besso Lominadze, and convene a meeting of the interim Politburo.

Lominadze arrived in Hankou on July 23. Of Georgian descent and a protégé of Stalin, he was only twenty-eight years old and entirely unfamiliar with Chinese affairs.[13] This newcomer was bound to pale in comparison with the all-powerful revolutionary strategist Borodin, who came to China with years of practical experience. Lominadze's apparent strong point was that in the continued heated atmosphere in the

Soviet Union where Stalin's policies, especially those concerning China, were being ravaged by the Trotsky faction, Lominadze remained a staunch supporter of Stalin and Bukharin. Thus Stalin could trust him not to obstruct or twist his policies and directives while operating in China. Key Chinese leaders clearly were not impressed with Stalin's choice. After an early meeting with Lominadze, Zhang Guotao and Qu Qiubai—the latter soon to become the new Party head—expressed their despair over Lominadze's youth and inexperience and especially his hesitation to handle practical matters, particularly the urgent and thorny matter of a Nanchang uprising.[14]

By this time, in late July, the earlier peaceful separation of the Communists from the Kuomintang had become a policy of active expulsion, with more and more Communists being executed or driven underground. Exasperated by the increasingly bitter environment, leaders of the KMT Left who opposed both Wuhan and Nanjing, such as Song Qingling (Madame Sun Yat-sen) and Deng Yanda, left China. The recently established Front Committee, under Zhou Enlai's direction, made final plans for an armed rebellion at Nanchang on July 30. And finally, Lominadze received his awaited instructions from Moscow concerning the proposed uprising.

On July 26 a secret meeting was held in Hankou to discuss mainly the Nanchang Uprising. It was attended by Qu Qiubai, Zhang Guotao, Li Weihan, and Zhang Tailei of the Central Committee; Lominadze; the Russian advisers Galen (Vasily Bliukher) and Fanck; an unidentified representative of the Young Communist International; and two interpreters. General Galen opened the meeting by supporting the conservative approach that the Communist forces move back to Guangdong under the protection of Zhang Fakui's armies, rather than separating from these forces by remaining to carry out an uprising in Nanchang and then returning to Guangdong independently.[15]

Next, Lominadze reported his instructions from Moscow, which stated that no funds were available for the proposed Nanchang insurrection and that Russian advisers were prohibited from taking part in it. Finally, he noted that the Comintern telegram stated that "if the insurrection had no hope of success, it would be best not to launch it. The Communists in Zhang Fakui's army could be withdrawn and sent to work among the peasants."[16] Stalin's attitude regarding the Communists' relationship to the Kuomintang was already on record. He was counting on CCP work among the KMT "masses" or the KMT revolutionary base to produce a wave of popular support for eventually removing the traitorous Wang Jingwei and replacing his leadership with reliable allies. Stalin was not inclined, therefore, to expend efforts and resources to back a provocative Communist-led military revolt at this time.[17]

Lominadze selected Zhang Guotao to transmit Moscow's decision to the Front Committee in Nanchang. Zhang expressed strong reservations about undertaking this mission, claiming that he had helped plan the uprising and, together with other Central Chinese leaders, had approved carrying it out. Nevertheless, he stressed that Lominadze informed him that Moscow was really ordering the uprising halted, and as a Comintern directive this had to be obeyed.[18] Zhang said the meeting concluded with general agreement in line with Comintern policy to follow General Galen's recommendations for cooperating with KMT General Zhang Fakui, and Zhang prepared to leave for Nanchang that evening.

The following morning he arrived in Jiujiang and met with leading Communists to discuss Moscow's instructions. He found their response to be unanimous, saying that the uprising plan had to be executed and that it was indeed too late to turn back. Zhang said one member of the Front Committee, Yun Daiying, even accused the Comintern and Party Central leaders of "thwarting the Chinese revolution" and denied their continued leadership role in ongoing events. In response, Zhang claimed he also admitted to doubts about the continuing credibility in the movement of the Chinese Communist leaders.[19] Nevertheless, on July 29 he telegraphed ahead twice to the Front Committee in Nanchang saying: "It is better to be careful about a revolt, so no matter what, wait until he [Zhang] arrives and then decide."[20] The Front Committee leaders, frustrated over the terrible plight of the Communist movement and anxious to get on with their act of resistance, disregarded Zhang's cautions and continued making their plans.

Zhang arrived in Nanchang early on July 30 and met with the Front Committee members, which included Zhou Enlai, Li Lisan, Peng Pai, Yun Daiying, Tan Pingshan, Ye Ting, and Zhou Yiqun. He found the atmosphere tense and anxious, with few wanting to hear of Moscow and Hankou's pessimism about the chances for the uprising's success. Zhang first argued that an uprising could take place only if Zhang

Fakui agreed to support it. Zhou Enlai impatiently responded that Zhang Fakui was too closely allied with Wang Jingwei to agree to support the uprising. He fought Zhang's efforts to delay the uprising, which might give enemy forces the opportunity to concentrate their strength.[21] Zhang Guotao explained Hankou's position that the Communist forces should join the forces of Zhang Fakui and return in safety to Guangdong. In the course of lengthy and heated debate with Zhang Guotao, it was pointed out that knowledge of the uprising plan was now so widespread that Zhang Fakui was bound to learn of it eventually and then would no longer remain friendly to the Communists when and if they reached the south together.[22] In addition, there was sudden information that Zhang Fakui had decided to travel to Nanchang on August 1 to confer with his generals, He Long and Ye Ting. These circumstances apparently persuaded Zhang Guotao that, as Zhou Enlai argued, it was too late to cancel the uprising.[23] As Zhang reported: "It seemed that they had already 'mounted the tiger,' so it was too late to change their minds."[24] Indeed, Yun Daiying is said to have threatened Zhang that "if he continued to vacillate and undermine their resolve, they would expell him."[25]

The accumulation of devastating setbacks and losses experienced by the Communists from March 1927 on, which by late July was rapidly accelerating, created a collective mood of desperation for action and also revenge. As Zhu De explained, after the period of KMT–CCP cooperation ended in July, "a large number of Communist Party members were purged from the National Revolutionary Army. They had nowhere to turn. To salvage the revolution and cope with the pressing situation, we realized that an uprising was the only solution. . . ."[26] Or as Nie Rongzhen described the thinking just prior to August: "The Party decided to counterattack the Chiang-Wang betrayal of the revolution with an uprising at Nanchang."[27]

The Nanchang Uprising and Southern Expedition

The uprising was to begin before dawn at four o'clock on August 1 under the direction of Ye Ting and He Long. However, on the evening of July 31, one of He Long's Twentieth Army assistants informed General Zhu Peite's headquarters about the plans. Action now had to be taken in haste. Front Committee Chairman Zhou Enlai moved the time of the uprising ahead. At two o'clock the Communists began their attack and, within four hours, had subdued resistance, seized large quantities of weapons and ammunition, and occupied both the enemy military headquarters and the headquarters of the Jiangxi provincial government.[28] By noon business in the markets, shops, and restaurants had resumed with the townspeople understanding little of what had taken place, largely because the uprising did not ignite incidents of rioting, looting, or burning typical of the capture of cities during the warlord period.[29]

The Front Committee directed the military uprising at Nanchang, but once the city changed hands it was necessary to work out a formula of government that would satisfy the Comintern's authoritative political program to work with revolutionary elements in the KMT. What emerged was the Revolutionary Committee of the Chinese Nationalist Party (KMT). Party leaders, although disregarding Comintern directions not to stage the uprising, and launching their first military assault against KMT authority, still were constrained by policy to carry out their activities in the name of the KMT. The inclination again was to think in terms of orchestrating political change from above. The new Revolutionary Committee was charged with convening a KMT national congress for the purpose of reorganizing the KMT in favor of a Left KMT/CCP alliance and launching a punitive expedition against what would then be considered rebel centers in both Wuhan and Nanjing.[30]

The leadership composition of the Revolutionary Committee confirmed that while the methodology of government promised a legislated process of change, the Communists controlled levers of power. Tan Pingshan became chairman; Wu Yuzhang, general secretary; Zhou Enlai was to preside over military affairs; Lin Zuhan was to manage finances; Li Lisan was to head the Political Section; and Zhang Guotao was put in charge of the Peasant and Workers' Section.[31] To underscore the cooperative nature of the new system, a number of famous KMT leftists were added to the slate, including Song Qingling (Madame Sun Yat-sen), He Xiangning (Madame Liao Zhongkai), Deng Yanda, and even General Zhang Fakui. Including General Zhang among the twenty-five members provoked considerable resistance from some Communist leaders, but it was finally agreed that such a move might have the positive effect of keeping Zhang neutral to the uprising and its outcome, and perhaps even winning away more of his troops.[32] Of course, neither Zhang nor the other famous KMT members agreed to their appointment to the Revolutionary Committee or attended this meeting.

A military directorate was established, not surprisingly with He Long in command and Ye Ting as his deputy. Liu Bocheng became chief of staff and Guo Mojo was appointed head of the Political Department.[33] General He's forces maintained the name of the Second Front Army and continued to use the KMT flag.

The newly allied forces of Wang Jingwei and Chiang Kai-shek responded swiftly to the Nanchang events. A cable was sent from Wuhan ordering the capture of rebel leaders He Long and Ye Ting. Zhang Fakui and Zhu Peite were instructed to marshal their forces to "nip the revolution in the bud."[34] Zhang Fakui acted with haste to put down this revolt within his Second Front Army. The rebel troops were forced to withdraw from Nanchang on August 3, and the last units were disengaged on August 5.

The retreating rebel forces, comprising fifteen regiments, launched what became known as the Southern Expedition and resumed the plans to connect up with the peasant revolts taking place in Guangdong. The rebel leaders anticipated receiving Russian arms and ammunition through Guangdong port cities, and once they had assumed leadership over peasant revolts in the south, their ambitious plans included taking Guangzhou. With its surrender, the way would be clear for asserting Communist authority over all of Guangdong and using it as a base for launching a second Northern Expedition.[35] Needless to say, any previous hopes of receiving support from Zhang Fakui for these plans were dashed by the uprising at Nanchang.

Because the Nanchang uprising was a military revolt and hastily planned, little time or attention had been given to organizing mass support among the workers and peasants either in Nanchang or on the route south. The national Communist leaders did not coordinate their plans with local Jiangxi CCP leaders or organize, with their support, uprisings elsewhere in the province that might have tied down government troops. Instead, the Nanchang uprising, carried out in haste and with concern for secrecy, stimulated further conservative reaction in Jiangxi against Party personnel and organizations.[36] Southbound troops received no support from the peasantry in the form of porters for their huge supplies of ammunition captured at Nanchang, or even supplies of food or water. Li Lisan reported that "during only three days of march, we lost more than one-third of our actual strength, almost half the ammunition was abandoned . . . the soldiers who deserted or died of illness approached four thousand."[37]

After a three-day stay in Linchuan where much attention was given to improving the discipline and morale of the troops, the rebels continued on to Ruijin, the future Communist capital in Jiangxi Province, still experiencing very hostile actions from the peasantry along the route. In the campaigns directed at taking Ruijin, the rebel forces suffered heavy casualties, but finally defeated enemy forces under Qian Daqun's command in bloody engagements at Rentian on August 18 and nearby Huichang on August 24.[38]

The Revolutionary Platform and Policies

Following these military encounters, the exhausted Communist-led troops assembled at Ruijin. There attention finally turned to developing specific policies, programs, and strategies for the new government that first had been established at Nanchang. As early as the late July planning sessions at Jiujiang, the Party had decided to establish a Revolutionary Committee of the KMT. However, it was actually not until the committee's arrival at Ruijin that details concerning the form and objectives of the new government were developed. They reflected clearly Stalin's political direction that the CCP reorganize the KMT by filling its ranks with workers and peasants.

At Ruijin, it was envisaged that worker and peasant participation in the county, city, district, and *xiang* (administrative village) governments should reach a level of 90 percent, with several levels being presided over by a Revolutionary Committee. The Revolutionary Committee at these levels would supervise, using the new influx of sympathetic forces to reorganize the KMT "by the method of a left faction party purification."[39] The new forces would provide support to the Left against the Right in order to shift the focus of power toward the Communists. Party members would assume most of the positions on the revolutionary committees and through them control the functions of government. When enough Communists were securely in place, a Third Congress of the KMT could be called "for the purpose of contesting with Wang Jingwei and the others for the orthodox succession."[40]

By means of this gradual, legalistic approach, the Communists, still operating officially under KMT auspices, might plan for the legitimate transfer of power into their hands. In addition, the continued use of the title of the National Government might provide needed protection against possible hostile actions from the foreign powers and gain the neutrality of the KMT military commanders.

Another key issue addressed by the new revolutionary government at Ruijin concerned land revolution. The question of how much land to confiscate and from whom created heated discussions at the Jiujiang planning conferences in July. Li Lisan and Yun Daiying advocated taking the land of large landowners in order to bring about some degree of land revolution. Others, including Tan Pingshan, objected, fearing that such action would bring about a dangerous reaction and possibly further unify the landholders' power against the Communists. Some had reasonable fears that limiting land revolution might cause serious divisions among the rebel troops. When the Party Central finally acted on this problem, it recommended only that land revolution be the subject of propaganda slogans—in other words, that actual confiscation of land not take place.[41]

This policy changed immediately after the Nanchang Revolt, when the Revolutionary Committee's Peasant and Workers' Section, after heated debate over where to set the limit, passed regulations that landlords holding more than 200 *mu* (30.3 acres) of land be subject to confiscation. After all, it was now imperative that some land-confiscation policy be established because the Nanchang rebels had, in effect, advertised their uprisings by stating their intention to join the peasants in Guangdong to carry out agrarian revolution.

Guangdong peasant troops in the rebel armies severely criticized these regulations, pointing out that in Guangdong few landlords held that much land and thus "the tiller won't get his land." During the policy sessions at Ruijin, the new authorities, apparently fearful of potential disruption within their rebel ranks, amended the regulations, leaving only the instruction to "expropriate the land" and setting no limit on the amount.[42] This zigzag course demonstrated that there still was little consensus on this crucial issue of land revolution among top Communist leaders. One major obstacle was the political guidance to continue working with part of the landholding KMT. Further, the KMT had greater military resources to draw upon to protect their properties than the CCP had to seize them.

The land revolution was discussed again at Shanghang (Fujian), with individual leaders presenting their own observations and impressions. The majority favored unleashing the peasants by recommending complete expropriation of the land and giving to the peasants the key role of equalizing tillage rights in the countryside. Zhang Guotao, in charge of the Peasant and Workers' Section, disagreed with this radical position, and after pointing to the milder but detailed land program adopted and already implemented by the Guangdong CCP Provincial Committee, which offered some protection to small landholders, won acceptance of regulations "limiting expropriation to lands of 50 *mu* (7.5 acres) or more."[43]

While the land question had generated much debate and a variety of policy responses, it is significant that the problem of developing a policy concerning the workers received only passing attention. No clear approach was defined until the planning sessions at Ruijin, and then only after one discussion session. Certainly, leaders of the Revolutionary Committee such as Li Lisan already had extensive experience to draw on in planning and directing urban movements. Extensive spadework in this area had been done long ago. The more immediate and perplexing problem was that the recently proclaimed purpose of the Nanchang Uprising was to connect this urban-originated movement with peasant revolts in Guangdong, and yet the Party lacked even a cursory policy addressing the nature and extent of land expropriation.

As the Southern Expedition continued its march through Fujian and Guangdong provinces, it faced difficulties in raising revenues to pay expenses and in working out an approach toward the "counterrevolutionaries" encountered along the route. The Revolutionary Committee's Financial and Political Sections tried and discarded several policies to cope with these problems. The key obstacle was lack of peasant support. Active peasant support was absolutely essential for identifying and arresting large landlords and gentry in the areas transited. Once they were arrested, their lands could be confiscated or they might be heavily fined. Without peasant support, the rebel forces, rather than defeating the local establishment, found it necessary to compromise with its leaders in order to gain their cooperation in providing provisions and support. Unfortunately, this support often took the form of the local gentry conducting confiscatory levies against the peasantry, which in turn only further alienated peasant support for the newly arrived rebel forces.

No active peasant response materialized along the route mainly because Party organizations in most of these areas were never informed about the Nanchang plans and were also poor in quality or, in many places, nonexistent. Most of the active worker and peasant organizations had been crushed in the wave of conservative reaction. The absence of strong organizations precluded the Party's carrying out the necessary propaganda or organizational work among the workers and peasants.

The rebel forces arrived at the coastal city of Shantou on September 24. Their expectation that workers in Shantou, because of their protracted involvement in the previous Hong Kong–Guangdong strike activities, would actively support the rebel government was disappointed. The Russian aid, which had been one key reason for taking the rebel forces defeated at Nanchang on a southern march, had not arrived. The prospects of abundant Soviet aid coming through this port city had recommended Shantou to the rebel leaders as the logical provisional capital for their leftist government. The rebel leadership, now operating in Shantou, became even more apprehensive about the possible public disruption and retaliation that might result from their implementation of the policies worked out en route to confiscate the lands and fine those identified as local counterrevolutionists, especially in this setting of a coastal city, vulnerable to possible reprisals from the foreign powers. Under these circumstances, the rebels decided to abandon those policies.[44]

The trend toward moderation became even more apparent after the Nanchang forces reached the Chaozhou-Shantou coastal area. This was reflected in their response to calls for support from peasant leaders. Even before the rebel forces had reached Guangdong, the pockets of peasant activities west of Chaozhou and Shantou had been very successful, capturing the two cities of Haifeng and Lufeng. Peasant groups around Puning, just west of Shantou, called for rebel military support to help overwhelm the still successfully defended city. The Nanchang forces agreed to help the peasants capture Puning, but at the same time apparently emphasized their role as the proper, legitimate, or orthodox Nationalist Government of China. This pose of legitimacy caused them to refuse to allow the peasants to enter Puning to eliminate the power holders once the city was taken. Li Lisan claimed that when the Nanchang troops finally departed, no political power had changed hands in Puning, and the peasants became disillusioned with the rebels over this outcome.[45] In effect, the Nanchang troops appeared to take the side of the local forces that they were called to oppose. Like the local powers, the Nanchang forces did not permit changes to occur.

Members of the Revolutionary Committee, while in Shantou, again made contact with General Zhang Fakui, presumably to try to regain his favor and renewed support.[46] As incredible as this move might seem, the need for powerful military support was becoming increasingly urgent to the rebels, and Zhang's previous leftist sympathies still were fresh in their minds. In short, the pressing requirement for military strength precluded their being overly discriminating. After all, the military units at the Communists' bidding were not homogeneous and disciplined forces. At Nanchang they had consisted of various hastily assembled units unified mainly by their interest in joining the Nanchang revolt.

On September 26 Politburo member Zhang Tailei arrived in Shantou from Hong Kong with instructions from the Party headquarters.[47] During their march southward, the Nanchang leaders had been out of touch with the Party Central, which had recently moved from Hankou to Shanghai.[48] Zhang brought news of the major policy developments that had taken place in the interim. He instructed that new central policies required the Nanchang rebels to convert the Revolutionary Committee into a soviet government, thus dropping the title "The Revolutionary Committee of the Chinese Nationalist Party." Both Chaozhou and Shantou were to be abandoned, and remaining rebel troops were to be dispersed to Haifeng and Lufeng to support the rural peasant movements there by forming a Worker-Peasant Red Army.[49] In effect, the rebel leaders were told to discard the new government structure and revise completely their approach aimed at reaching accommodations with the left-wing and mainly urban forces in order to manipulate the political scene to favor Communist influence and control. By late September the Party's political line had changed considerably. The new emphasis was on providing military backing for agrarian revolution.

Zhang Tailei relayed orders that Zhang Guotao and Li Lisan were to report to central authorities in Shanghai, while Zhou Enlai was to supervise the local changes. In addition, he informed the Nanchang leaders that they had all been demoted by the central leadership. As the Party's review of Nanchang events developed, Tan Pingshan as chairman of the Revolutionary Committee came in for harsh attack. In November he was expelled from the Party for several alleged offenses, which became part of the central leadership's sharp critique of the Nanchang Uprising. In his presiding office, Tan became the "insignia" for all the Nanchang errors.[50]

As Zhang Tailei directed that these radical changes be made, the rebel forces were under increasing pressure from opposing armies and were preparing for a major battle at Tangkeng. The lengthy period that rebel leaders spent in Ruijin and other planning sessions, and at Shantou and Chaozhou, had allowed the enemy forces of Wang Jun and Qian Dajun time to concentrate their forces for a major assault. To Zhang Guotao, this hardly seemed an appropriate time to break up the troops and disperse them among the peasants. Lamenting the turn of events that spelled the end to the labor of constructing the new government and its platform which he favored, Zhang contended "that a radical change in the thick of battle was like having an actor dismantle his own stage."[51]

The rebel forces were utterly defeated on October 1 at Tangkeng,[52] outnumbered 5,000 to 15,000. After the battle the retreating rebel forces split up. Ye Ting, Nie Rongzhen, and Zhou Enlai, the latter being carried on a stretcher, boarded a small boat and escaped to Hong Kong. Surviving forces of the 24th Division joined Peng Pai to establish a base at Haifeng and Lufeng.[53] A unit of the 25th Division commanded by Zhu De and including Lin Biao and Chen Yi traveled north to Hunan Province and, in January 1928, working with the Hunan Party organ and Peasant Self-Defense Corps, carried out the year-end South Hunan Uprising. It resulted in the establishment of a five-county (*xian*) soviet that lasted three months. In April 1928 Zhu De and Chen Yi joined Mao Zedong in the Jinggang Mountains in Jiangxi province, near the Hunan border, where they established the famous Jinggang Mountains Base Area.[54]

Reasons for the Rebels' Failure

The Nanchang Uprising and Southern Expedition underwent a formal review at the Party's November plenum. The Provisional Party Politburo on November 14 issued a "Resolution on Political Discipline," which enumerated the mistakes made by the Nanchang rebels.[55] Of course, by this time Party leaders already had met in August to form a new leadership and had made significant headway in working out policies to fit their status as independent of the KMT. The new CCP leadership had learned valuable lessons from both the Nanchang leaders and those who led the subsequent Autumn Harvest Uprisings. Participants presented detailed reports on their Nanchang experiences to the Party Central in Shanghai.[56]

When the Nanchang Uprising began, the Party's leadership was being reorganized and its general policies reviewed.[57] Thus efforts to consolidate a direction or plan faced difficulties. The Nanchang rebels found themselves developing policy on a plan-as-you-go-south kind of basis. By the time they reached Ruijin, they finally got around to clarifying the shape of the new government and developing some specific policies to meet the rural circumstances they had encountered.

Development of a stable policy concerning the confiscation of land, the treatment of counterrevolutionaries, and a means of provisioning the troops were new matters that were studied. But without a clear and workable political program concerning land revolution and the status of local power holders, mistakes were inevitable. Uncertainty about the amount of land to be seized and a reasonable hesitancy to confront the powerful establishment by eliminating "counterrevolutionaries" or taxing the local gentry reflected the Communists' continued quandary of how to deal with such issues, especially without peasant support, which never materialized. When the rebel forces reached Shantou, a large port city, the more rural-responsive programs developed in Juichin were significantly moderated or abandoned as leaders inclined in this urban setting toward making compromises with the functioning government and municipal establishment, even agreeing to forced confiscations from the peasants to provision the rebel forces.

The Party in November condemned rebel errors that included Communist attempts to reconcile with KMT generals and the selection of a route south whose alleged promise was mainly safety from enemy attacks. Besides reflecting the uncertainty of the Party's current political direction, these choices were dictated to a large degree by the fact of the rebels being greatly outnumbered, isolated, and dwindling in numbers. Finding the safest route and additional military support became something of a necessity when the supporting forces were reduced to 5,000 troops, many of them wounded, and yet Party Central's plans called for the eventual capture of Guangdong Province.

At the November plenum, Zhang Guotao was charged with distorting the contents of Stalin's telegram concerning the Nanchang Uprising. Rather than recommending against initiating a military coup, Moscow's instructions were now interpreted as favoring such action "unless there is no chance at all of victory," a situation that presumably no one would support.[58] Of course, by this time Stalin had changed his official position, being grateful for anything resembling a Communist success in China. Rather than condemning the uprising, he praised it.[59] Under these new circumstances, the Party leadership could hardly admit, as Zhang charged, that it had actually directed Zhang to go to Nanchang to discourage the uprising. Zhang lost his posts as an alternate member of the Provisional Politburo, to which he had been appointed in absentia in August, and as a member of the Central Committee.

In retrospect, it was the threat of mutual annihilation that brought military forces and the Communists together at Nanchang. The dangerous circumstances precipitated the decision to undertake a joint armed uprising. At Nanchang some of the great future military leaders of the Communist movement became associated with the Party's leadership. They led an armed uprising under independent Party direction against both the Wuhan and Nanjing KMT leadership, in defiance of Comintern orders. There were initial difficulties in asserting Party influence over its new and rather motley military components, as well as large-scale troop defections, but still the forces were joined. There is evidence that the CCP, in order to unify the thinking and instill revolutionary purpose and discipline, made preliminary efforts to institutionalize Party control by introducing Party representatives and political sections into military units. Ye Ting's Eleventh Army apparently became a prototype for placing Communist military forces under Party direction.[60]

The implication of these major developments was that from this point on the Communists and the Kuomintang leadership became engaged in a direct armed struggle for power and territorial gain, the outcome of which would not be settled definitively for the next twenty-two years. The key issues yet to be addressed decisively by the Communists included the role of the peasant movement and land revolution in a Party-led armed struggle for survival and expansion.

Chapter 3. The August 7 Emergency Conference

As the Nanchang rebels began their southward retreat, Communist leaders met secretly in Hankou on August 7, 1927, to reorganize the Party leadership, develop a new political framework and program, and determine ways to restore and strengthen the battered CCP organizations. This meeting marked the beginning of Communist efforts to consolidate their remaining forces in preparation for challenging the KMT authorities in a series of armed struggles for power. Comintern direction over policy and guidance played the key role in the proceedings, but it is also clear that CCP leaders with field experience voiced their observations and even criticisms concerning immediate and past policies for the Communist movement. While the full substance of these comments was not incorporated into the political program produced at the conference, the comments were brought into the arena of high-level policy circles and made part of the recognized experience and findings derived from carrying out revolutionary activities in China.

New Leadership Emerges

Following the Nanchang Uprising and Wang Jingwei's alliance with Chiang Kai-shek in Nanjing, the KMT Executive Committee on August 4 issued an order to KMT cadres and organizations to mobilize their forces to destroy the CCP.[1] Under these ominous circumstances, the interim Politburo established in July was no longer adequate to deal with the deteriorating situation. Formal action had to be taken to consolidate new leadership for the Party, redress the policy direction that, during Chen Duxiu's tenure, had led to the Party's severe political decline, and chart a future course for the CCP. Another consideration was the sinking Communist morale, since some had become so pessimistic about Communist prospects that they considered leaving the Party.

As a first step, Qu Qiubai held a planning session at Jiujiang, which the new ECCI Representative Besso Lominadze attended, for convening a Party conference. Following these talks, Qu and Lominadze both arrived in Hankou on July 23, 1927, and began making immediate preparations for the conference. Lominadze conveyed Comintern instructions requiring an extraordinary conference of the CCP for the purpose of correcting the Party's political program and changing its leadership.

In Hankou, Lominadze, of course, refused to accept any blame for the Comintern's having misguided events in China or for erroneous policy development. Accusing the Party's central leadership of Right opportunism and of disobeying directives of the Comintern, Lominadze called for an immediate Party session to reorganize the Party Central Committee. His critical remarks reflected the formal position of the Comintern stated in its resolution of July 14. This document charged that "errors committed by the Communist Party of China should be made good at once."[2]

On July 29 the Party Central hastily attempted to get word out to the provinces to send representatives to the meeting. The dangerous conditions and poor state of communications frustrated these efforts, and only representatives from Hunan and the new Party secretary in Shanghai came. These were in addition to members of the Party Central and Communist Youth League Central Bureau and responsible officials from Hubei and Shanghai, all of whom were already in the Wuhan area. Representatives from Guangdong, Jiangxi, northern provinces, and those in Shanghai other than the new secretary could not attend.

The sparse attendance was exacerbated by the fact that interim Politburo members Li Lisan, Zhou Enlai, and Zhang Guotao had already gone south with the Nanchang rebel forces. This raised questions about meeting the necessary quorum for holding a Party congress and electing new leadership. In fact, in later years, charges were made that the conference, when it did convene, was illegal from the start.[3] Aware that their procedures were unusual, and apparently attempting to deflect charges that the meeting was not proper, the Party Central on August 27 issued Central Notice No. 1, explaining that the August 7 Emergency Conference had been convened in response to the Comintern's telegraphed orders to Lominadze, which had to be obeyed.[4] The point was that while the conference did not constitute a formal Party congress, its powers to elect new leadership and develop policy had the official backing of the Comintern.

The Emergency Conference was convened in the second-floor apartment of a Soviet agricultural adviser to China. He instructed the arriving participants that if the meeting were interrupted by strangers, the explanation should be given that it was a shareholders' meeting. Conditions were hot and crowded, with participants unable at any time to leave the building and limited to a diet mainly of dried food.

Twenty-three Communists attended the conference, including Central Committee members Li Weihan, Qu Qiubai, Zhang Tailei, Deng Zhongxia, Ren Bishi, Su Zhaozheng, Gu Shunzhang, Luo Yinong, Chen Qiaonian, Cai Hesen; alternate members Li Zhenying, Lu Chen, and Mao Zedong; Central Investigation Committee members Yang Pao'an and Wang Hebo; Chinese Communist Youth League (CCYL) Central Committee members Li Zifen, Yang Shannan, and Lu Dingyi; the Hunan Party organization representative Peng Gongda; Hubei Party organization representative Zheng Chaolin; the Party Central Military Committee representative Wang Yifei; the Party Central Organization Department member Deng Xiaoping; and Liu Changqun, who was a secretary of the Chang Jiang Bureau.[5] Li Weihan chaired the meeting, but Qu Qiubai actually presided over the conference, which elected a Provisional Politburo of nine members and seven alternate members. They were to serve until preparations could be made for convening a regular national Party congress.[6] The twenty-six-year-old German Communist and Comintern representative Heinz Neumann also attended.

There are several lists of the composition of the new Provisional Politburo, especially in regard to the full or alternate status of members. Qu Qiubai, having close ties and the full support of the Comintern, was chosen to head the new organ, which probably included Li Weihan, Xiang Zhongfa, Su Zhaozheng, Zhang Tailei, Li Lisan, Zhou Enlai, Zhang Guotao, Mao Zedong, Liu Shaoqi, Cai Hesen, Xiang Ying, Luo Yinong, Peng Gongda, Deng Zhongxia, and Peng Pai.[7] Some of the confusion arises from the fact that no formal minutes were kept of the day's proceedings, so that the member composition of the elected bodies is based largely on the recollections of participants.

Recently, conference chairman Li Weihan provided additional information concerning the new leadership structure that emerged from this meeting. His identification of the offices and officeholders is summarized as follows:[8]

Qu Qiubai	Provisional Politburo head and Standing Committee member; head, Peasant Committee and Propaganda Bureau; general editor, Party Organ (*Bolshevik*)
Li Weihan	Provisional Politburo Standing Committee member; head, Organization Bureau and CCP Secretariat
Su Zhaocheng	Provisional Politburo Standing Committee member; head, Labor Committee
Zhou Enlai	Head, Military Affairs Bureau; assisted by Wang Yifei
Yang Zhihua (Madame Qu Qiubai)	Responsible for Women's Bureau
Gu Shunzhang	Responsible for communications
Zheng Chaolin	Responsible for publications
CCP Northern Bureau (Hebei, Shanxi, Manchuria, Inner Mongolia and Shandong)	CCP First Secretary: Wang Hebo CCP Secretary: Cai Hesen CCP Committee members: Peng Shuzhi, Zhang Kundi, Liu Bozhuang, and a CCYL representative
CCP Southern Bureau* (Guangdong, Guangxi, south Fujian, and coastal area special branches)	CCP Secretary: Zhang Guotao CCP Committee members: Zhou Enlai, Zhang Tailei, Peng Pai, Chen Quan, Yun Daiying, Huang Ping
Chang Jiang Bureau (established in late September: Hubei, Hunan, Henan, Jiangxi, Sichuan, Anhui, and Shaanxi)	CCP Secretary: Luo Yinong CCP Committee members: Yi Lirong and Cai Zhende

*Until this bureau could be organized, a Provisional Southern Bureau was to be formed by Zhang Tailei, Yang Yin, and Huang Ping.

Qu Qiubai took charge of the Party at age twenty-eight, with impressive background experience. During his 1921–22 stay in the Soviet Union, Qu served as a newspaper correspondent for *Chenbao* (morning paper), translator of Russian literature, interpreter at major Comintern events, and lecturer to new Chinese arrivals. He began an intensive study of Marxism-Leninism, and upon his return to China became the leading Russian expert in the CCP. Qu taught at Shanghai University when it was a guiding center for the May 30th Movement, edited major Party journals including *New Youth*, *Vanguard*, and *Guide Weekly*, and lectured at the Peasant Movement Training Institute. In early 1927 Qu helped plan the Shanghai strikes of February and March and became a political instructor at the Wuhan branch of the Central Military Academy (formerly Huangbu Academy). With these strong credentials Qu became the logical successor to Chen Duxiu.[9] The writings of the late Li Weihan, a recent (September 1982) Politburo member and vice chairman of the CCP Central Committee Advisory Commission, indicate that a positive reappraisal of Qu has restored him to respectability in official PRC historical circles.[10]

General Policy Guidance

Lominadze intended for the August 7 meeting to produce an accredited leadership for the faltering Chinese revolution and to lay down a revised general policy line for its development. His report was the first item on the day's agenda, taking until midday to deliver. While the specific contents are unknown, the general topics covered included class struggle and revolution, the questions of the workers and peasants, relations with the KMT, and Party relations with the Comintern.[11] Antecedents for his comments existed in guidance and interpretations of the Chinese revolution that had been emanating from Moscow for some time. The Seventh Enlarged Plenum of the ECCI in November –December 1926 had concluded that "the agrarian question is the central question. The class that gives a radical answer to this question will be the leader of the revolution."[12] The proletariat, of course, was the Comintern's choice to fulfill that mission. At the Eighth Plenum of the ECCI in May 1927, by which time the Chinese Communists were coming under increasing pressure, Moscow called for using the lure of benefits from agrarian revolution and Communist urban programs to entice urban and rural masses to join the KMT, gain influence in local governing bodies, and eventually play a role in enabling the Communists to have controlling power in a new National Revolutionary Government. While the Trotsky Opposition called for the immediate establishment of soviets in China, Stalin described the soviets as organs established solely to overthrow the existing government and pronounced them inappropriate inasmuch as he still regarded the Wuhan government as a legitimate and useful force for developing the Chinese revolution.[13]

This investment in the revolutionary potential and convictions of the Wuhan leadership, and the ability of the Chinese "revolutionaries" to mobilize the urban and rural masses in large numbers, was epitomized in Stalin's June 1 telegram calling for unusual feats of reform and mobilization to be carried out by the loyal forces. But the catastrophic events in China forced Stalin and Bukharin farther to the left. In their predicament of mid-July, they had to find some way to counter the almost constant attacks from the Trotsky Opposition, who claimed that still another disaster in China had resulted from incorrect policies. At the same time, in order to maintain a sense of policy continuity and preserve the framework of definite incremental stages inherent in their theoretical approach, Stalin had to support a continuing alliance with the broad KMT, if not the KMT Wuhan government. Further, with prospects for building a substantial alliance from above greatly diminished by the defection of the Wuhan KMT leadership, the soviet form now emerged as a means of mobilizing support, especially KMT mass support, from below. But this concept had to be presented in a manner connected to Stalin's past policies rather than seeming to verify well-known Trotskyist positions. What emerged was the analysis that the CCP-led revolutionary forces, including the KMT, having cast off the burden of the traitorous Wuhan government, now had a clear path for developing the revolution to an even higher stage of development, at which point the introduction of the soviet form would be entirely appropriate. Having successfully denied Trotsky at least a public forum for his attacks, the Stalin faction apparently felt secure enough to adopt some of Trotsky's ideas, particularly the useful soviet concept. In a *Pravda* article of July 28 Stalin directed that the Chinese Communists begin to "popularize" the concept of soviets in China.[14] This meant that the Party ranks should be instructed in the meaning and function of soviets, but it was emphasized that the time was not appropriate for actually establishing soviets as a part of any Communist urban program.

Moscow defended its position concerning the current status of the Chinese revolution and the appropriate policy concerning soviets in August. Using arguments critical of Trotsky's positions, Moscow explained that at this new stage, when the Wuhan KMT government had "deserted the revolution," the Communists should shift to a policy aimed at converting the lower-level KMT Party organizations into active agents for pursuing agrarian revolution, building strong organizations of the workers and peasants, and forming from the latter an effective military force. Thus, while any further cooperation with the KMT government was out, the mass membership of the KMT Party organizations, where the CCP had active organizational strength and experience, was still regarded as a potential ally.

In support of these goals the Communists were directed to carry on an active propaganda campaign for the "idea of soviets." But, leaving room to maneuver, Moscow said, "Should the Communist Party's efforts to revolutionize the Kuomintang not meet with success, and should it be found impossible to convert the Kuomintang into a broad mass organization of workers and peasants, and if at such time the revolution is in the upsurge, then is the time to make the propagandist slogan of soviets a slogan of direct struggle and to proceed at once to the organization of workers', peasants', and artisans' soviets."[15]

This Comintern analysis and guidance concerning the Chinese revolution provided the background against which Lominadze and the CCP leadership at the August 7 Conference met to develop the policies and operational programs to continue and expand their revolutionary activities. Following Lominadze's lengthy report, and some discussion by conference participants, the key conference document, drafted by Lominadze and translated into Chinese by Qu Qiubai, was passed. This was "The Circular Letter of the [CC] (CCP central committee) to All Party Members."[16] It explained to the entire CCP membership that past policies no longer were to be followed, and that a major shift in direction was being developed for the role of the CCP in the Chinese revolution.[17]

The CCP in the future was to follow an independent course, developing a mass movement of workers, peasants, and lower-level KMT members, or, in other words, building the revolution from the base to the highest levels. To clarify this new stance, the "Circular Letter" cited specific incidents from the recent past that deviated from this path. In urban affairs, examples were noted of the Party cooperating with KMT authorities to work out legal and peaceful means to settle labor disputes. More direct or violent means such as strikes or struggle campaigns had been wrongly avoided by Party labor leaders and incorrectly condemned as worker "excesses" and "infantilism." Of course, there is a plethora of evidence that the Comintern had once advocated exactly that conciliatory approach. During the discussion period, Luo Yinong charged that the guidance provided by two Comintern representatives working in Shanghai in fact damaged work there and thwarted revolutionary activities. He described the Party as behaving like the guest rather than the host of revolution.[18]

More examples of Party compromises and protection of the existing order in rural affairs were cited in the "Circular Letter." Rather than supporting spontaneous peasant uprisings to confiscate the land, the CCP reportedly backed the conservative, order-preserving rural systems favored by KMT leaders. Details of the famous Horse Day (May 21) Incident in Changsha were presented as clear evidence that the CCP failed to provide decisive leadership to a spontaneous mass movement.[19] But in speeches during the afternoon discussion period, both Cai Hesen and the Hunan representative Peng Gongda pointed out that the Party's Fifth Congress had passed a good land resolution, but that the Politburo had prevented its implementation. At least implied was that the Politburo was acting under the Comintern's direction. Peng described the Party's past leadership in rural affairs as emphasizing peace and not struggle.[20]

In addition to citing these negative examples of past Party behavior, the "Circular Letter" supported the Comintern's decision to identify these "mistakes" with certain key individuals. With so many of the alleged mistakes committed by the Party in checking so-called peasant "excesses," it was inevitable that Tan Pingshan, the former minister of agriculture and interior in the Wuhan government, would be singled out for blame. Ironically, Tan at this time was chairman of the Nanchang rebel's Revolutionary Committee, helping to establish agrarian policies during the course of their southern retreat. In addition to thwarting the peasantry, Tan was condemned for recommending the treatment of "counterrevolutionary elements . . . in accordance with the provisions of the law."[21]

Chen Duxiu, as the Party's general secretary, was held responsible for having contributed most heavily to the development of "opportunistic" policies. These included checking the development of the workers' and peasants' movement, paying close attention to government restrictions in urban and rural communities in order to maintain discipline and public order, and advocating a moderate and gradual approach to realizing Party objectives. Stressing the key role of mass mobilization and agrarian revolution in the present stage of the Chinese revolution, the August 7 leadership now vigorously condemned the Party's behavior under Chen's supervision, using the historical record to document cautious and compromising attitudes.

Trotsky, in his again unpublished "Platform" for the opposition, railed against the Comintern leadership for laying the blame for its failed policies on the CCP leadership, calling this approach "superficial and contemptible."[22] Zhou Enlai, writing about the August 7 Conference in 1944, emphasized that by making Chen Duxiu, who Zhou says was barred from attending the conference, a target for criticism, those attending failed to give adequate attention to the causes, nature, and consequences of past errors, and thereby lessened opportunities for learning from their mistakes. Zhou claimed that establishing personal responsibility also promoted the approach of investigating and removing key individuals in different localities "as if they were opportunism itself," rather than delving into the roots and resolving the actual problems at hand.[23] Abundant evidence indicates that internal struggle plagued the Party for years, and no doubt was fueled by the precedent established at this meeting of assigning individual blame for policies that went awry.

At the same time that they faulted Chen and Tan, the new leadership praised the ECCI for illuminating past errors. They glossed over the fact that most of the new leaders were in charge of the very policies now being condemned. In addition, and here Lominadze's hand in drafting the letter is clearly apparent, the Party credited the ECCI with having advocated the now-correct policies all along. Indeed, it was explained that the Comintern had been obstructed from properly influencing the course of events because the CCP "would not admit its errors or obey the instruction of the CI (ECCI)."[24]

The "Circular Letter" directed the Communist membership to continue to regard the Comintern as the omniscient source of revolutionary policy. ECCI resolutions on China of May 26 and July 14 were presented as the basis for understanding the "correct" revolutionary policies, while the "Circular Letter" itself was to aid in educating the membership by describing past errors in carrying out policy. With full responsibility for these mistakes having been assigned to past leaders, the new Party leadership now could assert its authority and command the disciplined support of all Party levels for the new policies.

Qu Qiubai spoke to the conference, drawing upon recent events and explaining their impact on policy development. He claimed that by July 13, when the United Front with Wang Jingwei was collapsing, the Party had developed a new policy that was exemplified by the Nanchang Uprising. Contrary to the manner in which the Nanchang Uprising developed, Qu claimed that its objective was to draw strength from existing peasant unrest by carrying out land revolution, supported by military force. To continue to guide the Party in this direction, Qu stressed seizing leadership over revolutionary activities while exposing Wang Jingwei's false promises to the masses, building a strong Left faction, and establishing in the process a provisional revolutionary government.[25]

Qu's recommendations are reflected in a key conference document developed after the conference closing, the "Resolution on the Political Task and Policy of the Chinese Communist Party." It refocused CCP attention away from the "opportunistic" policies of the recent past, which it claimed had curtailed the development of the workers' and peasants' movements. The goal now was to deal with the clearly powerful forces, including the "reactionary bourgeoisie," militarists, landlords, and "their imperialist allies"—all of whom the Communists viewed as solidly arrayed against the Chinese revolution. The survival of the CCP depended on recognizing and dealing with this "objective" condition and the proposed solution to overcome this threat was the mobilization of the masses, under the leadership of the CCP.[26]

In the course of presenting a theoretical analysis of the Chinese revolution, the resolution pointed out that while the revolution was currently in the bourgeois-democratic stage, meaning that threats from the imperialist powers and feudal elements were paramount, the CCP's mobilization of the worker and peasant masses to form a "Dictatorship of the Workers and Peasants" could bring sufficient pressure on this system to transform it eventually into a socialist system.[27] The process would entail the abrogation of all foreign debts and the unequal treaties, nationalization of all land, the destruction and replacement of all oppressive national organizations beginning at the top, and the implementation of legal rights and economic improvements for workers. These elemental changes were predicted to break the power of bourgeois-feudal forces in the country and prepare the way for a socialist political and social system.

Lominadze's hand in drafting this resolution is reflected in the view that the transformation of Chinese society toward socialism, under the CCP's direction, was a "continuous, unceasing process."[28] The political organ identified to conclude this process and establish socialism or "the socialist dictatorship of the proletariat" was the soviet, composed of representatives of the workers, peasants, and soldiers. However, major developments still had to precede and prepare the way for the establishment of soviets. First, the CCP had to organize insurrections in areas where favorable conditions already existed for their success. The peasant movements in Guangdong, Hunan, Hubei, Shaanxi, and Henan were noted as having a promising foundation for development. In the course of the insurrections, revolutionary committees had to be established to direct the revolutionary activities. As noted above, a revolutionary committee had already been formed in the course of the Nanchang Uprising.

Key provisions in this statement of the Communist program were that the insurrections had to be organized under the banner of the left wing of the KMT, and that once the revolutionary committees were established, they were to include KMT participation. The Comintern still regarded the KMT lower-echelon leadership and mass membership as having a special affinity and potential allegiance to CCP policies and programs. As in the past, the Comintern hoped that association with this historic organization of national purpose would provide support for building a strong left-wing faction to guide the revolutionary movement.

During the conference's afternoon discussion period, Mao Zedong spoke seven times on issues raised. Regarding the new policy line elaborated in Lominadze's report requiring continued KMT-CCP cooperation, Mao called the relationship of the KMT and CCP a long-standing and unresolved question. According to him, the Party's big mistake was its failure to dominate the relationship. He likened the KMT to an empty house waiting to be occupied. The CCP, like a new bride, reluctantly entered the house, but never mustered the resolve to become its master.[29] Peng Gongda related that on August 18, while directing activities in Hunan, Mao expanded this point. Mao said flatly that when the United Front collapsed on July 15, the KMT died and became foul, having become merely a party of warlords seeking personal profit and gain. He claimed the CCP should fight on under its own flag and leadership.[30]

But according to the official policy, two possible sets of circumstances might lead to the successful establishment of soviets in China. One encompassed a broad insurrectionary movement, with significant mass appeal, and included extensive participation by the KMT Left under CCP control. Revolutionary committees established under those conditions would serve as transitional CCP organizations, allowing the Party to exercise control over the establishment of the soviets, which subsequently would bring about the realization of socialism. The second set of circumstances assumed that the CCP was unable to win support or participation from the KMT Left, but had success on its own in carrying out insurrections in areas favorable to their development. Under the latter conditions, the CCP could capitalize on this wave of successful support and independently establish soviets.

Neither of these sets of circumstances was believed to exist in August, so the policy concerning the soviets recommended only that the CCP begin immediately to develop "propaganda," or in other words educate its membership and followers concerning the role and purpose of the soviets in the course of the Chinese revolution.[31] Actual implementation of a soviet regime, of whichever kind, would have to await the further progress of the revolution.

Urban and Rural Differences

Communist-controlled organizations to be established in the countryside were to be formed in a different way from those established in the cities. Upon completion of a rural insurrection, the revolutionary committee, which was to precede the formation of the soviet, was directed to set up a peasant association and transfer all committee power to it. In the countryside all political power was to be concentrated in Communist-controlled, peasant mass organizations.

In the cities, on the other hand, the circumstances were presented as inherently more complex. Representatives from various organizations such as factories, trade unions, student associations, merchant organizations, and military units were to be popularly elected from the ranks, and then gather as a conference of representatives of the people to elect a Revolutionary Executive Committee of a particular city or county. This new body was to assume all political power at these levels. Representatives from all the new county-level organs were to meet to elect the leadership of a provincial-level political regime—the Provincial Provisional Revolutionary Government.[32] (Subsequent discussion of the establishment of soviet organizations will indicate important similarities between the purpose and procedures for establishing the soviets and those of these earlier revolutionary committees.)

It appears that the new political regimes to be constructed in the urban areas would necessarily be fairly diverse bodies, representative of the several trades, professions, and other urban constituencies that made up the county or city, and would take considerable time to form. In the villages, political power would be centralized in one broad organization, and given the simplicity of this arrangement it could presumably be elected rather quickly. It is not clear from this guidance, however, how this rural structure was to relate to the urban-based system. These relationships are more clearly defined in the policy discussions of the proposed soviet system that took place late in 1927 and in the spring of 1928.

Regarding both urban and rural operational planning, the political guidance from the conference emphasized caution in implementing revolutionary activities. It explained that "insurrection is an art and not something that one can play with and it should be carried out with the greatest of care and with complete preparations—technical, organizational and political—made beforehand."[33] Ideally, key decisions such as whether to launch an insurrection in an area and what would be the best timing were to be based on an objective, Marxist-Leninist appraisal of the local and general conditions that would impinge on its success. As we will see, during the succeeding months the implementation of the revolutionary program developed at this conference heightened tensions and conflict between the Party Central, adhering to the official political line, and those in the field, confronting chaotic, dangerous, and often unique local conditions.

Organizational Guidelines

Qu Qiubai introduced three major resolutions at the conference concerning Party organization, the recent peasant movement, and the recent labor movement. The Party organizational policies reflected the immediate transitional stage in that while Party leaders were now seeking to build a strong, independent organizational apparatus, Party organs still were required to function under the banner of the KMT and to concentrate on including participation from low-level KMT members in the new urban and rural revolutionary governments described above. The KMT imprimatur and participation remained essential components of the plans for revolution.

To support the Party Central in Hankou, the "Resolutions on Party Organization" required the establishment of a publications committee and an authoritative Party journal. The Northern Bureau in Hebei, the influential Shanghai Committee, and the Southern Bureau in Guangdong were to cooperate in efficient dissemination of Party directives and Communist propaganda materials. A secret communications organ was to build a network to perform the strategic function of providing various levels of the apparatus with needed intelligence information concerning the strength and activities of the opposition and existing conditions in different places. In addition, with the mounting KMT pressures aimed at exposing and destroying CCP personnel and organizations, the need to develop and implement security procedures became a matter of pressing concern. As the resolutions, passed on August 7, stated: "The most urgent organization problem now facing the Party is formation of solid, hard-fighting, secret Party organs."[34]

Organizational guidance describing Party organs below the senior levels displayed two notable characteristics. First, the guidance was rudimentary and preliminary, especially when compared with resolutions (to be discussed) developed later in 1927. Second, it revealed again the urban bias of the Communist leadership. Emphasis was given to the establishment of Party branch organs at the provincial, municipal, county, and district levels. Branches at each of these levels were to be organized secretly and a standing committee of three to eight members elected to supervise the functions of the branch. Each level was to follow strict Party discipline by abiding by the political guidance and organizational decisions originating at higher levels, including the approval or disapproval of the leadership composition of the branch standing committees. The importance of secrecy in branch organizations and operations was noted as indispensable.

The urban orientation of this guidance is indicated by several features. Party branches were to be organized only down to the district level, with Party leadership in small cities and towns being selected by the district branch membership. There was no mention of a village Party branch organ, as there would be later. Further, the importance of establishing cells, operating under Party branch supervision, in the trade unions was discussed, but nothing was said about Party organs in peasant associations or comparable rural organizations. Also, in stressing the need to screen and strengthen the membership of the branch organizations, the resolutions called only for upgrading worker members into the leadership ranks and weeding out "opportunist" elements.

According to the "Resolution on the Recent Peasant Struggle," Party and Youth League organizers were to be sent out to key provinces to prepare for "systematic, planned peasant insurrections, organized on as wide a scale as possible," particularly during the forthcoming harvest season when the peasantry would have increased economic and political leverage in their local areas.[35] Although such uprisings were to be carried out under the slogan of transferring all political power in the villages to the peasant associations, the vague but essentially moderate Party policies were not designed to bring about that result immediately. The guidance stipulated that "the land of large and middle landlords should be confiscated and distributed to poor peasants. Small landlords should be forced to lower their rents."[36] The Party's moderate stance regarding small landholders was grounded in calculated expediency: "this is based on the strategy of neutralizing the small capitalists and small landlords whose power is much larger than their numbers would indicate."[37] Recognizing the extensive influence of small landlords, the Party did not intend to alienate their possible support or, more likely, provoke their violent reaction through blanket land confiscations. Also the Communists had far fewer trained cadres with established influence than necessary for supervising extensive changes in landholding arrangements.

During the Nanchang Uprising and retreat southward, rebel leaders coping with actual conditions and events had to define in concrete numbers the acceptable levels of landholdings. The Party leadership at this policy and planning conference used their categories without numerical definitions. Mao, on the other hand, in one speech called for a 50-*mu* limit, above which all lands would be confiscated. He stressed the need to develop different regulations for different levels of landholding (self-cultivators, middle peasants, etc.), presumably to clarify and standardize rural organization work. He also said the peasants should be treated more like brothers than outsiders and that the Party should formulate a strategy on armed struggle rather than just require its use.[38]

Mao stressed the essential need for solid military support for the forthcoming Autumn Harvest Uprisings, using his famous phrase that political power comes from the barrel of a gun. He recommended that the conference and the new Politburo pay close attention to use of an organized military as it related to armed struggle. The conference guidance, however, focused on building military support for revolutionary activities from among the troops and noncommissioned officers of KMT armies. Any deserting KMT forces could provide essential support for strengthening the left-wing forces and constitute the basis for constructing a disciplined revolutionary army. Rather than developing a strategy for armed struggle, the guidance stressed finding ways to acquire arms for worker and peasant supporters.[39] As for Mao's points concerning military affairs and the land and peasant questions, Lominadze reportedly refused any further discussion of these matters.[40]

In sum, the August 7 conference, occurring at a time when the Party was on the verge of collapse, provided leadership and outlined a new course for the surviving membership to follow. The program, which still lacked much concrete guidance, emphasized armed, Communist-directed, workers' and peasants' insurrections, which if successful would include the development of new political forms—the revolutionary committees and ultimately the soviets.

Party leaders, not without considerable resistance, accepted the Comintern's direction to continue to work under the KMT flag and with lower-level KMT members, but at the same time they set down resolutions for developing and strengthening an independent and now clandestine Party apparatus. Limitations in its formulations were serious, in that they gave only vague and preliminary guidance for establishing disciplined Party organs that were expected to go into action immediately. There was no discussion of Party organs at the village level, even though the Party according to the new political platform was to have as a principal goal the organization and preparation of armed peasant uprisings. The key question of how to relate military support to the peasants' struggle for land was overlooked.

Finally, the Party leadership cautioned members always to make thorough and careful preparations for their work among the masses, especially in preparing and carrying out an insurrection. But to an important degree, this realistic counsel for a measured approach conflicted with the underlying but pervasive current of feeling apparent in CCP writings at this time and demonstrated during the Nanchang Uprising, that is, the desire to strike out and punish the bourgeois KMT for its numerous atrocities against the CCP. Zhou Enlai related that after the failure of the First United Front, "some of our people became indignant, vengeful and desperate. This was one of the factors giving rise to putschism."[41] Further, Lominadze's overly optimistic analysis of the Chinese revolution as following a continuous and "unceasing" process toward realizing socialism predisposed a radical approach by leadership cadres.

The policies and guidance developed at the August 7 conference provided a basis for action during the following months and also were preliminary to the eventual development of new Communist organizational forms, such as the soviets, a comprehensive Communist strategy entailing the mobilization of mass support, and other key tactics and procedures. On the negative side, the shortcomings of the policies, some of which were noted by conference participants, were at the root of the failures and disruptions that the Communists experienced during the Autumn Harvest Uprisings of 1927.

Chapter 4. The Autumn Harvest Uprisings

Implementing the political program developed at the August 7 conference required resolving several key issues that still eluded the central leadership in Hankou. Most important, what kind and degree of military organization might effectively support uprising activities and protect any successes? What specific terms of land revolution might be used to stimulate and also channel the peasant movement? Finally, a comprehensive strategy had to be formulated to integrate and coordinate Party urban and rural organizational work with uprisings and their essential military components, while taking into consideration the varying local operating conditions.

These were pressing matters that Party organizers sent to the field had to confront almost immediately in their attempt to build a full-fledged, Communist-led movement. As we will see, they dealt substantially only with the first issue, and their actions brought them into direct conflict with the Hankou leadership. Cadres sent to the field to direct the Autumn Harvest Uprisings found the military aspects of their circumstances to be the most obvious and urgent. Conflict developed over their attempts to organize substantial military power to fulfill the radical plans, and the Party Central's demand that they rely instead on the masses as the main element in an uprising.

Hankou's policy unrealistically called for organized revolts directed eventually at capturing key cities, with assigned regular military units playing only a supporting role. Adherence to this course brought inevitable failure, and cadres directing the uprisings, particularly Mao Zedong and Peng Gongda, managed to survive only by exploring military policies and solutions more attuned to the desperate local conditions. Hankou's failure to grasp the significance of these emerging developments, which was to be borne out by future field experience, reflected a central leadership committed to general policies and responsive to Comintern direction, but as yet inexperienced at integrating field information and findings into an ongoing policy process. Thus Hankou continued to overlook the central point that, without a lengthy period of Party mass-organizing work, substantial military support was mandatory, especially when uprising targets were garrisoned cities.

Operational Planning

While the August 7 Conference produced the general policy guidelines for agrarian revolution, specific plans aimed at directly challenging KMT authority through rural revolution had been in the making since early June 1927, in the form of the "Resolution on Hunan and Hubei." This document, drafted in response to Stalin's telegram of June 1, was also inspired by the successes of Communist rural organizers working in Hunan and Hubei following the launching of the Northern Expedition and afterward by the quality of peasant resistance during the Hunan May 21 incident.

Additional deliberations took place at the important July 26 Party meeting, which considered four provinces (Hunan, Hubei, Jiangxi, and Guangdong) as being a potential field for the development of insurrectionary activities and, most important, linked prospects for success to support and leadership from military forces. As has been shown, the Nanchang Uprising on August 1 marshaled considerable military support but lacked a working insurrectionary program to deal with situations encountered. Because the Nanchang rebels remained separated from Party Headquarters, their experience and resolutions regarding the implementation of their essentially ad hoc policies were not available for consideration in the ongoing efforts to develop a comprehensive operational program. Rather, certain preliminary plans, based on conditions in Hubei and Hunan and including slogans and an action program, were examined by the new leadership at the August 7 Conference and became important to the development of a general operational program for Autumn Harvest insurrections.[1]

The central leadership led by Qu Qiubai decided that agrarian revolution was to be realized through insurrections carried out on as wide a scale as possible during the autumn harvest season. Although initially limited to the forced confiscation of land from large and middle landlords and the reduction of small landlords' rents, the ultimate goal of the insurrections was to realize "the universal slogan of 'land to the tillers,' carry out the nationalization of the land, and proceed to the redistribution of land."[2]

While the ultimate success or failure of the uprisings would be determined by the Communists' ability to organize a nationwide insurrection to overthrow the central government, Party leaders recognized that under the existing uneven conditions within the provinces, more limited policies were required initially. Since some provinces were more advanced in their revolutionary experience and development than others, Party organizers were to use as a starting point those provinces that had already become centers of the peasant movement for organizing armed insurrections.[3] Again, the four provinces Hunan, Hubei, Jiangxi, and Guangdong were recognized as the most favorable for initiating this work.[4]

Jiangxi Province eventually was eliminated from the planning because it became evident during the course of the Nanchang rebels' Southern Expedition that Jiangxi lacked the substantial Party organization and developing mass movement essential for carrying out an Autumn Harvest uprising. In addition, the insurrection in Guangdong never materialized, although not for want of leadership or some mass preparations. Rather, it seems that the Guangdong Provincial Committee decided to delay their uprising activities and await support from the retreating Nanchang armies. With the defeat of those troops at Tangkeng, prospects for a Guangdong uprising quickly vanished. Thus only Hunan and Hubei became principal sites of the fall uprisings.

A crucial feature of the operational planning was the conviction that, while careful and thorough preparations were to precede the launching of an uprising, once a plan was adopted, "there is absolutely no half-way abandonment of such a plan; insurrections must be led to the very end; they must be carried out with courage and boldness without turning back...."[5] Thus the August 7 leaders regarded the adoption of an insurrection plan as setting in motion an inexorable process leading to the realization of their rural program. Just as they understood the transformation of the bourgeois-democratic revolution into a socialist revolution to be a "continuous, unceasing process," and the course of land revolution as beginning with controlled confiscation but culminating in "land to the tillers," they saw the adoption of an uprising plan as requiring adherence to and completion of all the points included therein. This very rigid and doctrinaire approach placed enormous pressure and responsibility on those charged with implementing the Autumn Harvest plans after they were adopted. Given the beleaguered state of the Party organization at this time, and its lack of experience in mobilizing a broad rural movement, it would have been nothing short of miraculous had the fall uprisings fulfilled those lofty aims.

Mao Zedong and the Party Central Differ

Concrete plans for the Autumn Harvest insurrections were not made final until late August. In the meantime, the Party Central dispatched key cadres to the provinces to begin preparing for insurrections. Mao Zedong was sent to Hunan Province. There he entered into a dialogue with the Party Central in Hankou concerning basic aspects of the Party's general insurrectionary program. At a meeting with members of the Hunan Provincial Party Committee on August 18, Mao proposed major alterations to the Party's operational strategy, assuming a stance more radical than Party Central. These changes were contained in a letter dated August 20 from Mao to the Party Central.[6]

Rural conditions in Hunan seemed to radicalize Mao. After consultations with peasants and observations of rural conditions in "two countrysides" of the province, Mao decided that the confiscation of land should be in no way limited but should entail all lands, "including the land belonging to the small landlords and owner-peasants, for public ownership."[7] Furthermore, Mao viewed China as having long ago reached its equivalent of the Russian 1917 situation and as therefore entirely suitable for the establishment of "soviets of workers, peasants, and soldiers."[8] He advocated the immediate establishment of soviets in the four provinces Guangdong, Hunan, Hubei, and Jiangxi, after which he predicted that a countrywide victory would follow quickly. He also advocated substituting the Communist red flag for the KMT flag when establishing soviets of workers, peasants, and soldiers.[9]

On August 23 the Party Central replied to Mao's letter, with criticism of the above-mentioned three points as well as commentary on the overall plans that the Hunan Party leadership had drawn up for the Autumn Harvest Uprisings to be carried out in the province. The central leadership declared that objectively China had not reached a 1917 situation or the conditions of a proletarian socialist revolution, and therefore Party leaders should continue to work under the Left KMT banner, not to establish soviets, but to develop "the democratic political power of the workers and peasants."[10] Regarding the land question, the Party leadership instructed that the "main slogan at this time" was to confiscate only substantial landholdings. Policy toward small landlords required only rent reductions. In other words, Party leaders restated their position on the land question contained in the "Resolution on the Political Tasks and Policy of the CCP" produced after the August 7 conference.

Commenting on other aspects of the Hunan plans, the Party Central noted that although the city of Changsha was a proper starting point for insurrectionary activity, the Hunan leadership was placing too much emphasis on the need for outside military force to seize this key city. In so doing, Hunan leaders were not placing sufficient emphasis on leading and organizing peasant uprisings in the districts surrounding Changsha. The Hunan Party was warned that such a course would result "in a kind of military adventure," and Mao's plans for an August 30 uprising beginning in Changsha were ordered to be canceled.[11]

The focus on Changsha, Party Central claimed, had also caused the Hunan Party to neglect organizing uprisings in the more southern Hunan counties (Xiangtan, Liuyang, Liling, Xiangxiang, and Ningxiang). In addition, uprising activities in Hunan were to be coordinated with those taking place in Hubei Province. Prior to the uprisings, the Hunan apparatus was to disperse its members to work among the worker and peasant masses in order to clarify the purpose and goals of the Autumn Harvest Uprisings and to prepare carefully for their initiation.

Mao made a brief but forceful reply to the Party Central's points. In a letter dated August 30, he contended that an uprising in Changsha, which he planned to begin on August 30, would mark "the starting point" of the Autumn Harvest Uprisings.[12] Because he judged the strength of the workers and peasants in the area surrounding Changsha to be "deficient," he maintained that it was mandatory for the two regiments requested in his August 20 letter to lead and accomplish the capture of Changsha. Although Mao gave the preponderant role to regular military forces, he was careful to phrase this as follows: "while we plan the main combative force to capture Ch'angsha to be the workers and peasants, we are going to dispatch a certain two regiments to storm Ch'angsha. . . .'"[13] Mao believed that to seize political power, the peasants needed the support of at least one or two armed regiments.[14] Indeed, Mao claimed that to act otherwise was to misunderstand the conditions in Hunan—a charge he made against the Party Central.

The issue in dispute between Mao and the Party Central leadership was the extent and kind of military support to accompany any mass uprising—a key matter that was still only partially understood and vaguely addressed within Party circles. Mao apparently envisioned the well-protected provincial capital of Changsha as the starting point of the uprisings and thus realistically determined the need for regular military troops, acting under the cover of worker and peasant agitation, to realize the goal of capturing Changsha. The Party Central, on the other hand, advocated the use of organized, propagandized, and armed workers and peasants as the basis for Autumn Harvest Uprisings. Existing peasant self-defense forces were to be used as a basis for arming and organizing a rural military force. Regular military units or bandit forces were to act only as auxiliaries to this main uprising force, organized in several counties. Hankou cautioned that to put regular forces at the head of the uprising was to engage in a military adventure.

What must have made the Party Central's position appear untenable to those like Mao who were charged with implementing the uprising plans was that whatever forces were available in Hunan had to be mobilized to seize the well-guarded provincial capital with only about two weeks of preparation time. Furthermore, the uprising plans were to be followed strictly and, once begun, could not be dropped or even changed because of unfavorable circumstances. Working with limited time and a formidable target, it is not surprising that Mao proposed to focus all existing strength in central Hunan. Accordingly, the Hunan Provisional Party Committee instructed forces in the counties of southern Hunan only to be ready to respond to the major events that were to occur in Changsha.

The Party Central responded again to the Hunan leadership. In a letter dated September 5 it reviewed Mao's letter and an oral report on conditions in Hunan, both delivered to Party Central by an individual "in charge of the Provincial Committee," probably Peng Gongda, the Hunan Party secretary.[15] Again the conflict centered on tactics and emphasis. Mao's charge that "not to pay attention to the military and yet to have the people stage an armed uprising are a contradictory policy" was forcefully refuted. The Party Central emphasized that "the people" were to be mainly peasants, armed and mobilized throughout the province. The importance of the two regiments of regular forces requested by Mao was denied emphatically. By concentrating on regular military forces, the Hunan leadership was accused of having let slip many opportunities "to develop uprisings among the peasants," including those in southern Hunan. Preparations in southern Hunan were considered essential to broadening the base of support for any uprising that might arise in central Hunan. Otherwise, the latter could not be sustained and would likely be quickly suppressed.

The Hunan Party leadership was further reprimanded in this letter for having "cast doubts on the Central's policy" regarding "the question of political power," the KMT, and land confiscation. Hunan leaders were instructed to follow the Party Central's resolutions absolutely and with no vacillation. The letter also notes that the recently completed "Central's Uprising Plan of Hunan and Hubei" had been sent to Hunan after the Party's previous correspondence of August 23 in order to correct the faulty tactics and emphasis on regular military forces and to serve as the further guide to action.

The Final Uprising Plan

The Party Central provided a full statement of its position concerning the operational purpose, strategy, and tactics of the Autumn Harvest Uprisings in this "Uprising Plan of Hunan and Hubei," which it sent to Mao.[16] According to the final plan, both provinces were fully ripe for insurrectionary activity. Party leaders in Hunan and Hubei were to use the land revolution to incite workers and peasants to carry out an insurrection aimed at overthrowing the Wuhan KMT government and replacing it with a "truly revolutionary political power of the common people."[17] The plan thus limited the initial target to the Hubei-based Wuhan regime of Wang Jingwei and General Tang Shengzhi—not Chiang Kai-shek's Nanjing government.

The increasing radicalism of the Party Central is reflected in its statement that in order to ensure the "unrelenting progress" of the revolution, the land program was to be "thoroughgoing" and include confiscation of "the land belonging to the big and middle landlords," resulting eventually in the confiscation of all lands.[18] In the course of implementing the agrarian program, all the "local bullies," bad gentry, and other reactionaries were to be killed, their property confiscated, and political power in the villages turned over to the peasant associations, while power in the cities would be turned over to the popularly elected revolutionary committees. Regarding the opposing military forces that were bound to resist these actions, the Party Central boldly instructed that these forces be completely annihilated, apparently by the unlikely means of being drowned in a sea of armed, rioting workers and peasants.

The strategy for realizing these ambitious goals was sketched only briefly in the plan. Initial preparations for the desired uprising were to begin in the villages "remote from the cities" and thus presumably safer from retaliatory pressures. In these remote regions, those such as gentry and landlords holding political power were to be killed. Rural support was to be mobilized through peasant mass rallies and various kinds of propaganda based on provocative slogans such as "Rise in revolt to give land to the tillers," and "Rise in revolt to return all political power to the peasant association." Other slogans called for the overthrow of the Wuhan government, resistances to rents, taxes, and levies, and the "destruction of landlords and other powerholders." The expectation was that these preparations would set the spark for a vast uprising targeted against the key city in the rural region.

According to the plan, in the course of this uprising local power holders were to be destroyed and replaced by the new political regime, the Revolutionary Committee. When this occurred in several regions of the two provinces, ultimately power would change hands throughout both provinces, thus setting the stage for the realization of a nationwide Communist revolution. The achievement of this final objective would produce the Revolutionary Committee of China. In the meantime, the uprisings in Hunan and Hubei were to be organized under the name of the "Hunan and Hubei Sub-Committee of the Revolutionary Committee of China."

From their vantage point in Hankou, the central authorities had much to say in the plan about what they saw as the proper role of the military in the course of carrying out uprisings. Their basic policy was stated succinctly: "the land revolution must depend upon the true mass strength of the peasants. Troops and bandits are no more than an auxiliary force of the peasant revolution."[19] Regular military forces were not to play the leading role, nor were organized peasant forces to expect the regular military units to begin the uprising. Instead, the spontaneous flood of peasant uprising would receive the backing of regular military units, to an ever-increasing degree as more successful uprisings were accomplished, causing more support to be mobilized in favor of revolutionary objectives. As the uprisings came to include key cities, which in the plan was to happen quickly, and ultimately the provincial capital, well-armed main-force military units would be dispatched to deal with the opposition forces entrenched in those cities.

Regarding the development of military forces, prior to the initiation of uprising activities worker pickets in the cities were to serve as the basis for developing the Workers' Revolutionary Army, while in rural areas the Peasants' Self-Defense Corps was to be organized into the Peasants' Revolutionary Army. When acting collectively, these two armies were to be known as the Workers' and Peasants' Revolutionary Army.

Policy statements in the plan regarding other existing military forces reflected a note of caution. Any sympathetic bandit forces were to be placed under the control of the peasant associations of the revolutionary committees and become part of the auxiliary military forces participating in insurrections. After the uprising, and no doubt depending upon their performance in it, bandit forces were to be reorganized and presumably assimilated into the Peasants' Revolutionary Army.

An even more cautious attitude was to be displayed toward existing regular armies that remained neutral in conflicts between the forces involved in Communist uprisings and opposing armies. An aggressive approach might be taken to propagandizing among their troops and to taking advantage of the uprising opportunities afforded by their commanders' neutrality. However, in dealings with these neutral commanders the Communists were cautioned not to compromise their basic revolutionary goals in order to attract military commitment or support. Past experience had indicated that these alliances often were temporary and based on commanders' jockeying for a more favorable position.

Perhaps the plan's most striking feature, and the aspect that best displayed the attitude and temper of the Party Central at this time, concerned the matter of initiating and pursuing the uprisings. Already the uprisings in Hunan and Hubei were said to have lost ground by failing to capitalize in a timely fashion on the existing peasant unrest. But while this was considered unfortunate, it was not prohibitive. Rather, the several uprisings within the two provinces were to begin immediately and to fulfill each stage of development resolutely and without hesitation. This was to be true even if conditions developed that caused one area of uprising to lose contact and therefore valuable opportunities for coordination with other uprising areas. As the instructions related, "Even if, after the uprising broke out, contacts were cut off with various places, we should carry on, as planned, unrelenting attack on the unsuccessful points as well as the successful points."[20]

As will be shown, this kind of dangerous and unreasonable rigidity concerning the implementation of the uprising plan, requiring total compliance regardless of the obstacles or conditions encountered, was at the heart of the plan's eventual failure. Only after the string of failed uprisings during the fall of 1927 and the disastrous Guangzhou Uprising in December did the central leadership begin to emphasize the critical importance of taking into consideration existing local conditions, including the nature and strength of encountered resistance, and making necessary adjustments in timing and in degree of support while planning and directing the course of uprising activities. This realization became evident in the discussion of Party Central planning by early 1928.

The operational plan provided to guide the progress of the fall uprisings in Hunan directed that the action was to take place in three main regions surrounding key county seats. Following the strategy contained in the plan and discussed above, developments in the southern region were to include laying the foundations for unleashing the insurrection first in the remote villages. Then the forces mobilized at this initial stage were to be used to attack the townships in the several counties included in the southern uprising regions. Next, the increasingly mobilized forces produced at this stage in the uprising were to be used to attack the important county seat of Hengyang. Preparations for an uprising in Hengyang were directed to begin on September 5.

In eastern Hunan, the same procedures were to be followed by three separate groupings of counties, with the emerging mobilized forces to be focused on initiating an uprising on September 10 "with Ch'angsha as the center."[21] On the same date the western region was to stage an uprising aimed at taking Changde.

The Party Central envisaged that the uprising activity in those three major regions would produce a mobilized force that then could, with the additional support of military units from Tan Xing (a pro-Communist KMT officer), dispatch its "main force" to attack the provincial capital of Changsha, where forces from within the city were scheduled to rise up on September 12 or 13. The result would be the overthrow of the Hunan Provincial Government and the establishment of a "Hunan Provincial Provisional Revolutionary Government."[22] In the meantime, some of the newly mobilized forces were supposed to stay behind and maintain the security of the insurrection in the uprising regions.

The Party Central's operational plan for Hubei divided the province into seven uprising regions. The action was to begin on September 10 in the southern Hubei region. At the same time uprisings were to be staged in central and western Hubei, which, when coordinated with the southern region, would become "an independent uprising base" to threaten Wuhan as well as Changsha in Hunan.[23]

It was hoped that an uprising could be launched in the northern region on September 10 and be supported by another pro-Communist KMT officer, Zhang Zhaofeng, who was currently operating in south-western Hunan province and supporting with two regiments the insurrection in north Hubei. If the insurrection in western Hubei were carried out successfully, Zhang would have the opportunity to move on Wuhan, where a large uprising "or at least a big riot also should be developing."[24] In the event that both the western and central Hubei uprisings were successful, Zhang's forces were to move down into Hunan or return to northern Hubei. Finally, after central, western, and northern Hubei all had unleashed uprisings, concerted attention was to be given to eastern Hubei and the Peking-Hankou Railway regions. The question remains as to how these rigidly timed, grandiose plans actually were implemented in Hubei and Hunan.

The Plans in Practice: Hubei and Hunan

The uprisings in Hubei were to be directed by a Special Committee sent out to each of the uprising regions and operated under the general supervision of the Hubei Provincial Party Committee.[25] While Hubei had been divided into seven uprising regions, only one—the southern region including the six counties just south of Wuhan—became the locus of significant uprising activity. Still, this region was strategically important because it controlled the railroad and waterway traffic between Changsha and Wuhan and thus had the potential for influencing both Hubei and Hunan, as was called for in the central plan.

The south Hubei region faced serious obstacles to carrying out even the preparatory stage for launching the uprisings. First, the Party organization there consisted of only some two hundred members, and even those were not considered reliable. Second, the region's peasant movement was weak and not well armed. Reportedly, there were less than three hundred available firearms divided unevenly among the peasant associations in the six counties when the uprising was scheduled to begin. To compensate for those crucial shortcomings in manpower and armed peasant support, the Special Committee looked around for reliable supporting allies, but again met with unfavorable conditions. Unlike other regions of Hubei, secret society strength was low in south Hubei and unsympathetic. In addition, other military units, such as the so-called "ragtag armies" in the region, were not responsive to the Special Committee.[26]

The operational plan called for the actual uprising to begin with the two well-protected county seats, Puqi and Xianning, after preparations for this stage had been made in the outlying villages. Inasmuch as the necessary armed peasant support did not exist to carry out even this preparatory stage, the prospects for mustering adequate forces for capturing the county seats by September 10 must have seemed dim indeed to those on the Special Committee. They thus took the logical step of requesting support for taking Puqi and Xianning from regular military forces thought to be still under Communist control. They also attempted to find local military allies. The Provincial Committee responded by branding their request for troops as opportunism and evidence of their lack of faith in the masses. Local morale must have plummeted even further when Hubei Provincial Party Secretary Luo Yinong paid a visit to the Special Committee just three days before the insurrection was to begin and issued an order for a purge of the local insurrectionary organization.

Despite these substantial problems, which were further compounded by a last-minute withdrawal of support by certain Party-controlled military units in the area, the insurrection was launched two days early—on September 8. On that date the opportunity arose to ambush a train heading for Changsha that carried weapons and a large amount of Chinese dollars being shipped from Wuhan to cover local militarists' expenses in Changsha. The insurrectionists succeeded in seizing the money and weapons, but they permitted the train to proceed on to Changsha, thus allowing the enemy authorities in Hunan to know of the insurrectionary incident within hours.

Most important, the Communists failed to take the two county seats early on in the uprising. Not surprisingly, their hastily mobilized forces were simply no match for the regular garrison forces (particularly in Puqi) protecting these towns. Under the circumstances, the insurrectionists had no choice but to retreat into the countryside. On September 12 they established a revolutionary government in the small mountain town of Xikeng in Tongshan county. This body probably became the first independent state organ established by the Chinese Communists in the remote countryside.[27]

Finally, one more dogged attempt by the insurrectionists to seize a county town—albeit of lesser stature than Puqi or Xianning—resulted in tragedy, with the whole Special Committee leadership falling victim to the treacherous machinations of a wily local commander. The Special Committee was dispersed, bringing the insurrection effort in Hubei to a close.

The course of events in Hunan entailed similar obstacles and defeats. Hunan had been the locus of significant peasant activity during the course of the Northern Expedition. It is well known that the young Mao made his famous observations about the powerful potential of the peasantry after his investigations of the rural scene in Hunan in early 1927. However, during the course of the May 21 Incident, the Party organizations active in rural organization work in Hunan were severely damaged. They were only barely restored in mid-August when Mao was sent by the central leadership to begin preparations for launching the Autumn Harvest Uprisings.[28]

The Party Central's operational plan called for uprisings in twenty-four counties in the three uprising regions of southern, western, and eastern Hunan. As it happened, only the eastern region, and within it some seven counties situated in close proximity to the provincial capital Changsha, became the scene of the uprising. Four military units or regiments were readied for action by the first week in September. The Hunan Provincial Party Committee designated these forces as the 1st Division of the First Army of the Chinese Workers' and Peasants' Revolutionary Army. Initially, the overall commander of these insurrectionary forces was Lu Deming, with You Shaidu as deputy commander; both commanders were Communists. The first and core regiment, often referred to as the Lu Deming regiment, originated as a garrison regiment attached to Zhang Fakui's Second Front Army in Wuhan and included more than one thousand troops. After several mutinies in the field, however, You Shaidu assumed command of the Lu Deming regiment and formed an alliance with other local forces. These forces, which became the division's second regiment, were made up of a "ragtag army" commanded by the former bandit Qiu Guoxuan. The third regiment, commanded by Su Xianjun, was made up of local recruits attached to the Pingxiang-Liling Self-Defense Corps. Many of these recruits were nonpeasant rural inhabitants with ties to local secret societies. The fourth regiment, under Wang Xingya, included mainly unemployed miners of the Anyuan-Pingxiang region of Jiangxi.[29]

The final plans called for the four regiments to engage in pincer blows against the county seats of Pingjiang and Liuyang on September 11. Just prior to this action Party organizers were to stir up the peasantry in the countryside around Changsha. Then on September 15, when the satellite towns had been taken and the rural masses were in revolt, the attack on Changsha could begin with the expectation that the city would fall into Communist hands the next day.[30]

The fourth or Anyuan regiment launched its march on Pingxiang, just west of Anyuan, on schedule. Failing to seize that well-protected county seat, it moved on up the rail line and succeeded in taking Liling on September 12. The capture of Liling was preceded, and presumably aided, by peasant uprisings in the nearby countryside, and once the city was taken, the Anyuan forces followed through by establishing a revolutionary committee, announcing a land program, and restoring the labor unions and peasant associations. Also, Zhuzhou, an important town on the railway to Changsha, was temporarily captured by Communists armed with only sixty rifles. A sense of panic arose in Changsha by September 13. The revolutionary tide appeared to be moving in the Communists' favor.

But the events of the next few days seriously set back the Communist efforts in Hunan. In the course of responding to the Hunan Provincial Committee's call to attack Pingjiang, the county seat north of Changsha, the combined forces of the first and second regiments met with disaster when the second "ragtag" regiment mutinied on September 15, causing heavy losses to the first regiment. This serious blow to the military capability of the Autumn Harvest forces was further compounded when on the same day efforts to bring about the desired peasant uprisings in the countryside surrounding Changsha failed.

The Hunan Provincial Committee, responding to these events as well as to misinformation about the current status of the Anyuan regiment, made the independent decision on the evening of September 15 to cancel the Changsha insurrection scheduled to take place the following day. During the next two days the third and fourth regiments, having failed to coordinate their drive on the county seat of Liuyang, found their forces isolated and surrounded. Survivors from the first regiment under You Shaidu and the third regiment retreated to the mountain town Wenjiashi in Liuyang county bordering Jiangxi Province. There they held a Front Committee meeting to review and discuss the recent failures.[31]

In this protected setting they were joined by Mao Zedong, who had been captured by local police after departing Changsha to join his troops. Mao only barely escaped execution at the hands of his captors and had completely missed the military phase of the Hunan insurrection of the preceding days.[32] Nevertheless, based on his observations and review of the Autumn Harvest Uprising in Hunan, Mao concluded that when confronted with powerful enemy forces, insisting on attacking a large city is like "knocking an egg against a rock, it is self-annihilation."[33] Rather, he stressed, the Communist military forces under those circumstances should retreat to the countryside where the enemy strength is weakest and conserve their revolutionary power.

Mao also raised the issue of the need to establish a base area to aid the pursuit of armed struggle and land revolution. He stressed that, backed by a secure base, armed forces might maintain the fluid operating style essential to support these revolutionary activities. Lands seized could be better protected and the peasants better mobilized.

Mao had critics at this Front Committee meeting who charged him with displaying a "mountain king" (*shan dawang*) attitude by advocating the establishment of a base area in the middle part of the Luoxiao Mountains. Mao retorted simply that indeed he intended to be a mountain king—a Red mountain king of an armed base area.[34] On September 19 Mao and the Hunan Front Committee overruled You Shaidu's defense of the Party Central's order to continue the attack on Changsha. Instead, Mao began a retreat southward toward the Jinggang Mountains on the Hunan-Jiangxi border.

On the same day that Mao was leading the retreating troops south, the Party Central met to revise the policy guidance developed at the August 7 Conference regarding working with the revolutionary KMT and establishing soviets. In a crucial decision they confirmed Moscow's conjecture that it might not be possible "to revolutionize the Kuomintang" and convert it into a mass organization.[35] They therefore directed Party organs to move beyond propagandizing the idea of soviets to the higher stage of establishing soviets, under the CCP's own banner. Just over a week later *Pravda*, hailing several temporary successes in China as evidence of a new revolutionary upsurge, ratified the CCP's policy of establishing soviets.[36] Following the Comintern's lead, the Party Central specified that soviets were to be established first in key cities "when we are sure of a decisive and firm victory."[37] Ironically, Changsha was named as one of those "key places," along with Guangzhou.

Thus on September 19, as Mao was heading south, the Party Central sent a brief message to the Hunan leaders condemning the Provincial Committee's decision of September 15 to cancel the uprising in Changsha for the following day. It based its position on a report dated September 16 from the Comintern adviser Ma Kefu, who was in Hunan trying to direct the insurrection.[38] "Comrade Ma" expressed bitter frustration over the cancellation of the Changsha uprising and accused the Hunan leadership of cowardly actions and falling into panic under conditions that were not all that unfavorable to a successful outcome. Ma was particularly severe in his appraisal of Hunan Secretary Peng Gongda, whom he charged with cowardice and deception. In two letters to the Hunan Provincial Committee on September 16 and 17, Ma directed the Hunan leaders to make immediate preparations for a prompt attack on Changsha in order to halt the ongoing retreat. In one revealing statement Ma made the accusation that the provincial leaders were basing their actions "entirely on the given situations as they arise at the moment" rather than, as he obviously preferred, implementing according to rigid schedule the plan for the Hunan uprising.[39]

In response to Ma's report the Party Central directed the Hunan authorities to mobilize their forces "to storm Ch'angsha on the one hand and to erupt immediately an uprising in Ch'angsha on the other."[40] In addition, Party leaders dispatched Ren Bishi to Hunan to see that the original uprising plan was faithfully carried out without any vacillation and to thoroughly investigate the recent actions. The outcome was that Ren arrived in Hunan, called an emergency meeting of the Provincial Committee, and apparently reorganized it.[41] But beyond this Party reorganization and investigation work, there was little Ren could do to reverse the collapsing situation in Hunan.

The Postmortem

Ren's findings in Hunan became part of the Party's review of the Autumn Harvest Uprisings, which continued throughout October and was formalized at its November plenum. In the Provisional Politburo's "Resolution on Political Discipline" of November 14, Party organizations and leadership in both Hunan and Hubei came in for serious criticism regarding their work in staging uprisings.[42] It was stressed that the Hunan Provincial Committee, even after Peng Gongda was warned about relying excessively on military forces rather than mobilizing the rural masses to lead the uprisings, continued to follow that course and deviate from the uprising plan. With this overemphasis on contacting "local bandits and a handful of motley troops," the Hunan leaders had neglected to develop a land program that could win over peasant support. Similarly, they had failed to destroy the local "village bosses and bad gentry" and to educate the rural population concerning new rural political structures.[43]

As punishment for their errors, all the leading Hunan Party officials were dismissed from membership on the Provincial Committee. Both Peng Gongda and Mao Zedong were removed as alternate members on the Provisional Politburo. Peng was even placed on probation or "under surveillance by the Party for half a year."[44]

The Hubei Party leadership fared better at the plenum. The leadership in southern Hubei was credited with having been successful at triggering some rural mass response. However, the Hubei leaders were admonished for displaying "distrust in the peasants" when they decided to cancel the attack on Puqi because in their judgment the peasants lacked weapons and sufficient strength to carry out the action.

The more serious errors were placed with the Northern Hubei Special Committee leadership. The entire committee membership was "given a warning," and its secretary, Lu Chen, was removed as a member of the Central Committee because of Special Committee policies that overlooked or devalued local peasant strength, instead emphasizing cooperation with and manipulation of local military forces.

Qu Qiubai, writing in Moscow at the Sixth CCP Congress during the summer of 1928, reported: "It can be said that the first period after the August 7 Conference was the period of hard labor in the birth of Bolshevism in China."[45] Certainly, one major reason for the hardship was that Party leaders were instructed to carry out ambitious plans for armed revolution with organizations that were still regrouping after the disastrous events of spring and summer 1927. Some organizations, like the Hunan Party, were even undergoing a purge, and all were faced with the obstacle of having now to operate clandestinely. Frequent complaints were lodged with the Party Central concerning the shortage of manpower for carrying out the required rural organizational work, even from the key provinces of Hunan and Hubei.[46] Many available local leaders were uncertain about how to carry out their responsibilities. As the Hubei secretary reported, "Comrades did not know what the struggle was all about...."[47] Even Mao himself claimed that he did not have any experience before the winter of 1927–28 with land revolution.[48] The same kinds of problems plagued the planned harvest uprisings in Jiangxu and Zhejiang, which were quelled before they could begin or just after they started.[49]

The rigid timetables and scenarios for the uprisings placed impossible demands on local cadres. For example, the North Hubei Special Committee was instructed that "even though there might be military changes, under no circumstances should there be changes in the political decision, that is, not to delay the uprising beyond September

12."[50] The point was made repeatedly that the local leadership was not to harbor doubts about the Party Central's instructions and was to execute them to the letter. Lacking in manpower, organization, and experience, local leaders not surprisingly turned to making arrangements with existing military organizations in order to have a chance at implementing the radical uprising plans, especially those that entailed taking key cities. In Hunan, Party leaders viewed the Red Spear organizations as potential allies, while in both Hunan and Hubei, contacts were made with various kinds of military forces, many of which later were found to have more interest in plunder than revolution. This distraction of effort toward forming military alliances provoked the Party Central to charge the local leadership with neglect in organizing the rural masses.

Having limited organizational strength, Party leaders, both at the central and local levels, invested their hopes in a "spontaneous" rising of rural masses, particularly in Hunan and Hubei, once an initial spark could be ignited in the movement.[51] In the absence of careful and extended Party work among the rural populations, however, the masses simply did not respond. The military forces that were to serve as auxiliaries were forced to retreat in the face of overwhelming opposition. In short, the Party Central, under Lominadze's direction, aspired to impossible goals, particularly that of seizing key cities. While Party organizational strength was weak, the opposition forces were formidable, and the Communists still did not understand the proper kind and degree of military force to use in support of agrarian revolution. A workable equation, balancing military strength against thorough and careful mass work, still had to be formulated and matched to the realities of local conditions.

Nevertheless, the Communists gained valuable experience from the Autumn Harvest Uprisings. The establishment of a truly rural government at Xikeng was a forerunner of the soviet governments to come. The concepts of retreat to protected mountainous areas when faced with insurmountable opposition, and formation of base areas, although only just raised at this time and implemented as tactics of last resort, later would become established Communist strategic policy.

Chapter 5. The November Plenum:
Policy Review and Development

The events that accompanied the failed Nanchang and Autumn Harvest Uprisings precipitated a full review of the policies, strategies, and tactics laid down at the August 7 Emergency Conference. To conduct this crucial business the Provisional Politburo met in a special enlarged plenary session November 9–10, 1927, in Shanghai.

The important new developments to emerge at the plenum were, first, the emphasis on Party organizational work at the grass-roots level and integration of lower-level organizations with the top levels of the Party. Eventually this would allow better reporting on actual local conditions to reach and influence senior Party levels. Second was the Party's recognition of the importance of guerrilla activities as an essential component of organized, rural, armed revolution. Guerrilla tactics emerged as the most suitable and effective solution to the pressing question of what kind of military force was essential for backing the program of agrarian revolution. Most important, this finding indicated that the Party Central finally was beginning to integrate the facts and potentialities of local conditions into its otherwise Comintern-dominated policy process.

The authoritative resolutions that resulted from the plenum's sessions included one providing an analysis of the nature and status of the ongoing Chinese revolution and including a general strategy based on that interpretation for its further development; a second addressing the key organizational tasks to be carried out within the Party; a third identifying serious errors committed over the summer and fall and meting out punishments to those responsible; and a fourth requiring the convening of a full Party congress (the sixth) during the first half of March 1928. Finally, the plenum produced a formal resolution on the labor movement. Regarding developments in the country-side, the resulting document was only a "draft program on agrarian problems," to be reviewed and discussed among the Party member-ship and finally referred to the proposed Sixth Party Congress for official clarification and ratification.

Defining the Nature and Future Course of the Chinese Revolution

Those present at the plenum included Qu Qiubai, Li Weihan, Su Zhaocheng, Ren Bishi, Gu Shunzhang, Luo Yinong, Xiang Zhongfa, Zhou Enlai, Zhang Tailei, Li Lisan, Deng Zhongxia, Cai Hesen, Ren Xu, and Comintern representative Lominadze.[1] Notable in their absence were Mao Zedong, who was in the Jinggang Mountains at that time; Peng Pai, who was in south Fujian; and Zhang Guotao, who by his own account remained in hiding in Shanghai from October 1927 to May 1928 and was excluded from Party policymaking circles. After being disciplined for his role in the Nanchang Uprising, Zhang came into sharp disagreement with Qu Qiubai over the Party's uprising policies, which he considered "wrong and harmful."[2] Li Weihan reported that on November 14, just after the plenum, the Provisional Politburo Stand-ing Committee was enlarged from three to five members, with the additions of Zhou Enlai and Luo Yinong. Luo apparently replaced Li Weihan as head of the Organization Bureau that, once established, was supposed to result in the dissolution of the Northern, Southern, and Chang Jiang bureaus.[3]

Policy guidance concerning the proper direction of the Chinese revolution continued to be a major issue in the fierce struggle in Moscow between Trotsky and the leading faction of Bukharin and Stalin. Trotsky's position was deteriorating rapidly in relation to the now firmly entrenched leading faction, but the China issue remained one of the few promising areas left for his maneuver. Bukharin and Stalin continued to espouse the official position, transmitted through the Comintern, that in the stage of bourgeois-democratic revolution, a democratic dictatorship of two classes — the workers and peasants — would lead the Chinese revolution in an unceasing fashion directly to socialism. In contrast, Trotsky writing in September assumed a position to the left of the leading faction, having already telescoped past the stage requiring dictatorship of the proletariat and peasantry to "the task of establishing a dictatorship of the proletariat supported by the rural and urban poor."[4] Trotsky argued that the entire bourgeoisie, after Wang Jingwei's betrayal in July, had become a reactionary force, and stressed that the only hope—and he was still optimistic —was for the Chinese proletariat, under CCP direction, to lead the poor peasants in agrarian revolution and begin to create a revolutionary army.

He defined the agrarian revolution in China as an antibourgeois revolution because of the unique bonds between the bourgeoisie and land ownership. Therefore, the task of agrarian revolution, so central to all revolutionary plans for China, was properly the preserve of the dictatorship of the proletariat and not, as Bukharin maintained, a task for the bourgeois-democratic stage. Summing up, Trotsky pronounced that "the Chinese revolution at its new stage will win as a dictatorship of the proletariat, or it will not win at all."[5]

As an examination of the key resolutions produced at the November plenum will demonstrate, the positions taken by Trotsky and those espoused by Moscow's representative in China Lominadze actually were becoming perilously close—so much so that when the events of the fall were reviewed at the ECCI's Ninth Plenum in February 1928, Lominadze would be accused of having characterized the Chinese revolution as a permanent revolution, a charge associating him with Trotskyism. The following discussion will show the basis for that charge.

At the heart of the problem was how to define the Chinese revolution: as a bourgeois-democratic revolution, even though the bourgeois were no longer recognized key participants, or as a socialist revolution that carried the uneasy burden of having as a principal focus agrarian revolution? The latter, according to Marxist-Leninist theory, was an exclusive goal of a bourgeois-democratic revolution. The November plenum's authoritative "Resolution on the Present Situation and Tasks of the Communist Party," drafted by Lominadze, provided an awkward and rather perilous resolution of this problem by requiring a combination of both categories of revolution.[6] The organized forces of workers and peasants were to take upon themselves the task of the democratic revolution by ridding the country of feudal land relationships, warlordism, and the influences of imperialism. But this phase of the struggle was described as bound to advance beyond the limits of bourgeois democracy and quickly progress to a higher level in which, in urban areas, capital would begin to be eliminated, with worker confiscation and management of the factories, banks, railroads, and so on, thus ushering in the socialist stage of revolution. In accord with the Comintern guidance, the argument that emerged was that a democratic dictatorship of two classes — the workers and peasants — would lead the Chinese revolution directly to socialism.

The basis for this position had been established at the August 7 Conference, but at that time only the national bourgeoisie was identified as "reactionary." The aid of the lower level or petite bourgeoisie still was to be solicited in order to bring about continuous progress toward a bourgeois-democratic revolution — a framework that made familiar Marxist-Leninist concepts and analysis somewhat more applicable. But when it became clear by September that the Party could not win over sufficient or dependable Left KMT support, and thus the Party turned to the new organizational form, the soviet, the need became pressing to revise this theoretical treatment of the Chinese revolution.

Thus the "Resolution on the Present Situation and Tasks of the Communist Party" explained that the Chinese bourgeoisie was not strong enough to carry out the heavy responsibilities of the bourgeois-democratic revolution and would, on acquiring power, turn that authority over again to the more powerful landlord and warlord forces.[7] This argument was used to explain the conflicts and failures leading to the dissolution of the First United Front. Under these circumstances, the revolutionary forces had to move quickly through and beyond the bourgeois-democratic stage toward the more favorable socialist stage. Qu Qiubai explained that this could be accomplished because the bourgeoisie and the feudal landholding interests in China were inseparably linked. Because of this linkage, carrying out the first stage, namely agrarian revolution — a bourgeois-democratic task — necessarily would lead directly to overthrowing the bourgeoisie itself — a socialist obligation.[8] This process was to progress through specific stages, and so far the pace had been exhilarating. In the course of four months the Comintern had gone from a position that first advocated a four-class alliance, including the national bourgeoisie, the petite bourgeoisie, workers, and peasants, to a three-class alliance, and finally one based on workers and peasants only.

The November plenum leadership, under Lominadze's advisement, assessed the continued political chaos in the country and repeated incidences of revolutionary activities, in particular the October peasant uprisings in Jiangxi, Hebei, and Shandong provinces, and concluded optimistically that all of China was in a "direct revolutionary situation."[9] Although he conceded that the duration of the directly revolutionary situation might be measured not in months but possibly years, Lominadze stated that the revolutionary development had the characteristics of "uninterrupted (*wujian duande*) revolution," or what Marx termed a permanent revolution with "no clear demarcation between the democratic and the socialist revolution."[10] In seeming contradiction to the admissions that the directly revolutionary situation might last for years and that the responsibilities of the temporary bourgeois-democratic stage had not been resolved, the Party declared its expectation that the revolution would advance toward socialism "in rapid progress." Further, according to the Party's assessment of immediate prospects, the Chinese revolution "has already transcended the scope of democracy and is progressing rapidly. Inevitably, it will thoroughly resolve its democratic responsibilities and turn quickly toward the socialist path."[11] Qu Qiubai slightly qualified this analysis, however, by emphasizing that although the Chinese revolution was uninterrupted in character, it was not yet purely a socialist revolution, but then it was not a purely democratic revolution either.[12]

In keeping with the projected tone of an uninterrupted and progressive development of the revolution, the immediate goals set at the plenum assumed a radical turn. In the cities bourgeois enterprises were to be subject to seizure and nationalization, with workers put in charge of managing the factories. In addition, bourgeois property might be seized and distributed among the urban poor in order to raise their living standards. In the countryside the position taken under the slogan of "land to the tillers" was "to confiscate all land and distribute it to the poor peasants for cultivation through the Soviet of the peasants." According to the "Draft Resolution on the Land Question," all debts, rents, and tax arrangements were to be abolished and a guaranteed livelihood provided to the old, sick, widowed, and disabled.[13]

In other words, the goals set for the Chinese revolution required that in the cities the workers under Party leadership were to carry out an unrelenting movement toward a socialist revolution. Concurrently, the Communists working in rural areas were to organize and guide a movement aimed at the direct and immediate realization of land revolution to eliminate feudal relationships in the countryside.

Indeed, it is difficult to discern a real difference in substance between Trotsky's conception of the demands of permanent revolution, which included full-scale agrarian revolution, and Lominadze's "uninterrupted revolution," except that the latter made a claim to completing fully concrete stages—at a rapid pace—in the course of making a historic transition or "growing over" into socialism. In fact, the two views were so close that it would become easy and efficacious for the Comintern in February 1928, when explaining still more failures in China, to charge a good share of the blame to Lominadze and his alleged Trotskyist concept of "permanent revolution."[14]

Developments in Operational Strategy

In addition to participating in the plenum's discourse charting the future course of revolution in China, the Party Central provided the basic operational strategy for carrying out future insurrectionary activity. This was the guidance that was to aid cadres on the scene in charge of implementing the new policies. In this regard the firsthand experience gained during the Nanchang and Autumn Harvest Uprisings contributed significantly to the task. As the "Resolution on the Present Situation and Tasks of the Communist Party" stated, "the masses, through the experiences of defeat, learned revolutionary struggle."[15]

Although fully subscribing to the concept of "uninterrupted revolution," the plenum's leadership stressed the practical importance of careful timing in staging insurrections. Specific conditions favoring success were explained, and adherence to them expected of Party cadre. Cautionary guidance was given to make the level of activity, whether urban or rural, suit the actual operating environment and degree of popular support and not outpace existing conditions or underrate them.[16]

In the cities Party cadres were to develop a following among workers by gradually leading them from attention to daily economic problems of immediate concern to a focus on broader political matters. In the countryside Communists were to focus mainly on gaining leadership over the existing spontaneous peasant movement. Reminiscent of statements during the Autumn Harvest Uprisings, the two tendencies identified as having the most dilatory effects on the revolution so far were first, relying too heavily on military forces to implement revolutionary programs or "not trusting mass power but trusting military power," and second, rather than developing an effective and aggressive mass policy, adopting a "wait-and-see" approach or even restraining spontaneous movements where they occurred.[17]

To remedy these ills, the Party Central worked out a general strategy and stressed that preparations for the urban and rural revolutions were to be closely related. The strategy was threefold: "(1) unleash and organize the latent, spontaneous uprisings of the peasants as far as possible, (2) unleash an extensive economic struggle in the cities and lead it to a revolutionary high tide so as to make armed insurrection possible, and (3) combine the insurrectionary forces of the workers and peasants in order to seize political power."[18] The convergence of the urban and rural insurrections would set the stage for a general uprising.

The organization, officially endorsed by the plenum, that was to consolidate political power in both urban and rural areas was the soviet. When the Party Central announced its commitment to the establishment of soviets in September, it specified that "the organization of soviets should be effected first in those key places like Canton [Guangzhou] and Ch'angsha [Changsha] when we are sure of a decisive and firm victory; before these key places are taken over by the revolutionary insurgents we should resolutely refuse to organize soviets in small cities."[19] Regarding the inauguration of new organs of political power in small cities, the Politburo stated that guidance developed at the August 7 Conference should direct these efforts.[20] In other words, political power in small cities was to reside in the popularly elected revolutionary committees. In the countryside organized peasant associations were to act as governmental bodies, with their elected representatives chosen on the basis of the election regulations of the peasant associations.[21]

At the November plenum, however, the concept of the soviet was given broader definition and powers. It was described as a council of representatives of the workers, peasants, and soldiers, popularly elected, and charged with carrying out the revolution. Upon completion of a successful insurrection, the soviet, rather than a revolutionary committee or peasant association, was to serve as the new governmental organization in both urban and rural areas and was charged with seeing that all points in the general revolutionary program were realized. In other words, the action slogan became "all power to the soviets."

Cities Are "Guiding Centers."   The policy of establishing soviet political power through armed uprisings of workers and peasants continued to focus on urban insurrections. The priority of urban uprisings is clearly stated in the "Resolution on the Present Situation and Tasks of the Communist Party," which claimed that without the leadership and support of the workers, the peasant uprisings could not succeed. The urban uprising was to become the center and point of leadership of spontaneous peasant uprisings. It was described as the "predetermining condition" (*xianjue tiaojian*) of a secure and successful general uprising.[22]

Four specific preconditions were spelled out for a successful insurrection in a city, while none were developed for rural areas. The urban preconditions were (1) the intensification and expansion of the daily economic struggle into a general political struggle; (2) the likely collapse of the regime of the ruling class; (3) the city dwellers at large hating and opposing the ruling class and favoring its downfall; and (4) the technical preparation and organization of the revolutionary force of the working class.[23] Regarding the urban labor movement, the plenum set up an ad hoc committee for its development and adopted a resolution providing extensive guidance to responsible cadres.[24]

Even in the "Resolutions on Recent Important Organizational Tasks," passed at the plenum, a comparatively lengthy and detailed section dealing with labor union organization was followed by a very brief statement concerning the problems of peasant organization, which concludes with the following guidance: "Those peasant organizations will become Soviets or councils of peasant representatives *as soon as* the laborers seize political power during the high tide of the revolution" (italics added).[25] Accordingly, the workers, upon seizing power, were to establish an urban soviet, which would then signal the peasant associations that a rural soviet was permissible and desirable. Clearly, the operational strategy developed in November called for making "cities the guiding centers of spontaneous peasant insurrection."[26]

Provincial reporting in November indicated that the priority set on attacking the cities was widely followed. The Shandong Provincial Committee leadership instructed a major county committee to "seize urban political power, and establish a revolutionary regime," even if that new regime could remain in existence for only a short time.[27] In addition, Cai Hesen, recollecting events during the fall, claimed that an active debate had taken place at a meeting of the Northern Bureau, which he chaired, and at the Hebei Provincial Committee, in early November just prior to the plenum. At issue was the validity of attacking cities, including county seats. In the course of the proceedings, Cai drew overwhelming opposition for his criticism of what he called the "'attack-city' doctrine," pursued at the neglect of more modest goals. Unable to win support for his position, Cai had to settle for a statement of his views criticizing the majority, which he disparagingly claimed "knew nothing but a cry for uprising and thus tended to neglect small daily struggles."[28]

No doubt the pervasive push for urban uprisings was motivated at least in part by a desire to prove that the Communists still represented a continuing force in the country. The most visible way to accomplish that end was to successfully establish a revolutionary government in an urban area, even if, as was frequently stated, that new regime could last only for a short time. Certainly one important dividend from such a success would be a boost to Party morale, the lack of which is reflected by the fact that by the November plenum, Party memberships had declined to 10,000 from a figure of 50,000 just six months earlier.[29] Of course, a large measure of this membership decline should be ascribed to effective White Terror campaigns.

Former Party Secretary Chen Duxiu in a letter dated November 12, 1927, criticized the strong trend toward attempting to seize political power through uprisings, particularly in cities. He maintained that such a radical policy communicated to the population that a Communist "uprising was merely a power struggle between C (for Communist Party) and K (for Kuomintang). . . ."[30] In words that were prophetic of the eventual emphasis of Communist strategy in 1928, Chen counseled that Communist policy and propaganda should be more attuned and responsive to the real economic needs of the population and not so singularly concerned with staging uprisings directed at seizing power.

Finally the official view of the existing situation in China as requiring "direct revolution," which should make rapid progress in surpassing the more limited goals of the bourgeois-democratic revolution and switch on to the socialist path, spurred Communist cadres to extend their insurrectionary programs to the limit. Anything short of consolidating a "guiding center" or urban revolution might bring against them the damning charge of opportunism. It appears that a significant part of the autumn trend toward carrying out premature uprisings without regard to the objective operational environment arose out of this widespread, residual fear of being branded as opportunists.[31]

Guerrilla Tactics. The events as they unfolded propelled the Communist leadership to find ways to counter force with force in the battle to survive. The Communists did face formidable opposition. At the top, the KMT looked seriously divided, with key factions in both Nanjing and Wuhan, internecine warlord conflicts, and the recent but temporary resignation of Chiang Kai-shek. Below that level, however, were the vast numbers of politically active leaders of the local and regional Chinese establishment who opposed radical social change. The KMT had achieved popularity with this conservative group by defeating warlords during the Northern Expedition. The new militarists (Tang Shengzhi, He Jian, Xu Kexiang, and others) who emerged out of this milieu represented powerful and committed opponents to the continued survival of the Communists as an effective organization and movement.[32]

Reflecting again a responsiveness to the events of the fall and these existing conditions, the plenum leadership discussed guerrilla tactics as a vital part of the new operational strategy to be employed in armed insurrections. Guerrilla tactics were not discussed at the August 7 Conference but had been widely used during the course of the Autumn Harvest Uprisings. On October 29 the Party's Chang Jiang Bureau claimed that guerrilla warfare was the main form of struggle in China.[33] The plenum confirmed and also defined this viewpoint. Guerrilla activity was described as appropriate only in rural areas, but guerrillas were assigned the key role of propagandizing, organizing, and arming the peasants preliminary to their staging local uprisings.[34] The goal was to produce a growing body of support for Communist objectives and coalesce opposition to the hostile local establishment. The following illuminates the preparatory mission of guerrilla warfare: "Guerrilla warfare is, when there is yet no prospect of victory to seize political power through uprising, the kind of struggle to spur the peasant masses, whence it is to develop right into an uprising."[35]

Militarily, guerrilla warfare units were not to be aimed at taking a county seat or major urban center, but were to act as a small, solid, armed force in surprise attacks against more powerful local government and landlord forces. Eventually, after chipping away at the local establishment's power, Communist-led forces, through these guerrilla tactics, could gain control over large areas.

In December Qu Qiubai identified these areas of guerrilla control as "revolutionary districts" (*geming dicheng*). But, responding to the exigencies of the Comintern's "uninterrupted revolution," Qu instructed that once this level of development was reached, it must proceed forward and could not stay in the guerrilla stage. Rather, as stated in the plenum's guidance, the guerrilla tactics were to lead to the establishment of the rural soviet.[36] The latter, when coordinated under the guidance of the urban soviets, would progress to the establishment of soviets in several counties, and then a provincial-level soviet, and ultimately a general insurrection.[37]

At the November plenum, then, the policy of agrarian revolution introduced at the August 7 Conference was expanded from an initial focus on four provinces to a focus of general scope. Faced with a seriously weakened military position following losses during the Nanchang Uprising and Autumn Harvest Uprisings, and the need to counter local oppression by building broad influence and support in the countryside, the Party had to turn its attention to developing the concepts and tactics of guerrilla warfare. This was a key step in the Party's development in 1928 of a comprehensive strategy for mobilizing powerful rural support. In late 1927 the development of guerrilla warfare marked the beginning of the Party's integration of its own experiences and findings concerning making revolution in China into the policymaking process. It also increased the tension between Lominadze's authoritative insistence on urban-centered revolution and the growing recognition emerging within Party Central that conditions in China required other solutions.

Strengthening Primary Communist Organizations

The implementation of the policy of agrarian revolution and the formation of soviets required strong, disciplined, primary Communist organizations, namely Party and Youth League bodies, at all levels, and particularly at the basic village and factory branch levels. These bodies were needed to organize, propagandize, train, and arm a mass following responsive to Communist programs. With the onset of widespread conservative reaction against the Communists, organizational work rose in importance and demanded a tighter, more disciplined, and now clandestine structure operating in the urban and rural areas. Communist organizers could capitalize on spontaneous urban and rural movements, but by the fall of 1927 a professional revolutionary organization was essential for leading and directing this work.

Numerous primary organizations were damaged during the Autumn Harvest period. The key Northern Bureau was destroyed, and several provinces reported little or no organizational strength with which to carry out their programs.[38] Addressing this problem, the November plenum leadership issued guidance and requirements for building primary organizations beginning for the first time at the base, where the most effective mass contacts could occur, and building to the highest levels.

Whereas the Party, while in collaboration with the KMT establishment, had concentrated its energies on building influence within the county and provincial administrative centers, it now shifted the focus toward building strength at those basic levels that would offer the greatest opportunity for reaching the masses of workers and peasants. The November plenum's organizational guidance emphasized the importance of strengthening Party branches and pointed out: "there are still very few Party cells in many large factories, business establishments and particularly in the villages and armed units. Strictly speaking, there is almost no Party organization in the villages."[39]

Party organizers cited "our experience" in concluding that having Party branches and sections in the villages would not only provide opportunities for better organizing activities at that level but also would allow the Party to exert more control. Without the presence of branch- or cell-level personnel, peasant insurrections were found to be "entirely spontaneous and of anarchical characteristics."[40] Thus branch-level organs were essential not only for gaining opportunities to organize mass support but also for channeling it in desired directions. At the same time, in the course of developing peasant mass support, care was to be taken not to exert undue restraint and obstruct mass activity, thus preventing revolutionary change in the countryside.

By late December, and in accordance with two notices on organizational reconstruction issued by the Party Central after the November plenum, the priority given to establishing branch-level organs was emphatically stated: "we should implement reorganization from below to above."[41] The reorganization of the provincial-level Party organ would have to await the successive reorganization of all lower-level Party organs, beginning at the basic branch level. Thus by the end of 1927 the Party had developed an organizational policy that reversed attention away from strengthening mainly the administrative levels of the Party structure, which by nature were separated from direct contact with the urban and rural populations.

A second area of emphasis in the fall and at the plenum concerned the reorganization of the existing Party and League structures. In what was described as a "purification process," members who joined before September 1927 were to undergo reinvestigation and reregistration, during which time they would be examined for any residual "opportunistic" sympathies with the KMT, evidence of disagreement with existing key Communist policies, and slack participation in the ongoing programs. This was in fact a purge of the primary bodies to rid them of "non-proletarian intellectuals"—those most likely to be in opposition to the current radical Communist policies—and replace them with the more reliable "elements of the workers and peasants" in the leading organs at all levels.[42]

The plenum's organizational guidance and the notices that followed represented an extensive development of the general policies set down at the August 7 Conference. Detailed organizational guidance contained in the *Zhejiang Collection* defined the Youth League structure at each level, beginning with the basic branch level.[43] Because this was the first extensive description of the Chinese Communist organizational system as an independent structure, it is described below at length. The organizational chart in figure 1 was based on these materials. The succeeding organizational chart in figure 2 provides additional and comparable organizational information concerning the

Figure 1 Chinese Communist Youth League
Organizational Structure

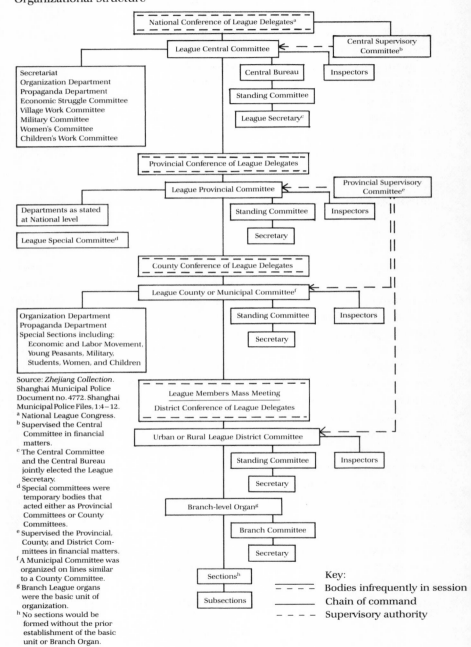

Source: *Zhejiang Collection*.
Shanghai Municipal Police
Document no. 4772. Shanghai
Municipal Police Files, 1:4–12.
[a] National League Congress.
[b] Supervised the Central
    Committee in financial
    matters.
[c] The Central Committee
    and the Central Bureau
    jointly elected the League
    Secretary.
[d] Special committees were
    temporary bodies that
    acted either as Provincial
    Committees or County
    Committees.
[e] Supervised the Provincial,
    County, and District Com-
    mittees in financial matters.
[f] A Municipal Committee was
    organized on lines similar
    to a County Committee.
[g] Branch League organs
    were the basic unit of
    organization.
[h] No sections would be
    formed without the prior
    establishment of the basic
    unit or Branch Organ.

National Conference of League Delegates[a]

Central Supervisory Committee[b]

League Central Committee

Secretariat
Organization Department
Propaganda Department
Economic Struggle Committee
Village Work Committee
Military Committee
Women's Committee
Children's Work Committee

Central Bureau   Inspectors

Standing Committee

League Secretary[c]

Provincial Conference of League Delegates

Provincial Supervisory Committee[e]

League Provincial Committee

Departments as stated
at National level

League Special Committee[d]

Standing Committee   Inspectors

Secretary

County Conference of League Delegates

League County or Municipal Committee[f]

Organization Department
Propaganda Department
Special Sections including:
    Economic and Labor Movement,
    Young Peasants, Military,
    Students, Women, and Children

Standing Committee   Inspectors

Secretary

League Members Mass Meeting
District Conference of League Delegates

Urban or Rural League District Committee

Standing Committee   Inspectors

Secretary

Branch-level Organ[g]

Branch Committee

Secretary

Sections[h]

Subsections

Key:
- - - - - Bodies infrequently in session
———— Chain of command
- - - - Supervisory authority

CCP included in the Party constitution adopted in 1928 by the Sixth Party Congress. It shows how the League fit into the larger framework of Communist organization by 1928, noting particularly its relationship with the CCP.[44]

At the heart of this organizational system was the concept of democratic centralism provided by the Comintern. In essence, this principle required a hierarchical system beginning with a subdistrict branch and going up to district, county (xian) or municipal (the two were similar in authority), provincial, national, and ultimately to the pinnacle of authority, the Comintern leadership.[45] As the chart indicates, the leadership at each level was to be elected by a conference of delegates from the general membership at that level. After election, however, the key leaders were to be approved by a higher level.

Special note should be taken of the branch-level organization, for it was the basic unit of organization and the new focus of attention. All Communists were required to belong to a branch organ. In urban areas branches were to be formed mainly according to a trade affiliation or productive employment, resulting in factory branches, mine branches, seamen's branches, railway branches, and so on. For those such as manual workers and house servants falling outside a general category, street branches were available. In the countryside, a village branch was the basic Communist unit.

The branch level was the level at which practical work was to be carried out. This work included recruiting and training new members, holding meetings to explain and lead discussions concerning basic local issues and ongoing Communist policies, seeing that all policies emanating from on high were implemented, guiding actual economic and political movements in the area, and contacting and reporting to higher levels on the local situation.[46]

The branch-level organ elected a secretary and standing committee to supervise and administer the routine work of the branch. Also, when branch members were more than seven, they were required to organize sections or cells to specialize or concentrate the work on specific targets such as a particular factory or mine.

The district-level organization was to include representatives from the most important branches in the district. The secretary and standing committee of the district organ were to supervise the work of the various branch organs, help organize new branches, and through dis-

Figure 2 The Party and League Organizational Relationship

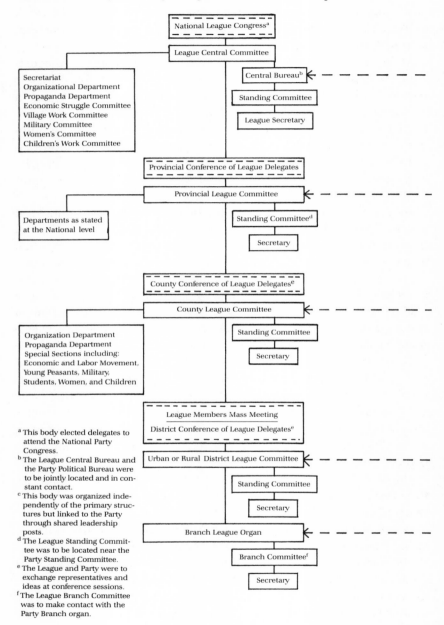

National League Congress[a]

League Central Committee

Secretariat
Organizational Department
Propaganda Department
Economic Struggle Committee
Village Work Committee
Military Committee
Women's Committee
Children's Work Committee

Central Bureau[b]

Standing Committee

League Secretary

Provincial Conference of League Delegates

Provincial League Committee

Departments as stated
at the National level

Standing Committee[d]

Secretary

County Conference of League Delegates[e]

County League Committee

Organization Department
Propaganda Department
Special Sections including:
Economic and Labor Movement,
Young Peasants, Military,
Students, Women, and Children

Standing Committee

Secretary

League Members Mass Meeting

District Conference of League Delegates[e]

Urban or Rural District League Committee

Standing Committee

Secretary

Branch League Organ

Branch Committee[f]

Secretary

[a] This body elected delegates to attend the National Party Congress.
[b] The League Central Bureau and the Party Political Bureau were to be jointly located and in constant contact.
[c] This body was organized independently of the primary structures but linked to the Party through shared leadership posts.
[d] The League Standing Committee was to be located near the Party Standing Committee.
[e] The League and Party were to exchange representatives and ideas at conference sessions.
[f] The League Branch Committee was to make contact with the Party Branch organ.

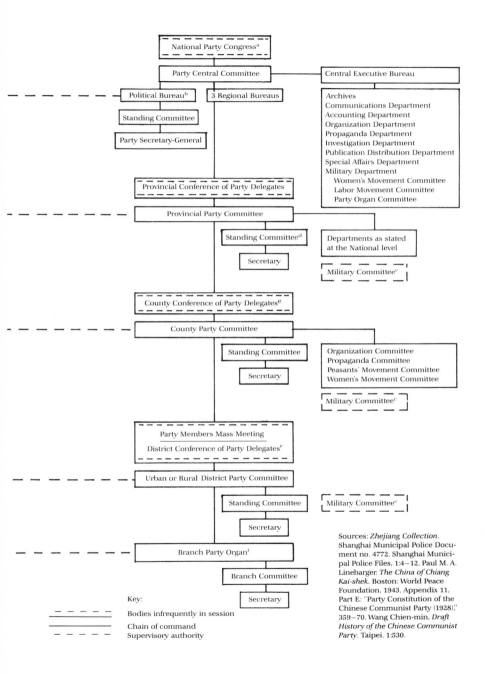

Key:
- - - - - Bodies infrequently in session
——— Chain of command
- - - - - Supervisory authority

Sources: *Zhejiang Collection*. Shanghai Municipal Police Document no. 4772. Shanghai Municipal Police Files, 1:4–12. Paul M. A. Linebarger. *The China of Chiang Kai-shek*. Boston: World Peace Foundation, 1943. Appendix 11, Part E: "Party Constitution of the Chinese Communist Party (1928)," 359–70. Wang Chien-min, *Draft History of the Chinese Communist Party*. Taipei. 1:530.

trict inspectors provide close supervision and guidance regarding issues and problems within a branch.

At the county or municipal level (the latter applied to a sizable urban area), the elected county committee, having representatives from key districts, was to supervise and guide the work within its larger geographic scope. Because of its broadened authority, the county committee was to include specialized departments to strengthen efficiency and the quality of work. These included departments of organization, propaganda, economic and labor movements, young peasants, the military, students, women, and children. The county-level leadership, of course, was to report on the actual work being done in these areas to superior organs on a regular basis. In addition, roving inspectors appointed by the county committee were to insure that the orders, plans, and policies of higher organs were being carried out by the branches.

The provincial-level committee was to include representation from the most important provincial organizations, including delegates from the leading industrial and trade branches. Being responsible for the supervision of work throughout the province, it was to maintain close contact with subordinate levels, often assigning members to participate in lower-level work, run a publishing organ to clarify policy issues, inspect the work of lower organs, report regularly to the Central Committee, maintain a bank of specialized bureaus, and perform other supervisory and administrative tasks.

At the top of the Communist organizational system was the Central Committee, elected from a National Conference of Delegates. The chief responsibility of the Central Committee was to elect a Central Bureau and secretary for the League and Political Bureau for the Party. The Politburo in turn elected a Standing Committee, which exercised direct authority over Communist affairs. The Central Committee, no doubt with decisive influence by the Politburo, elected the Party's general secretary. In the Party system the Central Committee was to supervise and manage the various regional bureaus, including the Northern Bureau, the Southern Bureau, and the Chang Jiang Bureau. Specialized departments and committees were to guide and develop corresponding ones at the provincial and county levels.[47]

This central level provided, under the direction of the Comintern and its representatives in China, the general political guidance that defined and guided the work at subordinate levels. This was facilitated by an authoritative publishing organ, which was to disseminate major policy resolutions, instruct specific Communist organs, report on experiences around the country, publish important lower-level reports and resolutions, and so on. Where special circumstances arose, special commissioners were to be dispatched to guide and attempt to improve a particular important situation.

Certainly a very close interchange of information and results between the lower levels and the top was essential for keeping policy guidance, which by theory had to emanate from the top, in line with the practical realities confronting the branch leaders who implemented policy below. The frequent lack of working communications between the various levels, poor security measures, and, indeed, the absence of working organs, particularly at the basic levels, often seriously impeded the workability of this system during the period under study. Nevertheless, because this plenum endorsed and defined this system, it thus opened the way for field- or branch-level cadres to communicate more effectively and thus exert greater influence at the policymaking levels of the Party.

Such was the basic framework of the Party organizational system. In operation it was to function under the Leninist principle of democratic centralism. Its leaders were to perform in a "democratic" fashion by involving the broad Party membership in discussions of practical issues in order to awaken each member to the larger social and political dimensions of his experience in the matters under discussion. Once decisions were made final, however, under the principle of "centralism" there could no longer be any dissenting members, whether they agreed with the decisions or not. The aim was to awaken political consciousness and at the same time inspire and instill ideological solidarity within the general CCP membership.

Although the guidelines for the development and proper functioning of a strong Party apparatus were available by fall of 1927, the conditions for their implementation still were not good. Reports concerning the weakness of Party organizational structures within the provinces were widespread. One major contributing factor was that during the course of the Northern Expedition many Party organs had been assimilated into the KMT structure. Therefore, with the break in that alliance, it was necessary to reregister all Party members and screen them for any collaborationist or "opportunistic" leanings. By the fall and winter several provinces were describing their attempts to cleanse and reorganize their existing Party organs as well as establish new ones.[48]

The official line at the November plenum concerning organizational tasks was to carry out a thorough "bolshevization" of the Party apparatus. This meant a reorganization of the Party leadership at all levels so that the majority of Party leaders would come from the worker and peasant ranks. Also, work was to begin on the formation of a system of random inspections at the various levels of the Party apparatus to ensure that the transformation of the Party leadership actually occurred. This comprehensive reorganization process was to be accomplished at all Party levels before convocation of the Sixth Party Congress, which was set for six months later.[49]

Developing Security Procedures

The Party faced the immediate and pressing concern of how to operate covertly in order to ensure the survival of Communist personnel and organizations. Certainly in the area of military work, where the dangers were especially high, there was an obvious need to maintain a closely guarded secret relationship between Communist bodies and soldiers' cells operating in opposing military forces or between cadres attempting to train and arm willing worker, peasant, or soldier groups. On a number of occasions in the fall of 1927, imminent military plans and operations had been leaked, resulting in their failure.

The need for good security was a central concern at the August 7 Emergency Conference, reflected in the regulations developed there and during the fall. Examples of proper security procedures were included in the "Resolutions on Organization," developed at the November plenum.[50] The question arises as to how the Chinese Communists suddenly developed such an impressive body of knowledge concerning security matters. Again, the Comintern's contributions were paramount. Just as it had shaped the CCP and even KMT organizational design and development, the Comintern provided the theory and practices for developing security procedures to be followed in all areas of operation, including personnel, organizational matters, preparation and handling of documents, and the holding of meetings.[51]

In organizational matters, the Russian concept of democratic centralism was the cardinal principle. Now, in matters of security, the Comintern originated the principle of compartmentalization. This meant segmenting the information available to members of the organization into small parts, so that the defection or revelations of one member would not result in extensive damage to the entire organization. By the fall of 1927 practical application of this principle required that Communist activists know the identities and residences only of those absolutely essential to their work. The locations of other Communist organizations were not to be widely known, and the most secret offices, such as the communications units and archives, were required to change their locations frequently in order to minimize the chances of discovery by police. In fact, a "second-defense line," or backup string of secret communications offices, working offices, and archives, was supposed to be identified and ready for activation in time of emergency.

Document security dictated that naming individuals or organizations in correspondence was to be avoided. Identities were to be conveyed through secret characters or codes, which were to be changed frequently to protect their secrecy. An organization known as the Central School periodically issued a list of "pronouns" or false terms designating key Communist organizations. One notable example provided in the guidance explained that an invitation to attend a "wine party" meant that the recipient was being informed to attend a district committee meeting.[52] The Central School also was active in providing secret writing techniques, using invisible inks and codes, to support document security. For example, if a letter were received that concluded with the characters for "happy" (*kuaile*), the recipient would know that a hidden message had been written with ferrous sulfate and tannic acid and could be treated in an appropriate way to reveal the hidden text.[53]

Meetings of Party members or organs were to carry heavy security arrangements. In general, meetings were to be limited in attendance. Documents were not to be brought to meetings unless absolutely essential to the proceedings, and then the means for their quick destruction were to be readily available. A cover story to explain a gathering was to be devised at the start of any meeting. For example, language books might be distributed to create the appearance of a foreign language class in session. Finally, the appointed time for meetings was to be calculated five hours previous to that given in the notification of the meeting. Thus a meeting reported to be planned for 6 P.M. would actually begin at 1 P.M. Meetings were to be brief, and, once adjourned, members were to leave separately and at different intervals.

In sum, increasing Communist discipline and good security procedures were policies developed in response to the dangerous operating conditions and numerous failures experienced after mid-July. To realize the proclaimed goal of establishing soviets, the Party shifted focus to building primary organizations at the basic branch level in order to promote the building of Communist strength among worker, peasant, and armed mass groups. The "spontaneous" actions by these groups were to be assisted by auxiliary military forces, following the new tactics of guerrilla warfare.

Communist planners, however, still lacked a clear sense of the role each of the components was to play in the overall design for making the revolution and how best to develop and coordinate these roles. What was to be the specific function of the Peasant Association in preparing the countryside for a change in power? How did it relate to the urban struggle, which still was to guide the overall revolutionary situation? When, what degree, and what kind of military force was to be applied? The biggest question was: How were primary Communist bodies to develop, manage, and coordinate each component in order to create a controlled and effective movement that could realize the goal of political and social change?

The experience of the fall clearly was invaluable to the development of new policies. But the Communists continued to operate under Lominadze's theoretical conception that the Chinese revolution would follow an unrelenting and continuous course toward the realization of socialism. With the membership down to 10,000, communications between Communist organs often nonexistent and poor at best, a continued urban bias growing in part out of past experience, lack of organizational strength at the basic targeted levels, a commonly expressed misunderstanding of what the focus and goals of the revolution really were, and, most important, the strength and preponderance of the opposing forces, the Communists were in for difficult times. This was especially true when, as we shall see, goals were again set to seize power in heavily protected urban centers.

Chapter 6. The Guangzhou Soviet: Failure Brings Restraint

A recent Communist source claims that from August 1927 to the end of 1929 more than two hundred armed uprisings occurred.[1] At the Party's November plenum the focus on agrarian revolution shifted Communist attention to the countryside, but the Party continued to emphasize the cities as being the hub or guiding center of revolutionary activity. As this chapter will show, the impact of the plenum's pronouncements was momentous.

Plans for General Uprisings

The principal planning and action aimed at staging general uprisings took place in the four provinces of Jiangsu, Hubei, Hunan, and Guangdong. In Jiangsu the provincial Party leadership pointed optimistically to short-lived peasant uprisings in Wuxi and Yixing counties west of Shanghai in southern Jiangsu. They interpreted these events as clear evidence that a provincewide peasant uprising had begun in Jiangsu and that preparations now were in order for staging an uprising in Shanghai.

In an urgent draft resolution passed on November 9, the Jiangsu Provincial Party Committee ordered that a provincewide peasant uprising be carried out "before November 15," and that plans also be made to prepare a worker uprising in Shanghai to serve as the guide for a Jiangsu general uprising.[2] To speed developments in Shanghai, the Party had to dispatch organizers to the factories to coerce the apparently unwilling workers into staging strikes.[3] With so little time and owing to the strength of the entrenched establishment in Shanghai, nothing came of these revolutionary plans for Jiangxu, including the strike efforts.

Qu Qiubai later described the period between the August 7 Conference and the December defeat of the Guangzhou Uprising as one displaying a dangerous new tendency that he called "blind actionism" (*mangdong zhuyi*). He cited as evidence the fall events in Hubei Province.[4] The situation in Hubei developed around signs of serious division within the KMT, a condition that seemed to offer the Communists opportunities. Tang Shengzhi, the KMT military leader at Wuhan, initiated a rebellion against the recently unified KMT regime in Nanjing. The latter responded by dispatching forces to subdue Tang on October 24, 1927. Hearing of these developments, the Communist leadership in Hubei debated whether Tang could survive this rebuke and, if not, to what extent should the Party take advantage of these cleavages and Tang's weakness to stage a general uprising.[5] A further question was, in the event of Tang's fall, should the Communists act immediately to stage an uprising, or merely increase their efforts at making thorough preparations for an eventual uprising? At issue were the timing and degree of preparation necessary for staging a general insurrection leading to the establishment of an urban soviet. As the events unfolded, members of the Party and League leadership in Hubei came into direct conflict because of their opposing views on these key issues.

On October 25 the Hubei Provincial Party Committee met, with participation by members of the Youth League, and concluded that Tang's forces would likely fall, and that when that occurred, a worker uprising should be staged to establish a soviet in Wuhan, while at the same time expanding guerrilla warfare in the nearby countryside. Youth League member Liu Changzhun and two others drafted a resolution passed by the Standing Committee entitled "Resolution on the Current Urgent Struggle." It set forth a radical action program calling for a general uprising and establishment of a Wuhan soviet and for the intensification of rural guerrilla warfare aimed at establishing separate independent areas in the countryside. It directed revolutionaries to "kill and expropriate the property of all village bosses, bad gentry, big capitalists, counter-revolutionaries, and government officials; confiscate the land of landlords; loot and burn reactionary agencies; raid prisons and set free prisoners; occupy factories," and so on.[6] Hubei Youth League members maintained that even if a Wuhan soviet were established for a few days only, this accomplishment would be very meaningful.[7]

However, when Luo Yinong, a member of the Provisional Politburo and secretary of the Chang Jiang Bureau, returned to Hankou on October 28 he injected a measure of restraint into the proceedings. Luo expected Tang's forces to hold out for some time, and, as explained in the "Yangtze [Chang Jiang] Bureau's Recent Political Resolution," he proposed using that lead time to initiate a moderate program of action aimed at preparing the way and strengthening Communist forces for eventual participation in a general insurrection. The Hubei Provincial Party Committee accepted Luo's resolution and action program on October 30. Thus it abandoned the earlier League-sponsored radical program aimed at a direct seizure of power in Hubei and based on the conviction that Tang's forces would collapse quickly.

The situation in Hubei again became fluid when it was learned that Tang Shengzhi's forces were no match for the attacking Nanjing army. On November 12, as his forces were withdrawing from Wuhan, Tang resigned. Judging conditions at that moment to be particularly advantageous, the Communists responded quickly by planning among other things a general strike for the next day. However, on such short notice and with little or no preparatory work having been done among the Wuhan workers and nearby peasants, the strike failed and resulted in the capture and execution of some Communist cadres. Nanjing forces subsequently took Wuhan on November 16.

Luo Yinong had departed for Shanghai earlier on November 4 to attend the November plenum. At the plenum the warring conditions between Wuhan and Nanjing were given serious attention and taken as reason for encouragement. After all, one of the prerequisites developed for a successful urban uprising was evidence of "the imminent collapse of the ruling class." Against the background of recent events in Hubei, the Party Central on November 15 produced instructions for the Hubei and Hunan Provincial Party committees to mobilize and make preparations for uprisings to occur within a short period. Once started, they were to converge into a general uprising and produce a soviet. Luo was designated to direct and prepare for uprisings in the two provinces.

Luo returned to Wuhan on November 25, just nine days after the city had changed hands. In contrast to his earlier moderate stance, but in response to Party directions, Luo at an expanded meeting of the Hubei

Provincial Committee explained the spirit and policies of the November plenum. He related the instructions that "within one month" political power in Hubei was to be seized and cadres were to immediately begin the necessary preparations for uprisings.[8]

With conditions in Wuhan much less favorable now, Youth League leaders Liu Changzhun and Han Guanghan responded to the new orders by making charges to the Party Central that Luo "and others" had behaved in a cowardly manner and acted opportunistically at the time of Tang Shengzhi's initial rebellion, when chances for effective action were much better. They demanded that in the spirit of the November plenum's resolution aimed at "strengthening political discipline," a full investigation of the circumstances and events surrounding Tang's rebellion and the Hubei Party's responses be undertaken.

Evidently impressed, the Party Central reacted immediately to the League's charges. On December 4 it organized a Special Committee consisting of Su Zhaozheng, Guo Liang, and He Chang to investigate the alleged mistakes of the Chang Jiang Bureau and the Hubei Provincial Committee. On December 9 the committee arrived in Wuhan and immediately suspended the authority of Luo Yinong and the Hubei Standing Committee. Luo was ordered to proceed to Shanghai.[9]

For almost the next two months Party authorities at several levels discussed and debated the Wuhan events and circumstances. At the Hubei Provincial Party Conference, held on December 14–15 at Hankou, both Youth League members and the Special Committee dispatched by the Party Central to investigate the situation blamed Luo for miscalculating Tang's quick defeat and for issuing orders that curbed the insurrectionary mood of the Provincial Committee. Luo Yinong earlier had admitted that he had misjudged Tang's weakness, but claimed that this was of no importance because all the conditions essential for a general insurrection, as stated at the November plenum, were not present anyway.[10] He firmly maintained that the principal effort should have been to create the required conditions and not to take any immediate action toward insurrection. Like other Party leaders charged with staging uprisings at this time, Luo was struggling to resolve the dilemma of how best to manage the dangerous conditions that the Communists confronted, and at the same time support and maintain the revolutionary momentum that Party authorities, particularly at the

November plenum, claimed existed. Luo knew that to avoid or ignore the latter would expose him to the dread charge of right opportunism. The result in Hubei was confusion, vacillation, and conflict within the leadership ranks.

After tense debate and much confusion, this Provincial Conference concluded by issuing a resolution recommending disciplinary action against Hubei leaders considered guilty of serious errors. Luo Yinong was to be dismissed from membership on the Central Committee, as was Provincial Secretary Chen Qiaonian. Several members of the Provincial Standing Committee were to lose their posts, while League Provincial Secretary Liu Changzhun was to be given a severe warning (apparently to show impartiality).[11] After such a stormy gathering, entrenched differences of opinion remained, particularly on the part of Luo Yinong, who in the meantime was presenting his side of the story to the Party Central in Shanghai.

In late December the Party Central met to examine the thorny Hubei question. From the charges, countercharges, reports, and documentation submitted for its review, a resolution on Hubei was adopted on January 3, 1928. It sorted out the evidence from the charges and dealt directly with defining what had emerged as the most workable methods and tactics to be followed at all Party levels, under the dangerous and increasingly threatening conditions produced at Wuhan and by now at Guangzhou, with the failure there of the Guangzhou Soviet.[12]

The Chang Jiang Bureau, under Luo Yinong, was faulted for having miscalculated Tang's retreat and therefore for not having taken better advantage of the war situation between Wuhan and Nanjing to provide extensive guidance to cadres concerning work to be done among urban workers and peasants in preparing for an insurrection. At the same time the resolution clarified the point raised by Luo that the timing of a general insurrection depended on the creation of the conditions required for its initiation. Since this preparatory work had not been done in Wuhan, Luo was correct in not ordering an immediate insurrection when the only destabilizing factor present was that Tang's forces had begun their withdrawal.

The Party Central's resolution criticized the Standing Committee of the Hubei Provincial Committee for its policies vacillating between calls for immediate insurrection and recommendations for more preparations during the course of events in Wuhan. Responsible members were ordered dismissed from the Provincial Committee. The League Provincial Committee of Hubei was reprimanded for its orientation toward favoring an "immediate insurrection," and the Special Committee was censured for becoming embroiled in Party and League conflicts and failing to deal with the actual issues and work plans in Hubei.

The Party Central, however, did succeed in generating consensus among Party and even League leaders on one key point. This was that armed insurrection aimed at the establishment of a soviet required careful preparations, and the timing of its initiation and its location required that certain preconditions be fulfilled. Of course, to date the Party Central had worked out, at the November plenum, only what specific preconditions were essential for initiating insurrections in urban areas.

With so much turmoil within the Hubei leadership ranks, the uprising plans there never materialized. The results in Hunan were no more favorable. Luo Yinong, upon returning to Wuhan on November 25 with instructions to carry out a two-province uprising, informed the Hunan Provincial Committee leadership by letter of the Party Central's orders. In response, on December 1 the Hunan leadership issued instructions for a general mobilization of cadres at all levels to draw up and implement uprising plans. The Provincial Committee's plans included a massive worker and peasant demonstration to take place in Changsha December 7–10 and to lead to a state of general uprising in Hunan. As it turned out, no substantial mass uprising occurred, and because of the strength and preparedness of the opposition, what little mass activity did materialize was quickly put down.[13]

The Guangzhou Uprising

While general uprising plans failed in Jiangsu, Hubei, and Hunan, there was at least temporary, if costly, success in Guangdong. Qu Qiubai claimed that "the Canton Uprising was the direct expression of the spirit of the resolution of the November Enlarged Conference."[14] The successful completion of the plans for the Guangzhou Uprising were at the heart of the Party Central's plans for carrying out successful uprisings in one or several provinces, leading directly to a general uprising on a national scale. Qu reported that just shortly after the November plenum, Party Central leaders met with Zhang Tailei, head of the Provisional Southern Bureau and secretary of the Guangdong Provincial Committee, and on November 17 decided on a general uprising plan for the province.[15] According to this plan, which was to be implemented by the Guangdong Provincial Committee, Guangzhou was to serve as the guiding center and key point for a provincewide general uprising aimed at establishing a soviet.

Conditions in Guangdong looked favorable for the insurrection. In the countryside the Hailufeng Soviet, established on November 7, had taken control of six counties under the direction of the peasant leader Peng Pai. In addition, there was evidence of serious conflict between the controlling Guangdong militarists. Remnants of Zhang Fakui's Second Front Army staged a coup d'état on November 17 in Guangzhou and overthrew the ruling militarist, Li Jishen, who had been in power since April 1927. Hostilities followed, with forces allied with Zhang in pursuit of those loyal to Li. Hoping to seize the moment, the Party Central on November 17 directed the Guangdong Provincial Committee to "utilize the opportunity of civil war . . . to expand the uprisings in the cities and villages . . . to agitate among the soldiers, to stage mutinies and revolts, and in the time of war swiftly to link such uprisings into a general uprising for the establishment" of soviets.[16] Zhang Fakui was forced to send increasing numbers of his troops out of Guangzhou to pursue and check Li Jishen's forces, thus weakening Zhang's hold over Guangzhou.

On November 26 the Guangdong Provincial Party Committee met to review the current situation and accepted the Party Central's instructions regarding insurrections in Guangdong. To implement these plans, a Revolutionary Military Council of five was created with Zhang Tailei as chairman and Ye Ting as commander in chief. The Comintern's representative on the scene was Heinz Neumann, who reportedly brought Comintern funding for the revolt from Shanghai.[17] With their organization in place and the knowledge that the peasantry in Guangdong had risen for the third time and had established a soviet government, the Communists felt that the time to strike was near. Most important, they had succeeded in heavily infiltrating Zhang Fakui's remaining 1,200-member Officers' Training Regiment in Guangzhou, commanded by Ye Jianying.[18]

On December 7 the Guangdong Provincial Committee set the insurrection date for December 13. Then came the shocking news that

Zhang Fakui, on orders from Wang Jingwei at Shanghai, was about to disarm the Communist-influenced Training Regiment and reinforce the Guangzhou garrison. Reacting to this threat, the Communists moved the uprising date up to December 11 at 3:30 A.M. At that time the soldiers of the Training Regiment were to disarm military units. At the same time hastily organized Red Guard forces, known as the Guangzhou Workers' Red Detachment and composed of some two thousand workers, were to disarm police and guard units, seize major military and police headquarters, free prisoners, and occupy government buildings and arms depots.[19]

If some factors appeared to favor the Communists' insurrection, the balance of fighting forces decidedly did not. A rough estimate of Communist strength totaled some 3,200 including the Training Regiment, Red Guards, and some guard and police support. Of the additional 1,500 armed peasants expected to participate, only 500 actually arrived, and those soon were bargained successfully out of their objectives. The strength of opposition forces exceeded 10,000 military and police troops within the city. In addition, anti-Communist trade union members far outnumbered those included in the Red Guards.[20]

Still, in the spirit of the November plenum, the Communists plunged ahead and initially were successful. By 3 P.M. on the day of the uprising most of the city had been brought under Communist control. Apparently unconvinced of the Communists' staying power, Ye Ting, the military commander who had arrived in Guangzhou only six hours before the revolt began, expressed caution over the course of events. At a meeting that evening Ye proposed that the rebel forces might best be withdrawn on the next day in order to preserve their strength. Huang Bing, a member of the Revolutionary Council, claims that Heinz Neumann criticized Ye's proposal and stated that the policy at that time should be one of continuous attack. He added that the Communist Party of the Soviet Union (CPSU) was about to hold a congress and that if Guangzhou could be held for eight days, its success would exert a great influence at that meeting.[21] The outcome was that Ye's proposal was voted down.

A soviet was proclaimed at the start of the Guangzhou insurrection, and a radical political program was set forth. The latter included a platform calling for nationalization of the banks and factories, the expropriation of bourgeois property, an eight-hour day with increased pay, and agrarian revolution with the land reverting to the tillers.[22] Labor leader Su Zhaozheng, who was in Wuhan at this time investigating the events surrounding the failed Hubei uprising, was named chairman of the Guangzhou Soviet. Until his return, Zhang Tailei acted in his place. Zhang also served as naval and army commissar. Other key offices and their holders in the Guangzhou Soviet were as follows:[23]

Yun Daiying	General Secretary
Ye Ting	Commander in chief, the Workers' and Peasants' Red Army
Xu Guangying	Chief of staff, the Workers' and Peasants' Red Army
Yang Yin	Counterrevolutionary Suppression Commissar
Peng Pai	Land Affairs Commissar
Zhou Wenyong	Labor Affairs Commissar; commander, Red Guards
He Lai	Economic Affairs Commissar
Huang Ping	Foreign and Internal Affairs Commissar
Chen Yu	Judicial Affairs Commissar

Plans called first for implementing the revolutionary program in Guangzhou and eliminating opposition forces there. The next step was to confront the remaining militarist troops throughout Guangdong province. Active peasant participation was to support this final stage, but this portion of the planning was sketched only in broad outline.[24]

From the start the Communists faced serious leadership problems. Ye Ting had only recently arrived in Guangzhou and thus was not adequately prepared or familiar with the disposition of forces or conditions for revolt. On the second day of the insurrection Zhang Tailei was shot and killed while returning from a meeting. Moreover, the Party Central in Shanghai had not been informed by the Guangdong Provincial Committee of the exact timing of the uprising and thus had no opportunity to organize outside support.[25]

Responding to the Communist threat at Guangzhou, Zhang Fakui and the other militarists quickly came to terms and joined forces to confront the Communist forces. Altogether, militarist forces numbered some 50,000 troops. The Communists could not even count on support from the neighboring peasantry, since the closest area of Communist strength in the Guangdong countryside was some 250 kilometers away in Hailufeng.[26] In their earlier mood of optimism the Communists had neglected to develop a retreat plan to shift their forces to the countryside in the event of defeat. Thus when the militarists counterattacked with support from foreign gunboats, the Guangzhou Soviet was brought to a bloody end after two and a half days, on December 13. About 1,500 Communists and their leaders were able to escape. Some under Ye Yong and Xu Xiangqian went to the Hailufeng area. Other units went to Hainan Island, Western Guangxi Province, Hong Kong, and Hunan.[27] In the White Terror campaign that followed, some two hundred Communists and over two thousand Red Guards and Red Army soldiers perished, according to the estimates provided by the Guangdong Provincial Committee.[28] In addition, five members of the Soviet Consulate in Guangzhou, who had been involved in the uprising, along with several Chinese, were marched about the city past the extensive, burned-out ruins before being shot in front of the Bureau of Public Safety. The latter had been the headquarters for the Guangzhou Soviet Government.[29] The Russian Consul, who had been taken prisoner, was expelled by the KMT authorities, and all Russian consulates and trade missions in Nationalist territory were closed. On December 15 the Nanjing government broke off diplomatic relations with the Soviet Union.[30]

One of the best statements, often quoted, illuminating the apathy, confusion, and even hostility that greeted the Communist uprising at Guangzhou was made by its military commander, Ye Ting. Ye lamented the lack of mass participation or even sympathy for the Communists' campaign—a momentous change from previous years when hundreds of thousands participated in Communist-led strikes in Guangzhou:

> The great masses did not take part in the insurrection at all. . . . All the shops were closed, and the shopworkers showed no desire to support us. . . . Most of the soldiers who had been disarmed simply dispersed around the city. The insurrection was not related to the troubles that had arisen among the workers of the three railway lines. The reactionaries were still able to use the Canton-Hankow line. We did not pay sufficient attention to the fleet, which remained in enemy hands. Our party did not do what was necessary to support the base organization of workers. The armed detachments of the engineering union, wearing white armbands, chased their red brothers and shot them. The power station work-

ers put out the lamps, and we had to work in the dark. The workers of Canton and Hong Kong, like the seamen, under pressure from the British imperialists did not join those who were fighting. . . . As for the river transport workers, they shamefully put themselves on the side of the Whites, who they helped to cross the river while we for our part were unable to find even a small number of boats. The railway workers of Hong Kong and Hankow transmitted the enemy's cables and transported his soldiers. The peasants did not help us to destroy the railway, and did not try to prevent the enemy from attacking Canton. The Hong Kong workers did not show the least sympathy for the insurrection.[31]

On December 14 the Party Central, obviously unaware of the failure of the Guangzhou Soviet and still clinging to extravagant assumptions about what might result from taking Guangzhou, issued a Central Notice calling the Guangzhou Uprising the beginning of a province-wide uprising and a signal for a nationwide uprising to seize political power. The notice instructed Communists to launch a Guangdong provincial uprising to secure the victory in Guangzhou, carry out a general uprising in both Hubei and Hunan provinces, and establish an area of separate Communist strength in the territory adjoining Jiangxi and Hunan provinces. The latter, when united with the ongoing uprising in Hubei province, was to further guarantee the success of the Guangdong Uprising. Collectively these events then would "expand the whole country's general uprising."[32] As it turned out, of course, with the failures in Changsha, Wuhan, and now Guangzhou, these overly ambitious and unrealistic plans had to be discarded.

It has been asserted that the Guangzhou Uprising was organized in direct response to Stalin's orders so that he could use a "victory" in China to vindicate his theoretical position and soften the impact of his crushing the Trotsky Opposition at the CPSU Congress.[33] The congress met in Moscow December 2–19, 1927. This assertion fails to recognize several overriding factors. First, Stalin's position at the Fifteenth Congress already was solid, and there was hardly any way to distract attention away from his blows to the opposition. Trotsky had been expelled from the CPSU in November and had subsequently been abandoned by key followers, such as Zinoviev, as the Trotsky Opposition crumbled.[34] Immediately after the congress 1,500 oppositionists were turned out of the CPSU, and 2,500 signed statements of recantation.[35]

Second, the CCP leaders were hardly such puppets of the CPSU that they would obligingly plan a major Chinese uprising merely to influence the progress of a Moscow power struggle. Rather, the November plenum under Lominadze's guidance had already called for staging general uprisings guided by those in major urban centers. The events in Hubei had followed such a course, with the emphasis there being on taking Wuhan. In Hunan the focal point was an uprising in Changsha. Even the radical slogan that "taking Guangzhou for a short period of time would have important significance" had been repeated in Hubei with regard to Wuhan. In other words, developments in Guangzhou were part of an established policy trend that emanated from the November plenum and were not an isolated response to Moscow's direction.

In addition, there is evidence that Zhang Tailei required no prodding to carry out the Guangzhou Uprising plans. Zhang was so optimistic about the success of the uprising that when the suggestion was raised that a retreat plan should be drawn up in case of failure, he responded that the rebels could not fail.[36] Indeed, a criticism eventually leveled at the Guangzhou rebels was their lack of an escape plan. Thus while a Communist victory in Guangzhou might have been useful to Stalin, the event itself developed from established Communist policies and out of the conditions and course of events already taking place in China.

The Party Central Modifies Revolutionary Tactics

Qu Qiubai described the period of the Guangzhou Uprising as a time "when blind actionism made itself manifest in a number of provinces . . ." and noted that "various provinces at the time were busy setting the date for the uprising." Further, he claimed that "there did prevail in the Party a general feeling that the Party was moving toward the left."[37] Reflecting this sentiment at the provincial level, the Shandong Provincial Committee instructed its county committees on November 29 that: "The action this time should start with economic struggle leading right up to a mass uprising, killing scabs, occupying factories, capturing counterrevolutionaries, and disarming the army and police. Our purpose in this uprising is to stir up the revolutionary sentiment of the masses and provide them with the practical knowledge of managing factories and seizing political power, not merely to get them organized."[38]

To counter this dangerous trend, the Party Central pointed out key tactical errors that had occurred at Guangzhou as well as in the course of the other uprisings during the fall and ordered that they not be repeated. It stressed that preliminary organizational work among the urban and rural masses had to be developed to a very high degree before an uprising aimed at seizing political power could be launched. In Guangzhou, for example, the peasant masses in the city's suburbs had not participated in the uprising. Several key labor unions had not been mobilized and some not adequately propagandized.[39]

The Party stressed that close attention should be given to the objective conditions at the uprising site. The Guangzhou rebels had not taken into account the numerical and military superiority of the opposition's forces or penetrated its armies. Existing conditions had to satisfy certain prerequisites such as the four identified in November for staging an urban insurrection. Cadres had to establish a solid basis of support backed by strong worker and peasant organizations and an effective Party organ; otherwise they would be engaged only in "playing with revolution." Party instructions to the Jiangsu cadre on January 1, 1928, criticized the commonly held position that establishing a soviet even for a few days was meaningful.[40] Of course, just two days later the Party Central issued the already discussed decision concerning the Hubei events, which largely exonerated Luo Yinong and contained observations similar to those above concerning mistakes made in Hubei.

Another common error ascribed to cadre in Wuhan and elsewhere was the tendency to regard any sign of struggle as evidence that a full-scale uprising was in progress. Often this provoked cadres to coerce workers to carry out strikes and demonstrations or to apply military force against peasants to follow Party directions. Not only did these methods fail, they usually engendered resentment and opposition. Finally, the Party Central criticized the tactic of killing and burning property on a broad scale during the course of uprisings.[41] The Guangzhou leadership came in for special admonishment regarding this mistake. In one incident during the course of the uprising, a large amount of cash contained in a warehouse and vaults was lost to the Communists after they set them afire.[42]

Thus by early 1928 the Party Central had come to recognize the

importance of carefully evaluating objective conditions and understood the perniciousness of certain tactical excesses. In the key January "Resolution on the Principles of Work in Various Provinces," which
Qu Qiubai explained "set forth principles of work for the whole Party,"
the Party Central's grasp of lessons learned from the experiences of the
fall and recent uprisings is clear: "It would be blind actionism if we
were to rely only on the bravery of a small number of Communists,
assassination of individuals, guerrilla tactics of murder and arson without mass participation, frivolous calls for immediate insurrections in
large cities disregarding the situation and conditions for a direct
uprising, insurrections by a small number of Party members, and other
actions that neglect the masses. This kind of blind actionism that plays
with uprisings . . . is also a crime against the revolution."[43]

At the same time this resolution shows that the Party continued to
hold the remarkable strategic view that prospects for establishing political power at least at the provincial level were good. As Qu reported,
"after the Canton uprising, an upsurge was evident in the Chinese
revolution."[44] This was in harmony with the argument that Lominadze
would make when he presented his prognosis of the Chinese situation
to the upcoming ECCI February Plenum in Moscow.[45] Thus plans were
included in this resolution to establish two key centers for seizing
power at the provincial level in one or several provinces. As in the past,
one center was to be established in Guangdong Province. The other
required coordinated developments in Hunan, Hubei, Jiangxi, and
southern Henan provinces, which on completion would produce a
second revolutionary guiding center in Wuhan.[46]

In discussing this resolution, Qu sheds some light on why CCP leaders continued to seek a base of strength from which to capture key
cities. Qu explained: "Meanwhile, the reactionary forces, which could
cling to the large cities and industrial and commercial centers of the
provinces, put up a desperate fight. They carried on a reign of white
terror and a vigorous anti-communist campaign. The struggle to take
over the cities became even more important to the proletarian party."[47]
Thus the impetus for seizing key cities arose in part from the pressing
concern to try to diminish the severe oppression emanating from
urban centers. Besides seeing their own survival at stake the Communists, having experienced frustrating defeats and losses at the hands
of KMT forces, no doubt were also eager to exact some revenge. Further,

some might even have questioned whether the alternative of a prolonged and rural-centered movement, separated from the urban
proletariat, could be considered a valid Communist movement. Finally,
there was concern to maintain the morale of Party members and followers after the fall defeats. In internal correspondence, the Party
instructed members to put the best possible light on its ongoing programs and policies: "At this moment when the revolutionary spirit is
at its ebb, we should put forth slogans of 'determined victory' for
our struggles in order to arouse the masses from their cowardly and
abject spirit."[48]

The ECCI's Ninth Plenum Orders Restraint

Trotsky called the Guangzhou Uprising a putsch and "an *adventurist*
zigzag by the Comintern to the left." He predicted that now the
Comintern would take a "longer zigzag to the right," especially regarding Chinese politics.[49] Indeed, the Comintern responded to the latest
disasters in China by shifting the emphasis of its earlier theoretical
interpretation and providing guidance to steady the course of events
there. It organized a Chinese conference to precede the ECCI's Ninth
Plenum, which met in Moscow February 9–25, 1928. At this conference
the issues and problems of events in China were debated heatedly and
at length. Besso Lominadze presented his interpretation that there
was no middle path for China. Either the country would become an
imperialist colony or it would move rapidly through revolution toward
a proletarian dictatorship. This view ran counter to the interpretation
presented by Bukharin and Stalin, coauthors of the important "Resolution on the Chinese Question," adopted on February 25, 1928, by the
plenum.[50] This document began with the authoritative statement that
"the present period of the Chinese revolution is a period of bourgeois-
democratic revolution which has not been completed."[51] It condemned
the characterization of the present phase of the Chinese revolution as
one that was already a socialist revolution, thus qualifying for government by a proletarian dictatorship. It blamed Lominadze for commit-
ting a Trotskyist error by characterizing the Chinese revolution as a
"permanent" revolution with a concomitant "tendency to skip over the
bourgeois democratic phase."[52] But in stating their position, Bukharin
and Stalin avoided dwelling on the concept that "this bourgeois-

democratic revolution has a tendency to grow over into a socialist revolution," which had been the ECCI's emphasis since July 1927.[53] Clearly the opportunities for confusing "growing over" with "permanent revolution" had already precipitated disastrous results in China. Bukharin and Stalin chose now to stress the more restraining side of their approach—that of fully completing each historical stage before moving on to the next—as well as the "national peculiarity" of the Chinese revolution.

The plenum declared that "the first wave of the broad revolutionary movement of the workers and peasants ... is over" and had involved "heavy defeats." It concluded that "at the present time, there is still no mighty upsurge of the revolutionary mass movement on a national scale," but noted the existence of certain promising signs such as the Guangzhou Uprising and especially the centers of peasant activity in Guangdong and other provinces.[54] The overall situation in China was characterized as following a pattern of uneven development: "The course of the Chinese revolution has underlined one of its peculiar features, that is extremely unequal development. It is developing unequally in different provinces. ... It has also until now developed unequally as between town and country."[55]

The expectation was that the revolution would advance more in the countryside than in the cities because of the extent of White Terror being waged against the workers. Under these conditions the basic tactical line required that: "all Party work must now be concentrated on winning over the worker and peasant millions, educating them politically, organizing them around the party and its slogans...."[56]

To a large extent this emphasis on careful planning, coordination, and strict attention to mass work had already been recognized by the Chinese leadership and included in its tactical guidance by late January. The Comintern warned, however, that special care was to be taken to carefully assess the strength of the mass movement and that of the opposition and to guard against any inclination "to break away from the masses, push too far ahead," and thus run the risk of becoming divided or defeated (as happened in Guangzhou).[57] At this stage, goals for the workers were to be limited to those of trade unionism, that is, an eight-hour work day, increased wages, and so on, rather than the earlier radical paths leading to seizing and managing the factories, appropriate only at the socialist stage.

In Lominadze's absence the Chinese leadership also provided a comprehensive analysis of the Chinese revolution that foretold the Comintern's main themes but included more discussion of the nature and key function of the soviet. In the January 16 editorial in the Party organ *Bolshevik*, probably written by its editor Qu Qiubai, the argument was made that the soviets were to serve as the transitional form of government between the two key stages of the Chinese revolution and involve the broad participation of the peasants, soldiers, and urban poor.[58] Only when soviets were widespread in the country could the revolution grow into an advanced socialist revolution and embark on establishing a proletarian dictatorship and realizing a socialist action program. When the stage was reached that a determined struggle for the socialist revolution had begun, the slogan calling for a proletarian socialist dictatorship could be substituted for the earlier, more limited one calling for a democratic dictatorship of the workers and peasants.[59] At that point conditions would be favorable for rising up again and seizing KMT-fortified cities like Guangzhou.

In retrospect, the Guangzhou Uprising, aimed at establishing an urban soviet, was modeled after the October 1917 Russian experience. With its decisive defeat, the Chinese leaders once again had to reassess their position. Some now stressed learning the facts and lessons of their own conditions and experiences. With the overwhelming strength of opposition forces concentrated in the cities, the view that began to emerge was that the only viable path to survival and growth lay in the countryside. As Ye Jianying reported, "The Guangzhou Uprising was not a complete failure . . . it demonstrated that we could not take cities and after the uprising, should have shifted quickly to the countryside and joined the vital Hailufeng peasant movement. There we could establish a rural base area and launch guerrilla warfare having as its central theme land revolution."[60] As we will see, the response becoming prevalent among those actively engaged in uprising activity was that experiences like that of the Guangzhou Uprising confirmed the immediate value and necessity of establishing armed rural base areas.

Chapter 7. Building Rural Soviets

Extensive planning and policy development took place during the early months of 1928. In January the Party Central issued the "Resolution on the Principles of Work in Various Provinces," which outlined policy on work for the provinces. In addition, the problem of how, when, or under what conditions an uprising should be staged reportedly was dealt with in a Central Notice entitled "On Armed Uprisings."[1] These policies emerged at a time when the Chinese leadership was operating without a key Comintern adviser, since Lominadze had not yet been replaced. The new policies regarding the soviet organizations, military bodies, and Party strategy and tactics emerged to a large degree from the lessons of the failures of 1927, and from the pervasive fear within the leadership that the Communist movement would disintegrate unless key changes were made in operational strategies and tactics to deal realistically with the working environment in China.

Defining the Soviet

The centerpiece of the Party's planning efforts concerned the nature and function of the soviets. The authoritative document on this subject was the Party Central's directive "Confiscate All Lands and Establish Soviets."[2] This undated document probably originated during February 1928, after which the Party Central is known to have ordered specific CCP provincial committees to establish soviets and independent rural bases, making reference to its own detailed published provisions as guidance.[3] The provisional Jiangxi CCP Committee already had developed a Provisional Soviet Organizational Law in November 1927, presumably following the November plenum's official endorsement of the soviet. The Jiangxi law explained that the Party Central still had not published a soviet organizational law that would unify existing laws and be applicable to the whole country, and that therefore a temporary or provisional law was promulgated in Jiangxi.[4] In addition, the Hailufeng soviet issued regulations in November on soviet organization provided, it seems, by the Guangdong CCP Committee.[5] The point is that the Party Central had at its disposal the regulations and directives developed by these and possibly other CCP provincial committees from which to formulate a central policy on the soviets.

Theoretically, soviets were to function as transitional social and political organizations, which could unite the antifeudal and anti-imperialist elements in a people's democratic dictatorship and move the revolution along the path toward socialism. Practically, they were the bodies that were to attract, organize, and mobilize support from three key segments of Chinese society—workers, peasants, and soldiers. Members of these groups were among the most vulnerable to the dislocations and economic hardships of the time and were thus potentially receptive to the Party's programs. The Party planned to use the soviets to galvanize support from among these groups into an effective movement that could preserve a degree of Communist power and influence in the face of continuing KMT anti-Communist campaigns.

The soviets had both destructive and constructive functions. In the Party's terms: "The Soviet is an organ to create disturbances and to start struggles, to massacre local bullies and gentries and to deal with the people's economic problem. It is also an organ of legislative and judicial administration. In other words, it is the government of laborers, farmers, soldiers, and poor citizens of China and is a real people's government for the advantages of a majority of the people throughout the country."[6]

The Jiangxi provisional law explained that a basic function of the soviet was to teach the backward workers and peasants the principles of democratic government and how it works. Once they had mastered its rules, the next step was to turn the soviets over to the workers and peasants to manage for themselves.[7] Peasants in some areas had previous organizational experience through their membership in peasant associations. But the concepts of holding and wielding organized political power certainly were foreign and posed a substantial intellectual challenge. Having experienced years of rural servitude, peasants were inclined to consult rituals, incantations, or secret societies to achieve their objectives. Thus the educative tasks of the soviet clearly were awesome, especially with the emphasis now on rural soviets.

Organizational guidelines for the formation of soviets throughout the country clearly reflected the policy of building rural support around the land issue at the basic rural levels. Of particular interest is the fact that the system was to be built with the village soviet as the basic initial unit. When two village soviets were established, a district soviet then could be formed. As organized support broadened, the process could expand to include county or municipal soviets and finally the provincial-level soviet.[8] Table 1 details the background of the participants and circumstances of formation of soviet organizations at various levels.

As examined in chapter 5, the new regulations for building Party and League organizations that came out of the November plenum emphasized starting at the basic or branch level. This approach was carried over into the building of soviets. But with the soviet organizational system, the basic level was to be the village soviet. This did not preclude preparatory work aimed at establishing soviets in urban areas. Rather, the latter was to be a concomitant goal once a foundation had been established in the countryside. Just as guerrilla tactics had been confined to units located in rural areas, the point of origin for the soviet organizational system was designated in the countryside. Both had emerged out of the Communists' experience in dealing with the new operating conditions that began in 1927, and their recognition that organizational support could be realized most successfully in the relatively secure rural areas.

Newly formed soviet organizations were to serve as "the direct political authority of the people." They were to be elected by a gathering at a public meeting or by a conference of local representatives, as indicated in table 1. The franchise and the right to be elected to serve in the new government were extended to both males and females of sixteen years and older who were not "oppressors of laborers, religious, or anti-revolutionary elements."[9]

Once established, the soviet was to assume all authority previously held by the peasant associations, labor unions, any other Communist bodies, and the Revolutionary Committee. This latter organization was to serve only as the ad hoc provisional body that would coordinate the

Table 1 Various-Level Soviet Organizations:
Circumstances of Their Formation

Level	When formed	Background of persons attending first conferences	Required number at conferences
Village soviet	When the masses of the village in question arise.	Representatives of farmers, laborers, and soldiers.	At village and district conferences, one representative for every 500 farmers. If the number of laborers and soldiers is less than 500, other suitable arrangements based on local conditions must be made to ensure their active participation.
District soviet	When two Village soviets have come into being in the district.	Representatives of farmers, laborers, and soldiers.	
County soviet	When the urban labor movement is well-established and when two district soviets have been formed.	At least 30 percent of persons present should be laborers, 5 percent soldiers.	For county, municipal, and provincial conferences, the number of representatives depends on local struggle conditions.
Municipal soviet	When disturbances have been occurring throughout the province, then a municipality becomes the center for struggle and the establishment of a soviet.	70 percent of persons present should be laborers, 15 percent farmers and soldiers.	
Provincial soviet	When disturbances are occurring through the whole province.	40 percent of persons present should be laborers, 10 percent soldiers, and 50 percent farmers.	At least 40 representatives need to be present at the provincial conference.

Source: *Zhejiang Collection.* Shanghai Municipal Police Document no. 4772. Shanghai Municipal Police Files. 3:45–48, 50.

military, communications, and financial matters involved in actually carrying out the armed uprising leading to the soviets' existence. The previous responsibilities of these organs for education, propaganda, economics, and military matters were all to be centralized in the soviet.

A primary task of the newly established soviet was to oversee the thorough implementation of the land revolution, the key goal of the bourgeois-democratic revolution. The outcome of this work would be the complete annihilation of the social, political, and economic foundations of feudalism, which exploited the peasants' labor power and denied them any political role. The old rural power structure was to be replaced with a new system geared to bring about a more equitable distribution of economic wealth in the soviet area and guarantee "the absolute political rights of laborers and farmers under [the direction of] the proletariat [CCP]."[10]

The charts shown in figures 3 through 6 describe the organizational system and offices of the soviets that were to support the revolutionary program at each administrative level.[11] One unique function of the soviets was to establish a new culture in the areas where they were formed to replace the previous feudal one. The soviet's Culture Committee was to eliminate practices such as opium use, gambling, and foot binding and other discriminatory practices against females. An office charged with raising the general cultural level was included at every level of the soviet system.

Another organizational precedent for the soviet system defined by the Party Central appeared with the short-lived Guangzhou Soviet. Its functional committees were similar to those of the provincial-level soviet shown in figure 6. Both were served by committees handling the following areas: navy and army, diplomacy, economics, land, justice, and suppression of counterrevolutionaries.[12] Only the Culture and Finance committees were omitted from this earlier soviet. However, the Guangzhou Soviet included a committee devoted to labor union affairs, which is not shown in figure 6. Probably the responsibilities for urban labor unions were to be covered by the Economics Committee of the provincial-level soviet. Lack of a labor union committee also suggests the broader, largely rural focus of this new provincial body. In any case, this new rural conception of soviets now supplied what the Guangzhou Soviet had lacked: the underpinnings of an established village, district, and county-level soviet system.

Figure 3 The Village Soviet Government Structure

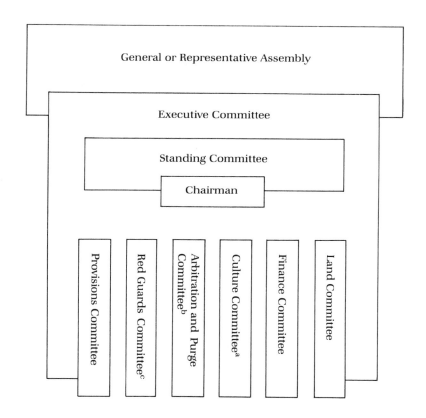

Source: *Zhejiang Collection*. Shanghai Municipal Police Document no. 4772. Shanghai Municipal Police Files, 3:52.

[a] This Committee was charged with education and propaganda work.

[b] This body was to arbitrate local disputes and handle local "reactionary" elements.

[c] This organ directed all Red Guard activities.

Figure 4 The District Soviet Government Structure

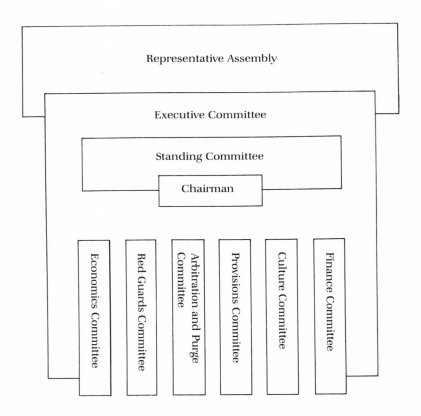

Source: *Zhejiang Collection*. Shanghai Municipal Police Document no. 4772. Shanghai Municipal Police Files, 3:53.

Figure 5 The County or Municipal Soviet Government Structure

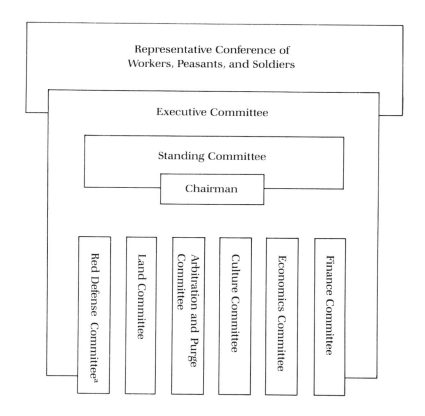

Source: *Zhejiang Collection*. Shanghai Municipal Police Document no. 4772. Shanghai Municipal Police Files, 3:54.

[a] The Red Army was controlled and mobilized at the provincial level, while the Red Defense Corps or Red Guards operated under the command of the county soviet.

Figure 6 The Provincial Soviet Government Structure

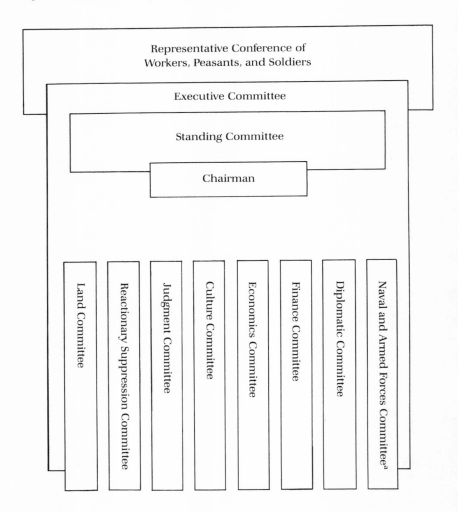

Source: *Zhejiang Collection*. Shanghai Municipal Police Document no. 4772. Shanghai Municipal Police Files, 3:55.

The internal staffing and operational procedures for each soviet level are given in table 2. The overriding concern was to maintain representation from the three social groups—workers, peasants, and soldiers. In contrast, guidance developed by the Guangdong CCP Provincial Committee (and approved by the Party Central in September 1927) to direct the work of establishing county and municipal government organizations required that county government committees be elected by 60 percent peasant representation, 30 percent worker representation, and "ten percent small merchants and poor intellectual elements."[13] The obvious lesson apparent by early 1928 was that, to be viable, the soviet governments had to include military participation as well.

Table 2 Internal Staffing and Operating Procedures
of the Soviets

	Executive committee members	Executive committee reserve members	Executive committee meetings	Standing committee members[a]	Standing committee meetings
Village soviet	5 to 7[b]	3	One a week	3	One every two days
District soviet	7 to 9[b]	5	One a week	3 to 5	Two a week
County soviet	11 to 13	7	One a month	5 to 7	Two a week
Municipal soviet	15 to 21	7	One a month	5 to 7	Two a week
Provincial soviet	21 to 27	11	One a month	7 to 9	One a week

Source: *Zhejiang Collection*. Shanghai Municipal Police Document no. 4772. Shanghai Municipal Police Files. 3:45–48, 51.

Note: If lacking worker participation, only a provisional county executive committee could be inaugurated. In villages a soviet might be established without assistance from municipal areas. A municipal soviet might be established at places that were not key industrial and commercial centers.

[a] At all levels, the soviet chairman was included in the number of standing committee members. He was to be elected by the executive committee.

[b] Efforts were to be made to elect laborers and soldiers to these executive committees.

According to general guidance provided by the "Central Government of the Communist Party" concerning the political, economic, and social roles that the soviets were to play in an area, the soviet at each level within a province had offices for handling any matters concerning the confiscation and correct public apportionment of lands and properties, dealing with local "reactionary" elements, scaling workers' wages and hours, and fixing tax levels in order to provide necessary government revenues.[14] These services are reflected in the four soviet organizational charts of figures 3–6.

In carrying out these responsibilities the soviet leadership was to adhere to the tenets of centralism, with all subordinate-level cadres being committed to follow any instructions that emanated from higher-level soviet leadership. This is another obvious point of similarity between the emerging soviet organizational system and that of the Party organizational system. Further, at the Soviet Conferences of Representatives the democratic aspects of Party democratic centralism are found within the soviet system in that the soviet leadership was to seek to hear representative opinions on key issues and to discuss and shape opinion on key issues within this larger audience.

One aspect of the concept of centralism was at work in the regulations that governed the crucial question of land division.[15] Reportedly, all lands and family temples were to be confiscated and converted into public property for management by the local soviet. These operations, performed by the village soviet, were to be carefully supervised and assisted by representatives from the district soviet organ. Land was to be apportioned to individuals who were able to cultivate it. Their right to plow the land was to be verified by a land certificate issued to them by the county soviet government. The guiding principle was that land was to be divided according to the background and skills of the receiver and could not be influenced by monetary considerations. The regulations emphasized that lands could not simply be bought and sold. The removal of the verifying authority to a higher level provided a built-in guarantee that local land division would be managed according to the highest Communist principles and would be less apt to bog down in traditional local contests for power and influence between, for example, local lineage or clan groups. If a county-level organ had not yet been established in a province, verification of the right to work the land in a village was to be granted by whatever higher-level organ existed.

Another important point relating to local land management concerned the amount of land to be apportioned to an individual farmer. The general policy was that the amount would be based on the number of family members and the degree of fertility of the land. There was also the provision that families of those serving as officers and soldiers in the Red Army could receive land and hire farm laborers to work the lands. Back in November Peng Pai had won acceptance of similar, if more detailed, criteria for land division in Haifeng, Guangdong.[16]

The regulations gave special consideration to the problems of farm laborers. If, in addition to their regular responsibilities as farm laborers, a group of them wanted to farm additional land, a portion of land could be allotted them and responsibilities for working it shared among the group. In addition, certain regulations guaranteeing protection to farm laborers after the confiscation of local lands were to be promulgated by the soviets. The important points of those regulations provided "higher wages, improved treatment and shorter working hours" for farm laborers. Those same provisions were to be extended to other local manual workers and to coolies. Other sections ordered the village soviets to maintain a livelihood for helpless and indigent members of the village community, including those living alone and unable to work such as orphans, widows, and persons physically incapacitated by injury or illness.

The Party guidance contains some very sketchy information concerning a soviet system's tax structure.[17] All land tillers were required to pay the county soviet a tax from 10 to 25 percent of their total crop yields. The exact amount presumably depended on local conditions and the extent and quality of local crops. Of the total taxes collected, 20 percent was to go toward funding the operation of a central soviet government.[18] The provincial soviet was to cover its expenses with 30 percent, while the village soviet received 20 percent. The county soviet was to receive 30 percent of taxes collected, but out of that it had to cover the expenses of operating district soviets.

These regulations concerning the soviet organizations, like other major Communist organizational principles and guidance, assigned a key role to the county-level organization. In the case of the soviets the county-level organ had authority for administering the key revolutionary task—that of land division—as well as tax collection and distribution. In the next chapter the county level will be shown to play an authoritative role in several other Communist or Communist-influenced organizations. The county-level soviet had the additional feature of versatility in that it could be applied either to a county center of little industrial or commercial importance, or it could be applied to structure Communist support in a major urban center. Thus the county-level organization could serve as a potential coordination point for both the urban and rural revolutionary movements.

Soviets Established in 1927 and 1928

Communist planning originally envisioned establishing soviets in the key cities Changsha and Guangzhou. As discussed above, the attack on Changsha never materialized, and the Guangzhou Soviet lasted only about three days. The earliest soviet government, rather than being based in a major urban area, centered on the adjoining counties of Haifeng and Lufeng in Guangdong Province and became known as the Hailufeng Soviet.

The Hailufeng Soviet. The founder of the Hailufeng Soviet, Peng Pai, was also the founder of the modern peasant movement in China. As early as 1922 Peng was leading a full-fledged peasant movement in Haifeng County of Guangdong Province, establishing there the first peasant association during the summer. Recognizing the need to instill in the peasant movement both modern organizational skills and a supporting ideology, Peng became director and principal instructor at the government-sponsored Peasant Movement Training Institute, established on July 3, 1924. Its purpose was to train rural political activists for the fast-growing Guangdong peasant movement, particularly in the counties near Guangzhou.[19] Under Peng's guidance, by May of 1926 nearly 200,000 peasants had been organized into 660 peasant unions in Haifeng County alone.[20] Graduates of this peasant institute received military training at the Huangbu (Whampoa) Military Academy, became key peasant organizers, and were largely responsible for the rapid development of the peasant movement in areas under KMT control from the fall of 1927 on.[21]

The Hailufeng Soviet Government was established by November 21, 1927, after three Communist-led insurrections. The first began on May 1, 1927, and was aided by the Peasant Self-Defense Corps, renamed the

Workers and Peasants Save-the-Party (Left KMT) Army. It succeeded in establishing a "People's Government" and holding the town of Haifeng for ten days before being forced by invading Kuomintang forces to withdraw to the rural villages around Haifeng.[22]

The second insurrection began on September 1 after the encouraging news of the southward march of He Long's and Ye Ting's forces and the directive for the Autumn Harvest Uprising had reached the area. Following sustained fighting between peasant forces and landlord protective forces—the Peace Preservation Corps and rural militia—the CCP announced the establishment of a "Worker-Peasants' Dictatorship" on September 17 and gave as its "sole task the extermination of anti-revolutionaries."[23] Its radical mission, which called for confiscating the wealth of local landlords, merchants, and officials, and total land confiscation, gave the new body the characteristics of the soviet. But at this time, of course, the Communists still were bound to working in alliance with the KMT and thus could not use the soviet nomenclature. Expecting a strong counterattack when anti-Communist forces advanced toward Hailufeng on September 25, the Communists withdrew to a remote mountainous district. Once again the attacking forces recovered the towns of Haifeng and Lufeng, but most of the surrounding areas remained under Communist control.

The prospects of the Hailufeng revolutionary organization improved when news arrived that the peasants' idol, Peng Pai, was back in Guangdong, and that troops formerly under He Long and Ye Ting's command, rounded up after the Nanchang Uprising defeats, had joined the revolutionary military forces. These new forces were given food, clothing, and a heavy dose of propaganda and were reorganized into the 2nd Division of the Worker-Peasant Revolutionary Army in preparation for a third insurrection. Their opportunity came on November 1, 1927, when KMT forces withdrew from the Haifeng area to participate in the imminent showdown between Zhang Fakui and Li Jishen in Guangzhou. The peasant forces once again attacked and occupied Haifeng and succeeded in extending their control throughout Haifeng County by November 19. The Party's East River (*Dongjiang*) Special Committee established a Provisional Revolutionary Committee and ordered Party members "to exterminate all the landowners" and confiscate their land and property.

The formal Hailufeng Soviet Government emerged from the General

Conference of Workers, Peasants, and Soldiers held in Lufeng on November 13 and in Haifeng from November 18 to 21 to elect the leadership of a soviet government and determine its policies. In addition to the two county-level soviets, the combined Hailufeng Soviet system was composed of subordinate district- and village-level soviets.[24] The Party's East River Special Committee, under Peng Pai's direction as secretary, acted as the coordination point for integrating these various-level soviets.[25] In regard to policy matters the new Hailufeng leadership closely followed Party guidance. Hailufeng's now organized forces followed a radical course, calling for ruthless destruction of all counter-revolutionaries and confiscation of all landlord lands—the policy ratified at the Party's November plenum. The military force necessary for carrying out these activities was provided by the 2nd Division of the Red Army (about 800 men), the 4th Division from Guangzhou reorganized under Ye Yong's command (1,200 men), the Workers' and Peasants' Revolutionary Corps (over 1,000 men), and numerous Red Guards in the villages.[26]

Peng's forces were adequate for pursuing the radical programs and holding off opposing landlord levies. But in January 1928 regular, well-equipped KMT forces under Li Jishen and Zhang Fakui reunited and began a drive that over the next three months successfully expelled the Communist-led troops from the Hailufeng area and drove many of them into the mountains near the Fujian border. The Hailufeng Soviet fell on February 29, 1928, in the face of overwhelming military power. Peng, the consummate peasant organizer, correctly read the often violent aspirations of the rural peasant population. What he still failed to grasp, however, was the essential need for a disciplined, trained, Party-led military force, operating out of a base area, to protect and consolidate the peasants' revolutionary gains.[27]

The Southern Hunan Soviet Governments. After the defeat of the Nanchang forces in Guangdong Province, Zhu De gathered about two thousand survivors and led them into southern Jiangxi for reorganization, indoctrination, and training. Desperate to preserve and supplement this strength, Zhu convinced a Yunnanese general and former military school classmate, Fan Shisheng, to integrate these troops as a regiment of Fan's Sixteenth Kuomintang Army in November.[28] Thus Zhu became a regimental commander in a KMT army, with Chen Yi as his political officer and Wang Erzhou as chief of staff.[29] In December Zhu's forces were ordered by the Party Central to participate in the planned Guangzhou Uprising, but apparently the Shanghai leaders were unaware of the timing and progress of the uprising. Zhu's forces were ordered to be in Guangzhou by December 15, but when they arrived, of course, the uprising had already failed.

The Shanghai Party Central was not impressed with the possible advantages of the alliance with Fan Shisheng and on December 27 ordered Zhu to disengage from Fan's forces.[30] Zhu was directed to get in touch with Mao Zedong's forces and "make a joint plan to spur the masses, create an independent uprising base through these armed forces, and establish a Representative's Council of the Workers, Peasants, and Soldiers—the soviet political power."[31]

Zhu separated from Fan's forces in January 1928 and proceeded as a guerrilla force into southern Hunan Province. There he could take advantage of a favorable military situation, for KMT generals Bai Chongxi and Tang Shengzhi were at war with one another and thus diverted from their regular anti-Communist drives. Arriving near Yizhang county in southern Hunan around January 20, 1928, Zhu with local Party authorities planned to launch an uprising aimed at occupying the county seat of Yizhang.

The uprising began at noon on January 22, the last day of the lunar year and the time for settling accounts in rural areas. To ease their way, Zhu's forces reportedly disguised themselves as KMT troops and after gaining easy entry to the county seat seized control of the town. By late January the Yizhang County Soviet Government was established, which lasted three months and included subordinate soviets at the district and village levels. Zhu reorganized the Yizhang Peasant Army into the 1st Division of the Workers' and Peasants' Revolutionary Army and made preparations to carry this success to other areas in southern Hunan.[32]

Zhu's extensive experience as a troop commander was demonstrated by the fact that Xu Kexiang, the KMT commander at the infamous May 1927 Horse Day Incident, deployed six regiments to crush the Communists, but still fell to Zhu's forces. Zhu's army went on to capture the southeastern county seats of Leiyang, Zixing, Yongxing, Guidong, and Rucheng, and to launch uprisings elsewhere in southern Hunan. This successful wave was interrupted in late April, however, when regular KMT forces became reunited and jointly sent seven divisions against Zhu's positions. Again, overwhelming military power turned the tide, aided in this case by a growing apathy on the part of the rural populations. Unlike Peng Pai, Zhu had talents concentrated mainly in military affairs. Routed in battle, Zhu's surviving armies withdrew from southern Hunan to the security of the Jinggang Mountains. In an oral account of these events, Zhu said that on April 28, 1928, at Longshi in Ninggan County, on the grounds of the Dragon River School, ceremonies were held to mark the joining of his forces with Mao's.[33] In May their military forces combined to form the Fourth Workers' and Peasants' Revolutionary Army. Zhu became commander of this considerable force, Mao its political commissar, and Chen Yi head of the Political Department.[34]

The Jinggang Mountains Soviet Governments. The establishment of the Jinggang soviet area had begun in October 1927 when Mao succeeded in regrouping the decimated Lu Deming or Wuhan garrison regiment, which had been unsuccessful at Nanchang and defeated in the Hunan Autumn Harvest Uprising, along with various peasant troops fleeing the repression that followed the Hunan military defeats.[35] Once deep in the Jinggang Mountains, Mao augmented his forces from local power-holder-bandit troops. Yuan Wenzai, the leader of one contingent of local forces, had established his power through manipulation of the local political-military scene. He operated skillfully in a milieu that during the 1920s included competing bandit groups, landlord militia, warlord armies, units of the National Revolutionary Army, peasant self-defense forces, and right-wing KMT forces. The proliferation of armed units accelerated after the end of the First United Front, compelling local power holders like Yuan for reasons of survival to strengthen their position by any means available in order to withstand the constant challenges.

Wang Zuo, another local leader, was even more immersed in the bandit world. Upon arriving in the area, Mao was quick to recognize that these two leaders could provide his forces with experienced local contacts, additional armed strength, and some link to previous Communist-led mass movements in the area. Recognizing the mutual benefits to be gained, in mid-February 1928 Yuan's and Wang's forces

Qu Qiubai took over CCP leadership from August 1927 to July 1928.

He Long, a military commander who helped establish revolutionary base areas.

Pictured is Comintern Representative Adolf Joffe, who concluded the entente with Dr. Sun Yat-sen leading to the First United Front.

Members of the Party Central in Ruijin, capital of the Jiangxi Soviet, in November 1931. From right: Wang Jiaxiang, Mao Zedong, Xiang Ying, Deng Fa, Zhu De, Ren Bishi, and Gu Zuolin.

Chen Duxiu was the first General Secretary of the Chinese Communist Party.

Zhu De developed principles of guerrilla warfare and became the Red Army Commander.

combined into the 32nd Regiment of the 1st Division of the First Red Army.[36]

Writing about the Jinggang Mountains experiences in November 1928, Mao repeatedly stressed the importance of the location centered on Ninggan. It was sufficiently removed from major enemy political centers like Changsha, Nanchang, and Wuhan, but close enough to monitor evidence of any internal conflicts that might signal opportunities for Communist offensives either in Jiangxi or Hunan. Its location, in a high valley on the border, entirely surrounded by mountains penetrated by only a few easily guarded passes, made it a defensible military base, and also allowed quick access to either province once campaigns were launched.[37]

These crucial military and geographic features of the Jinggang base apparently were not appreciated or perhaps not understood by the Hunan Provincial Party leadership, anxious to expand Communist activities in the province. In March 1928 the Red Army was ordered to participate in the abortive uprisings in southern Hunan, thus leaving the way open for right-wing local forces to recapture territory in the area and reestablish influence during the Red Army's absence. But when the Red Army returned, its forces were significantly strengthened by the arrival in April of Zhu De and Chen Yi's retreating troops. With this added backing, the Fourth Red Army between April and July 1928 seized and expanded its territorial base, establishing soviet governments at the county seats of Ninggan, Yongxin, Lianhua, and Suichuan, presided over by the Hunan-Jiangxi Border Area Workers', Peasants', Soldiers' Government.[38] Once again, in July 1928, the Hunan Party leadership sent emissaries to the Jinggang soviet area to order the local Party leadership to prepare to lead revolutionary activities in southern Hunan. One of the emissaries, Yang Kaiming, ousted Mao as secretary of the Special Committee of the Hunan-Jiangxi Border Area. Yang began preparations for the disastrous campaign, which divided the Communist military forces, to be led by Zhu De. In Zhu's absence, Mao's forces failed to defend the base area against the attack of eleven KMT regiments, and Zhu also experienced heavy losses in southern Hunan. The 29th Regiment was routed in a battle with Zhu's former ally, Fan Shisheng. Subsequently Zhu's forces were joined by Mao's, and on August 23 they decided to return together to the relative security of the Jinggang Mountains. Mao later called this period the "August defeat."[39]

After August 1928 the Jinggang base area came under almost constant attack from Hunan or Jiangxi armies united in encirclement and suppression campaigns against the Communist base area. Mao explained that when the opposing White forces were divided or engaged in internecine wars, the Red forces could follow more adventurous policies and tactics while continuing to build a solid basis in the "central districts."[40] On the other hand, periods of stability among the White forces brought attacks involving sometimes as many as eighteen regiments against the base area. Late in 1928 the Fourth Red Army was temporarily strengthened by the addition of Peng Dehuai's rebel forces. Peng's military forces—the former 1st Regiment of KMT General He Jian's 5th Independent Division—had revolted at Pingjiang in northeastern Hunan province in July. In November the Hunan CCP Committee directed Peng's designated Fifth Red Army to join forces with the Fourth Red Army in the Jinggang Mountains.

Even with this added military strength, however, a severe winter, compounded by an effective enemy blockade, the continued lack of local mass interest or support, and renewed and formidable attacks on the base area, forced Mao and Zhu De to evacuate the Jinggang soviet area in December and march into southern Jiangxi and western Fujian. Peng Dehuai's defending forces also were dislodged but were reunited with the Fourth Army in April 1929.

The Pingjiang Soviet. Peng Dehuai's skillful and dangerous work at organizing the lower officer ranks and soldiers of the KMT army eventually produced the Pingjiang Soviet. Peng commanded the 1st Regiment of the 5th Independent Division, one of the units in General Tang Shengzhi's army during the Northern Expedition.[41] While serving as a KMT commander, Peng organized secret "Save the Poor" societies around popular and progressive themes, demanding an end to foreign encroachments, calling for aid to the poor, and opposing the ill-treatment of regular soldiers. During this period Peng was introduced to key works in Marxist-Leninist literature by CCP member Duan Dechang. Integrating these with his previous readings in early reformist Chinese literature, including the writings of Liang Qiqiao and Kang Youwei, Peng became optimistic about prospects for deepening reform in China.[42] Subsequently he turned his "Save the Poor" societies into nuclei for organizing Communist soldier committees within the KMT ranks.

Peng joined the CCP in April 1928, sponsored by Huang Gonglue who, like Peng, studied means to subvert the KMT military from within.[43] Huang managed to become de facto head of a new Party military school for training lower-level KMT officers, while Peng worked at turning the 5th Independent Division into a secret CCP organ in the KMT army. Peng's opportunity came in the spring, when units of the Independent Division were transferred to Pingjiang, an area with a revolutionary tradition, near the borders of Hunan, Hubei, and Jiangxi provinces.

Before and after arriving in Pingjiang, Peng, as part of his KMT military duties, engaged in the ongoing anti-Communist "village-purification" campaigns. Troops under his command witnessed firsthand the slaughter of peasants like themselves. Peng reported using these graphic occasions of violence to educate his peasant troops about oppressive rural conditions, which he explained needed to be changed. Through intensive political education, he attempted to instill in his troops a clearer understanding and heightened consciousness about local political affairs. His favorite political education slogan stressed, "the rice we eat is produced by peasants, and the clothing we wear is made by workers. We must serve workers and peasants."[44]

In July 1928 Teng Daiyuan, a representative from the Hunan CCP Committee, arrived in Pingjiang to inspect local conditions. He made plans for the establishment of a CCP Hunan, Hubei, Jiangxi Special Committee to provide Party guidance and direction to the developing revolutionary activities. Teng found local conditions, including the strength and allegiance of local Communist forces, favorable for uprising. In the meantime, word reached Peng Dehuai through KMT channels that Huang Gonglue and his Party associates had been discovered. Further, Teng Daiyuan received instructions through CCP channels that the Party's involvement in the 5th Independent Division had been uncovered. Peng withheld this news from all but trusted supporters. Nevertheless, he and Teng decided that, under these circumstances, they had to act immediately.[45]

Staging an armed revolt demanded painstaking preparations, and Peng responded with characteristic resourcefulness. For example, to strengthen his forces, he asked his Hunan KMT superiors to send additional personnel, funds, and ammunition to Pingjiang, claiming that the 5th Independent Division's very successful and intensive village-purification campaigns had involved extensive fatalities and losses of equipment.[46] A final planning session set the date for the uprising on July 22 and produced a list of ten political goals to be accomplished by the uprising. These included the disbandment and capture of the local armed and political opposition, especially the hated militia and village-purification forces; the establishment of a formal Red Army and soviets; the cancellation of rents and debts, and division of the fields; and the implementation of measures to improve the conditions and livelihood of mainly the soldier ranks. If initially successful in Pingjiang, Peng planned to join with Zhu De and Mao Zedong and form a presiding border-area soviet government.[47]

Peng used the issue of back pay to galvanize his forces. This issue was crucial with the largely peasant ranks of the KMT armies, because senior KMT commanders commonly siphoned off funds meant as wages for the soldier ranks. In Pingjiang soldiers had not been paid for some time, and the more active among them had been demonstrating concerning this issue since early July. Just prior to the outbreak, Peng made a rousing speech to his prospective soldier revolutionaries, putting on a red tie to signify their revolt. Well-organized and motivated, the revolutionaries reportedly occupied the city of Pingjiang after only two hours of fighting.

The next day the rebels celebrated their success, and at a joint meeting of the soldiers' committees elected Peng as commander and Teng as Party representative of the new Fifth Red Army.[48] At a mass meeting on July 24 the Pingjiang Workers, Peasants, and Soldiers' Soviet was formed and its leadership elected. The first order of business for the newly elected soviet became the identification and execution of key opposition leaders, mainly leaders of the village-purification units. Soviets established at lower levels carried out similar operations.[49]

The Pingjiang events spawned uprisings and the establishment of soviets in bordering provincial areas. To oversee the expanding developments, the CCP established a temporary Hunan, Hubei, Jiangxi Border Area Special Committee with Teng Daiyuan as secretary. The broadening scope of Communist activity, especially with prospects of the Peng-Teng Fifth Red Army joining forces with the Zhu-Mao Fourth

Army, provoked the KMT into retaliatory action. KMT forces engaged in an intensive campaign to prevent this merger. The Fifth Army, for all its resourcefulness, could not meet the powerful KMT challenge. Thus Peng devised a strategy to divide the Fifth Army into five units, with three staying behind and two moving on to join the Zhu-Mao forces. In mid-December, after five months of bitter struggle, Peng and Teng's forces reached the Jinggang Mountains, and, as noted above, the Fifth Army joined the Red Fourth at Ninggan.[50]

A major reason for the short existence of the Pingjiang Soviet was its exposed location between the KMT strongholds of Wuhan, Nanchang, and Changsha. Peng admitted that no base area had been established for Pingjiang. He also reported that his troops were unfamiliar with the local terrain and customs, and that he himself did not yet understand the guerrilla concepts of protracted warfare.[51] Nevertheless, Peng and others gained valuable practical experience and broke new ground in the field of organizing popular participation and mobilizing support from among established regular military forces.

Northeast Jiangxi Soviet Area. The prominence of the Jinggang Mountains Soviet in the literature on the soviet can be attributed to Mao's later role in the Chinese Communist movement. Also, he left a record of its existence in his widely read "Struggle in the Jinggang Mountains." Often overlooked, however, is the fact that there were other soviets established during this early period, which were at least as important as the Jinggang Soviet, and which, along with the Hailufeng, Pingjiang, and Southern Hunan soviets, contributed to the general body of knowledge and experience being funneled through the Party Central. Deserving of special attention was the Xin River Soviet in Northeast Jiangxi Province, established by Fang Zhimin, Shao Shiping, and Huang Dao.

Whereas Mao found it essential to build alliances with local bandit power holders to help build a viable local movement, Fang Zhimin took a different approach. He exploited the rich legacy of extensive peasant activity in impoverished northeast Jiangxi, which included numerous peasant associations and active peasant self-defense forces. Fang, as a native of Yiyang *xian*, understood these developments, which he had in fact directed since 1924, when he became head of the Jiangxi Provincial Peasant Association.[52]

After hearing about the new policies developed at the August 7 conference, Fang returned to the Yiyang-Hengfeng (Yiheng) *xian* area to put his considerable organizational talents and extensive peasant experience to work in implementing the Party Central's new guidance.[53] On November 25, 1927, Fang became secretary of the Yiheng Party Work Committee, which became the leading organ of revolt in the area.[54] Members of this new committee, assuming aliases, set out to make contact with active members of the peasant associations and organize the Peasant Revolution Corps (*nongmin geming tuan*).[55] The Peasant Revolutionary Corps was an innovation on Fang's part. It was a military-styled structure starting with three peasants organized into a team, ten in a squad, and thirty in a group. Like Peng Pai, Fang had an intimate understanding of the local folk traditions and local conditions. Using this knowledge, he was able to attract local peasants to join the Corps. Participants were introduced to modern concepts of discipline and a revolutionary program.[56] The Corps organizations provided the basis for the subsequent development of local Party branches, Red Guard forces, local Red Army organs, and eventually soviet organizations.

The incident that sparked revolt occurred on December 10, 1927. Tax officials came to Loudilanja in Yiyang *xian* to collect taxes against the local coal business that the peasants were running to supplement their meager subsistence from the soil. Unable to dissuade these officials with explanations of their dire circumstances, the Peasant Revolution Corps disarmed the tax officials of their one rifle and drove them off.[57] Fang Zhimin, informed of the incident, called a meeting of the nine Peasant Revolutionary Corps heads. It was decided to stage an immediate armed uprising. Although the Corps was equipped only with homemade knives, weapons, and ropes, the uprising was well organized and expanded Communist influence beyond the Yiheng area northeast to Dexing *xian*. Along the way, peasant armed forces invaded landlord homes, seized and burned the land contracts, and confiscated grain and property. Looking back on the events, Fang explained that this impoverished area "was just like a powder keg, and frankly speaking, I was the one who ignited the fuse, setting off an immediate revolutionary uprising."[58]

In February 1928 a Yihengde Central *xian* Committee was established from the leadership of the three participating *xian*, with Fang Zhimin as secretary. In directing its activities, Fang left no group or activity without organization. Soviet organs were in place at the village, district, and *xian* levels, the so-called counterrevolutionary judgment and suppression work was started, and land division initiated.

The success of these endeavors, which reportedly involved over 100,000 peasants, soon provoked powerful retaliation from landlord-allied forces. In response, the Central *xian* Committee met, with Fang presiding, to determine its strategy. A vigorous debate ensued around whether to bury the weapons, dissolve the organizations, and go to the cities for underground work, or to stay and continue to preserve and build the existing revolutionary movement to the extent possible.[59] It was finally decided to conserve the main forces and withdraw to the mountainous area of Mopan in order to regroup and engage in a guerrilla struggle against the enemy. As a precaution, Huang Dao was sent south to the Guixi, Yujiang, and Wannian districts to establish another base as a fallback position in case Fang's forces could not survive. In the mountains Fang's forces concentrated on strengthening the Party organs, derived from the old Peasant Revolutionary Corps, to serve as the local nucleus of armed-struggle activities. Red Guards and local Red Army forces were built and strengthened, and out of the experience Fang formulated principles of armed struggle, based on the relative strength and weaknesses of the enemy forces, that were strikingly similar to those being proposed by Zhu De and Mao Zedong derived from their Jinggang Mountains experiences.[60]

Fang's local Red Army forces eventually became the Northeast Jiangxi Red Army. Besides these trained regular forces, Fang regarded the entire population as an armed force in various stages of readiness. The Red Guards and local Red Army were in a constant state of training and indoctrination in order to serve eventually as regulars in the Red Army. Distinctive of Fang's style in setting up armed base areas were his skill and concern over providing a pervasive organizational framework binding politics and the military under Party leadership and his emphasis on continual military training and development.

In December 1928 the Xin River Soviet was established, uniting eight counties including the nucleus counties of Yiyang, Hengfeng, and Dexing. One year later, at its first congress, the soviet passed temporary land laws, labor laws, soviet organizational laws, Red Army and Red Guard regulations, and so on—all condensing the experiences of the past two years. Red Army forces grew by 50 percent. The Xin River

Soviet and its presiding organ, the new Xin River CCP Special Committee, came to exercise authority over areas of Fujian, Zhejiang, Anhui, and Jiangxi provinces and involve more than 400,000 people.[61] It provided the organizational base for the key Northeast Jiangxi Soviet Government established in August 1930.[62]

The E-Yu-Wan Soviet Area. The foundations for the strategic E(Hubei)-Yu(Henan)Wan(Anhui) Soviet or E-Yu-Wan Soviet were laid in late 1927. The East Hubei CCP Special Committee carried out successful uprisings in Hong'an and Macheng in northeastern Hubei Province. The pattern, now familiar, repeated in that strong counterattacks forced the revolutionary forces to evacuate and flee into the nearby Dabie Mountains. There the rebel forces reorganized into the Seventh Army and began practicing guerrilla tactics.[63]

In 1928 the Seventh Army was able to retake the Hong-Ma region, and this time established a base at Chaishanbaoqu on the mountainous Hubei-Henan border to use as its revolutionary foothold. Its strength grew, and in July the army was reorganized as the 31st Division of the Eleventh Red Army.[64] By early 1930 the Communist forces had expanded into western Anhui and consolidated their presence in the three provincial areas with the formation of the Hubei, Henan, Anhui CCP Special Committee. Under its direction the armies were united into the First Army of 2,100 troops, and the E-Yu-Wan Soviet was established.[65] Eventually, this became the second largest soviet base during the period before the Long March, under the leadership of Xu Xiangqian and Zhang Guotao.

The Xiang-E-Xi Soviet Area. Another key base area that contributed to the general body of knowledge and experience concerning how to carry out effective rural mobilization backed with armed force was established by He Long, Zhou Yiqun, and Duan Dechang. Eventually this became the Western Hubei-Hunan or Xiang-E-Xi Soviet.

Having participated in the Nanchang Uprising and fought in almost continuous engagements during the fall of 1927, He Long was well qualified for his work when, in January 1928, he and Zhou Yiqun were sent by the Party Central and the Hubei CCP Committee to Jianli *xian* on the Hubei border with Hunan to carry out a year-end uprising.[66] During the following two years He and Zhou worked at broadening their base of support and carried out guerrilla warfare based on principles similar to those being developed out of conditions elsewhere, notably by the Zhu-Mao forces and Fang Zhimin.[67] By 1930 the Second Red Army was consolidated from among their forces, and He's control over at least six *xian* in the Hengfeng-Sangzhi area of western Hubei and Hunan was combined with Zhou's ten *xian* in the Lake Hong vicinity in Southern Hubei to form the Xiang-E-Xi-Soviet.

Other Soviet Areas. Mao reported soviet activity by spring of 1928 in southeastern Jiangxi and western Fujian provinces.[68] Zhang Dingcheng, who studied at the Peasant Movement Training Institute, founded a soviet in August 1928 in the Xi'an district of Yongding county in southern Fujian Province.[69] One account claims that by 1930 soviet armed strength reached 63,736 participants and included 124 *xian*.[70]

The map indicates the location of base areas formed during 1927 and 1928.

The Soviets' Military Support Structure

The emerging rural soviets became experimental areas operating under extreme pressure and focused on developing practical solutions to the problems of physical survival and the continuation of the revolution. An obvious lesson learned from the failures of the fall uprisings was the essential need for the development of military support and protection. In May 1928 the Party Central provided guidance entitled "On the Military Work" which instructed: "The Party should not only correct its past errors in military affairs, but it should devise ways and means to destroy the enemy's force, to enlarge the armed labor and peasant force and to inaugurate a Red Army. The military affairs question is now the most important."[71] The discussion of the military focused on the improvement and strengthening of two major military organizations: the Red Army and the Red Guards, or Red Defense Corps. According to the Party Central's guidance, the army to be established in the independent base areas was to assume the formal title of the Red Army and drop the previous name, the Workers' and Peasants' Revolutionary Army.[72] This was a significant change, indicating the Party Central's shift away from its earlier focus on activist, mass-based military bodies to more formal, disciplined organizations of military professionals. In a real sense the Red Army was to play mainly a defensive role. It was to

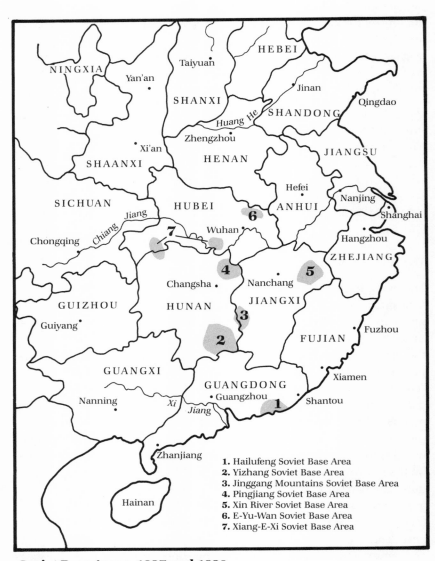

1. Hailufeng Soviet Base Area
2. Yizhang Soviet Base Area
3. Jinggang Mountains Soviet Base Area
4. Pingjiang Soviet Base Area
5. Xin River Soviet Base Area
6. E-Yu-Wan Soviet Base Area
7. Xiang-E-Xi Soviet Base Area

Soviet Base Areas, 1927 and 1928

protect the process leading to the formation of the soviet government, including the uprising and suppression of counterrevolutionary forces, land division, and election of soviet officers. In addition, Red Army forces were to safeguard the soviets once they were established from attack by KMT military suppression and encirclement campaigns, and guarantee their continued successful consolidation. The precious Red Army forces were not to be squandered in minor campaigns against landlord levies, and instead their units were to be conserved, trained, and strengthened to hold off the formidable and inevitable attacks from regular army forces.

The organizational arrangement for the Red Army under experiment during the spring of 1928 was the so-called 3-5 system, based on three squads composed of twelve men each. Working upward, three squads comprised a platoon, five platoons a company, five companies a regiment, and five regiments a division of 4,500 troops, as indicated in figure 7. According to the Party guidance, this system was patterned after the Taiping system and was selected "to accommodate the needs for guerrilla warfare." The "independent bases in various provinces" were to experiment with this system and to determine its usefulness "on the basis of the actual experiences."[73] Reportedly, the future course of Party policy on this aspect of the military would be responsive to reported local results.

A Red Army division received Party direction through political commissars "dispatched by the Soviet to supervise its officers and to take charge of implementation of the political work," including propaganda and organizational work.[74] Political commissars were to ensure that officers and men received equal treatment, and that there be no visible distinction by rank. Party authority within the Red Army was a feature borrowed from the KMT National Revolutionary Army System, which had been built on the Russian military model.[75]

Since the Red Army was to protect uprisings while they were taking place and safeguard the soviets once established, the Party planned for the Red Guards to operate as a localized militia force with heavy political responsibilities. Members of the Red Guards were to be active both in the cities and countryside, stimulating struggle campaigns, secretly organizing the military activities of workers and peasants, and providing military training and intelligence support. In cities their activities were to focus on the techniques of effective street fighting, sabotage of

Figure 7 Red Army Division: Organizational Structure and Party Relationship

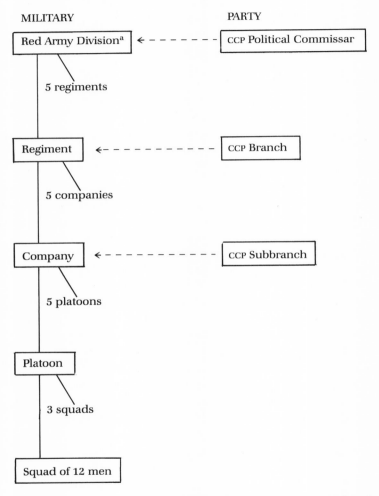

MILITARY   PARTY

Red Army Division[a] ← – – – – – – – CCP Political Commissar

5 regiments

Regiment ← – – – – – – – – – – CCP Branch

5 companies

Company ← – – – – – – – – – – CCP Subbranch

5 platoons

Platoon

3 squads

Squad of 12 men

– – – – – – – – Supervisory authority   Sources: Hyobom Pak, ed. and trans. *Documents of the Chinese Communist Party, 1927–30*. Hong Kong: Union Research Institute, 1971, 445; *Zhejiang Collection*. Shanghai Municipal Police Document no. 4772. Shanghai Municipal Police Files. 3:18–19.

[a] Attached to the division are Investigation Corps for reconaissance work, a Medical Corps, and a Communications Corps.

communications sites, demolition, and espionage; in rural areas the focus was to be on guerrilla tactics. Overall, the objective was "to militarize the broad masses of the workers and peasants."[76]

The suggested organizational frameworks for the Red Guards was based upon different sources, depending upon whether the Guards were to be urban or rural based. Urban Red Guard organizations were to be patterned after the strike picket corps, successful in Guangzhou, which gave special attention to how workers were already organized by various trades in certain key blocks in the cities. The aim was to set up parallel military organizations to bolster their local strength. The recommended organizational model given for the rural Red Guards was the Peasants' Self-Defense Corps, or "Peasant Self-Defense Army."[77] The regulations governing the organizational structure of soviets indicate that the Red Guard committees were to exercise jurisdiction over this work at each level below the provincial-level soviet. However, command authority over these levels and their activities resided with the county- or municipal-level Soviet Red Guard Committee (see figure 8). The Red Army was controlled by the provincial-level soviet.

The Red Guards were to function as an independent organization that worked closely with leaders of the Red Army. When the Red Army was engaged in field maneuvers, for example, this activity was to be supervised jointly by leaders of the Red Army and a high-level representative from the Red Guards. In time of war, however, the commander in chief of the Red Army exercised full authority over the Red Guards.[78] In addition, members of Guard units who performed well under attack or during operations were to be selected for service in the Red Army, making the Red Guards a major talent pool for the regular forces. As noted earlier, Fang Zhimin envisaged every Communist follower as a future Red Army member.

In all important aspects the Party was to play the key role in organizing and overseeing local Communist military affairs.[79] The prime instruments for exerting Party control were the military committees, which were to be formed by the Party's provincial committees, the special committees and the county or municipal committees, particularly in areas where an uprising was imminent or already taking place. As shown in the discussion of the emerging base areas, during this period, when communications were poor and soviet areas were forming in provincial border regions, the special committees played a particularly important leadership role. The military committees were the approving authority for the formation of a Red Army and Red Guard units. Further, these committees were to ensure that the Red Army and Guards were developed through training programs into effective fighting organizations, and most important were the loyal instruments of Party programs and policies.[80]

Any substantial plans or programs related to military work in an area first had to be examined and approved by the regular local Party organ before implementation. It is essential to note, however, that an overlap in leadership between the Military Committee and the regular Party organ at the same level was a basic feature of the system. For example, the post of secretary of the Military Committee was to be held concurrently by the secretary or by at least a member of the Standing Committee of the Party organ at the corresponding level.[81] This arrangement had several benefits. It made consultations with the authoritative Party apparatus simple, unbureaucratic, and therefore quite efficacious. Very importantly, the security of the regular Party organs was protected because there was no concrete organizational link between these organs and the military committees and, by extension, the Red Army and Red Guards, which were special targets for enemy raids and attack. Thus the military committees were organizationally independent of the regular Party apparatus.[82] The link between the two was formed only by a few selected individuals, who served in high-level capacities in both organizations. This feature, of course, had the effect of concentrating real power in the hands of a very few cadres. There is evidence that this condition created insecurities at Party Central when political authority in certain areas was backed by armies, thus potentially placing these areas beyond Shanghai's control.[83]

The typical Party Military Committee might consist of from three to five persons, with the League assigning some representatives to assist in the work. In addition, the Party dispatched so-called Military Affairs Specially Assigned Officers to support ongoing military activities that required extra, specialized help in crucial counties, districts, and particularly the key provincial cities.[84] Often these officials were sent to important areas that did not yet have a full Military Committee in operation in order to perform those functions in that area. Sometimes

Figure 8 Suggested Organizational Framework
for the Red Guards

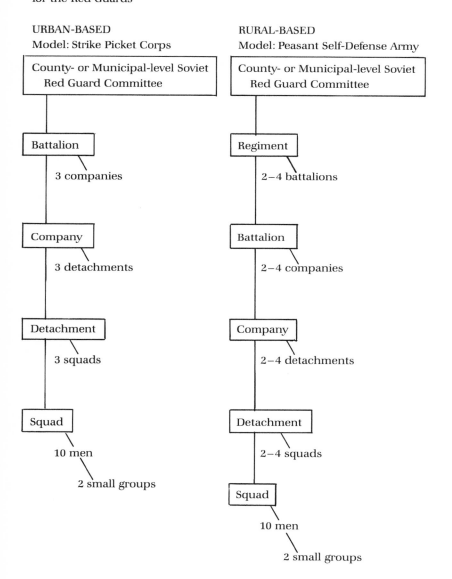

URBAN-BASED
Model: Strike Picket Corps

RURAL-BASED
Model: Peasant Self-Defense Army

County- or Municipal-level Soviet
Red Guard Committee

County- or Municipal-level Soviet
Red Guard Committee

Battalion

3 companies

Company

3 detachments

Detachment

3 squads

Squad

10 men

2 small groups

Regiment

2–4 battalions

Battalion

2–4 companies

Company

2–4 detachments

Detachment

2–4 squads

Squad

10 men

2 small groups

Source: Hyobom Pak, ed. and trans. *Documents of the Chinese Communist Party, 1927–30.*
Hong Kong: Union Research Institute, 1971, 439–440.

these special deputies were also experienced commanders in the Red Guards, just as the Military Committee leaders sometimes served concurrently as officers in the Red Guards.

Soldiers' committees were to be established among the Communist military forces, with extensive support from the League.[85] As noted above, Peng Dehuai pioneered in the use of these committees to carry out political education and agitation among the KMT soldier ranks. As with Peng's groups, the principal function of soldiers' committees was to encourage and lead frequent discussion sessions among the troops concerning outstanding problems and issues that concerned soldiers in their areas of operation. The effective performance of those tasks at the basic level was considered an essential part of the Party's general plan to exercise ideological and political control over members of the military forces. Reportedly, the League purposely was heavily involved at this level of military organizational work in order to induce them to participate more actively than in the past in work with soldiers.

Like the military committees, the soldiers' committees were independent organizational structures, but they maintained close Party affiliation through their leadership personnel. Communications, discussions, and meetings were limited to those between the soldiers' committee leadership and Party officials directly responsible for local military affairs. Any broader relations with the Party organs themselves were strictly prohibited in order that these organs could avoid the danger of discovery in the event of a raid on the soldiers' committee.

In sum, the task of establishing soviets carried with it important changes. It strengthened the rural focus, with the development of bases in protected provincial border areas away from key political cities. This in turn caused the Party to have to rely increasingly on ad hoc Party leadership organs such as Special Committees for the border areas, or Front Committees for times when the Red Army was establishing administration in new areas. It fostered an experimental approach and focused attention on the grass-roots level. Just as Party organizational work after the November Plenum emphasized building from the bottom up, the soviet system also followed this model. With a Party-military backed soviet organization assigned to lower and operational levels, the necessary basis for the early development of the mass line system materialized and the way was open for those in the field to exert decisive influence on CCP policy levels. Their pull would be in the direction of making the development of the Chinese revolution relate more intimately to actual indigenous conditions.

Establishing soviets also resulted in a general militarization of the prospective or actual constituent populations, with organizational forms being favored that best suited the development of guerrilla warfare and rural mass mobilization campaigns. The creation of formal Red Army organizations set the stage for the tensions that would develop among leaders concerning the appropriate mix of military power and mass action in supporting revolution. More important, it would strain relations between those holding legitimate power at Party Central and those holding real military power in the field. Finally, the Party's new role was to lead and coordinate all aspects of soviet-building. We will see that the accomplishment of that mission brought about important changes in the Party's organizational style and character by spring 1928.

Chapter 8. The Communist System in Transition

The work of carving out independent, armed base areas in China became the principal concern of Communist cadres from the central to the basic branch levels, involving a myriad of tasks and challenges. The central requirement for good results in this work was essentially the successful adaptation of the key concepts of bolshevism to existing Chinese conditions. These concepts had to be separated from their Russian context and made responsive to the exigencies of operational conditions in China.

Veteran cadres Peng Pai, Fang Zhimin, Mao Zedong, Zhu De, Peng Dehuai, and others demonstrated increasing awareness of this fact. They became intensely engaged, often in groping for solutions that might accomplish a transition. Their contributions from the field were seminal and became part of the policymaking process that directed the Communist movement. This chapter examines the Communist system as it was being defined during this critical period and reflects contributions from some of its leading cadres.[1]

Party and Youth League Internal Work

The work of the Communist system in China, as implemented by both the Party and Youth League organizations, was to fall into two categories. The first pertained to internal organization and methods of operation and was to be carried out in strict secrecy—an obvious necessity given the dangerous operating environment. This work consisted of building and operating the machinery of the Party and the League, training members, and implementing the policies emanating from senior levels. The second category, that of external work, concerned

Communist work among the masses and was aimed at increasing the strength and influence of the Party and League within the community. Work in the labor unions, peasant associations, and student and youth bodies fell in the category of external work. Whenever possible, this work was to be conducted openly in order to have the opportunity to influence and win broad public support for the Party and the League. Although there was to be a very intimate relationship between internal and external work, the two were emphasized as being two distinct areas.[2]

The distinctions become more apparent after we examine the differences in approach toward internal and external organizational work, both equally important to the life of the Communist movement. As had always been the case regarding recruitment for the Party or League, the official line stated that only the most advanced elements of the "proletariat" could become members of these primary Communist organizations. Selectivity and careful scrutiny of members for these organs were essential. Strict discipline had to be maintained by members at all levels of the organizational structures.

Regarding public bodies—falling under external organizational work—problems such as the effectiveness and responsiveness of individual members were not such serious questions. The basic requirement was satisfied even if members of public bodies were only receptive to general Party or League guidance. In fact, it was not necessary or even desirable for these bodies to function formally or mechanically under Communist direction. If all members of a public body, such as a labor union, became disciplined and trusted Communist followers, then the labor union would necessarily be converted into a Party or League organ and no longer perform the valuable functions of an open public body.

In recruiting for internal Party and League membership, heavy emphasis was placed on increasing the number of workers and peasants in the organizations. This was a theme that first became apparent over the summer and fall of 1927 when Party documents began to report that the principal shortcoming of the Party organizationally was that its leading cadres were not workers or peasants, but "petty bourgeois intellectuals."[3] Two serious problems sometimes developed, however, as this new recruitment policy was implemented. One was a tendency on the part of existing Party and League leaders to place peasant and worker representatives in figurehead leadership positions; another was for the leadership to conscript large numbers of peasants or workers into the organizations. These new members, it appears, were selected for membership only because of their apparent willingness to receive direction and offer sympathy and support.[4] This kind of mass-recruitment activity made for an impressive showing on membership rosters sent to higher levels, but it did not serve the organizations well because Party and League cadres failed to provide any training for new members, nor did they attempt to move them into positions of any significance in the organizations.

To remedy these problems, reforms were called for in all directing organs at the various levels. Worker and peasant members were to be appointed to key positions: as branch leaders, secretaries of *xian* and district committees, as a percentage of the standing committee memberships, and so on. In addition, regarding current members, "those hesitating, unfaithful, pessimistic, lazy, and unscrupulous elements should be mercilessly wiped off." Particularly singled out for dismissal were those described as "hesitating comrades" or "opportunists who lack courage to do the work. . . ." These were largely equated with the petit bourgeois or intellectual elements, who were no longer considered very reliable allies. In several places in Zhejiang the organization was described as being "terribly deficient" and in desperate need of reform and strengthening.[5]

Training activities were regarded as essential internal Communist organizational work. For example, new League members were to be given immediate basic instruction by the branch organ in the responsibilities of the League. This instruction also was to cover the following areas: (1) the differences between the League and the peasant association or labor union, (2) the differences between the League and the Party, (3) the basic tenets of Communism, (4) what comprises a branch organ, (5) what revolution can accomplish, (6) the nature and makeup of the district and *xian* committees, and (7) general instruction on how to become a good Communist. Upon joining the organization, all League members were bound by regulations to attend required meetings, pay membership fees, observe League discipline, participate actively in League business, and read thoroughly and promptly Party and League publications.[6]

As part of their training, new cadres were to be given opportunities to exercise supervision over actual work in progress. However, two important qualifications were placed on cadres in these and other leadership positions. One was that the work to be accomplished was always first discussed at length in Party or League meetings in order to maintain the key management principle that it is the body, rather than individuals, that decides and defines the basic tasks. Without these group discussions, the work was viewed as in danger of becoming too individualized, thus losing the spirit of the body. The second was the strong admonition against rapid promotion of the most able cadres into high-level permanent positions. The argument was that cadres who were moved up quickly in the organization were apt to lose their ties with the public, become lazy, and "adopt an official manner."[7] Rising new leaders were to maintain their close relations with the public—the condition that had first identified them to the top as potential leaders.

Another important facet of internal Party and League work was ensuring that communications between organs functioned well. The most important correspondence going through the various organizational levels was that which communicated the basic Party and League policy line set at the highest levels. Unlike the external propaganda line, which was to be much softer and veiled according to the degree of danger in a locality, the internal line was to be clear and specific. It stated the basic Communist goals, such as promoting the agrarian revolution, establishing soviet political power, opposing the imperialist powers, and overthrowing the KMT.[8]

In order to achieve the broadest possible understanding of these key programs at lower levels, the provincial committees were instructed to supply on a constant basis "propaganda and training material such as 'Political Correspondence', 'Outline[s] of Political Propaganda', strategical problems, answers to logical problems, material for practical struggle, etc."[9] These were to be used as the basis for political discussions down to the branch level. If the materials raised any further questions that could not be answered at the level where they were received, these questions were to be returned to the senior organs for additional explanations. The objective was complete understanding of the basic political program on the part of all members.

Procedures for transmitting the Party's basic policy line to lower levels actually allowed for certain adjustments in the line to occur.

Lower-level organs, upon receiving policy instruction from above, were to take into account local conditions before proceeding to transmit the new policy line: "When a Provincial Committee Notification is to be circulated, the *Hsien* [*xian*] Committee should not merely copy and forward it. It should be corrected to meet the local situation and written in the form of a *Hsien* Circular before it is sent to the branches."[10]

Basically, the above organizational concepts conform with recognized Leninist principles of organization. This brings the discussion to the consideration of the policies and mechanisms used by the Party and League in carrying out their crucial external work—the work that focused wholly on local conditions and the community at large. It is in this aspect of the work that some innovations occurred, for the purpose of accommodating the Communist organization to its real operational environment.

Party and Youth League External Work

To function properly, the secret Communist organizations were to channel their resources toward becoming powerful centers of influence within local communities. Their purpose was to win over the support of the local population, organize it into effective and responsive mass bodies, and then motivate it toward implementing the basic Communist political programs that had been formulated internally. This was to be a highly subtle and gradual process, often requiring tuning and adjustment to follow actual local conditions. The following passage suggests that the successful realization of such a process would very likely be accomplished by only the most sensitive and skilled Communist leadership: "The secret work of the Party and the movement of the masses should be clearly separated. The actual organization of the Party in a town or village should always be kept secret, but its actions should be directed toward the masses, thus constituting a link between the secret work of the Party and the public movement of the masses outside the Party."[11] A key point was that the community's acceptance of Communist policies and programs had to be won not through exhortation or command but by persuasion.

Within the Party and League organizations certain key mechanisms existed to support carrying out public mass work.[12] Two of the most important were the Provincial Propaganda Department and the Provincial Organization Department. To begin with, the leaders of the propaganda organs played important roles in the regular organization. For example, the chairman of the provincial-level propaganda organ served concurrently on the Standing Committee of the Provincial Party Committee. At the levels of the Special Committee, *Xian* Committee, and District Committee, a Standing Committee member was to be charged with overseeing propaganda work. The decision of whether to organize a propaganda organ at any particular level depended upon the scope of work in the area concerned. In other words, it depended on the strength of Party organization and the opportunities for exerting influence. A functioning propaganda organ was to include from three to five members, one of whom participated on behalf of the League.

Outlines setting the basic principles and propaganda themes were to be developed at the provincial level and disseminated to lower levels, where they served as primary guidelines for propaganda activities at those levels. One task basic to all Communist propaganda activities was the development of effective slogans. However, slogans were viewed as falling into two categories, requiring very different means for development and dissemination. One category, the so-called propaganda slogan, was characteristically broad and theoretical in content but always reflected the basic principles of the Party or League's fundamental line (for example, agrarian revolution, or realization of soviet political power), developed by organs at the highest levels. These slogans were to be used internally to enhance the spirit of the organization, or, in places where the Communists enjoyed considerable strength, they might be disseminated publicly, often through such media as wall posters, theatrical performances, posted cartoons, and publications.

The other kind of slogan was identified as the "movement slogan." These were to be developed specifically to suit certain local conditions. Rather than relying entirely upon guidance sent down from higher-level organs, propagandists developed movement slogans based on local conditions.[13] They were to be aimed at fulfilling the more obvious requirements of a specific target group. For example, the working conditions at a particular factory or within a certain village might serve as the focus for the development and tailoring of a set of movement slogans. To facilitate the process, the Party or League branch familiar with the target group might draw up an outline of certain practical demands broadly supported by the individuals concerned. This outline then served as the basis for propagandists' developing movement slogans for use among the specific groups. The Provincial Committee and its propaganda department became involved only in that it required lower-level organs to forward an information copy of that outline as it was developed in different areas of the province.

A number of publishing mechanisms were to support the larger propaganda responsibilities of the Party and the League. The provincial-level organ was charged with publishing a so-called "gray" periodical, or one that could not be directly identified with Communist organizations, but which would "criticize and reproach the 'reactionary' Kuomintang" while offering new programs and policies aimed at improving the situation of the provincial masses. The contents of this periodical were to include political commentaries, "logical articles," selected literature, and a section for reader correspondence.[14]

Besides publishing this formal periodical, the Party and League were instructed to work less formally through a publication known as the "mosquito newspaper." This was to be published either periodically or on specific, widely celebrated anniversaries, such as May Day, commemoration of the May 30th Movement, and year-end celebrations. The requirements for publishing this newspaper resemble those for the origination and dissemination of the movement slogans. The mosquito newspapers were to be produced and distributed by local organs in response to actual needs in a particular area. Often the newspapers included popular items such as well-known local songs, cartoons, and popular literature. Their overriding objective was to win the support of the workers or peasants in a certain locality by making cogent observations and commentary on their living conditions and livelihood. The provincial-level organ was not noted to be involved in this activity.

Fernando Galbiati explained that even before the Russians had established an active propaganda organ in Guangzhou, Peng Pai as early as 1922 was using propaganda methods directed at making an immediate connection with the rural masses. He wrote and staged theater productions portraying local injustices and designed to inspire revenge. Their ready appeal came from the fact that theater was an inherent part of the mainstream of indigenous folk traditions. Peng also produced cartoons focused on local themes, which he published in his magazines. He excelled at songwriting, taking old and loved folk songs and giving them new revolutionary content. Peng's methods became part of the techniques practiced by propagandists working in the Guangdong countryside.[15]

Propaganda committees in large counties were required to publish a weekly periodical or one issued every three days to carry out regular propaganda activities. At the branch level, propaganda groups were to be organized to work in labor unions and peasant associations. If it were impossible to carry on any of these activities, owing to very dangerous or unfavorable conditions, Party or League members were instructed to submit articles to existing, comparatively leftist publications with broad public dissemination in order to make some impact on the development of ideas within the community.

The other major area of Party and League external work concerned organizational activities aimed at increasing the influence and base of strength of the Communists within the community.[16] In areas where the Party and League were well entrenched, this work was to be carried on by a formal organization department. In areas of less strength, organization work was to be undertaken by individual members, specially trained in organizing different segments of the community into bodies that subsequently would be responsive to Communist guidance and influence. Actually, no group was to be excluded, so that the scope of organizational work included workers, peasants, soldiers, students, youths, women, and even bandits. By 1928 Communist plans and methods for influencing and organizing the labor movement were well developed.

Organizing a Labor Movement

After the Guangzhou rising, the Communist urban labor movement was in a perilous state. One report stated that "under the control of 'red' labour unions throughout the country, the number of organized workers is less than 40,000."[17] By comparison, in the summer of 1926 the Party claimed it had successfully organized 1.2 million workers.[18] Consequently the revival of the urban movement, particularly through the maintenance and development of any existing unions and formation of new ones, whether as regular Red unions or informal worker societies,[19] became a major duty of organizational personnel in various-level Communist organs.

Under the changed conditions, the foundation of the labor movement, like that of the Party and League organizations, had to be constructed from below.[20] Communist-influenced labor unions were to be organized into self-contained hierarchical systems, with the trade branch union forming the basic unit.[21] Moving up through the system (district-, *xian-*, and provincial-level trade labor unions), the presiding organization was to be the General Labor Union. Of course, each trade was to have its own organizational system so that the top ranks of the Chinese labor movement would include a Railway Workers' General Union, a Textile Workers' General Labor Union, and so on.

Party or League representatives or organs were to operate at each level within this system to provide direction and guidance to the labor organization's activities and to carry out training work. Their authority, however, was limited to directing only the activities of the labor union organization to which they were attached. In other words, the CCP organ of a Railway Workers' General Labor Union could not directly control the activities of labor organs at lower levels, for example, those of the various branch railway unions. The latter would be responsible only to the Party or League personnel or organs at their own immediate level in the union system and not to the higher-level Party or League labor organs. This was to provide these labor unions with some measure of organizational autonomy.

Party and League labor organs, however, were not completely cut off from exerting important influence at different levels within the labor union system for two reasons. First, the lower-level Party and League organs attached to labor unions were to follow the guidance and directives from higher levels. This allowed the Party and the League the opportunity to exert their influence indirectly, through their own organizational framework, at lower levels in the union system. Second, policy constraints made important independent action by any subordinate level difficult. Substantive policy concerning the goals, tactics, and activities of the labor movement, implemented by the Party or the League organs of subordinate-level unions, was to follow closely that laid out by the Party Central and supervised by the various levels of the regular Party and League apparatus.[22]

Figure 9 presents the structure that the internal organization of a labor union should follow, according to "Regulations Governing the Labor Unions."[23] The union leadership's principal task was to lead and direct the workers' struggle. This included investigating the needs and demands of the workers. The results were to be the subject matter for frequent discussion sessions with the union membership and the focus for organizing struggle movements and propaganda campaigns. Meetings with the membership also were to serve as a forum for "educating" the workers by pointing out the oppressive character of the gentry, landlord, and capitalist classes. Reaching a better understanding of the concept of class and the nature of class struggle was to be a major objective of union business, especially propaganda efforts. This was in addition, of course, to the constant primary objective of building stronger support for the Party and League programs.

In addition, Communist organizers were to establish workers' picket corps or military organizations of labor functioning under the guidance of the military affairs committees. Workers serving in these organizations were to be given secret instruction in street fighting and urban riot tactics. For the purpose of operating publicly, they might assume the seemingly harmless identity of an athletic corps or gymnastic society. Under conditions leading to the formation and preservation of a soviet, these armed workers would become the urban Red Guards. The union leadership also was to give special consideration to developing their influence within the youth movement and among female and child laborers. This was to be done by providing so-called "amusement resorts" to the union membership and to any other workers who might be attracted to the union through those means.

Under the extremely dangerous and difficult operating conditions, the Communists adopted an overall approach to organizing urban workers that emphasized caution, flexibility, and contact with the workers at the basic level. A key feature of their strategy was its emphasis on the united front concept. The Communists were to tune and adjust their approach to suit and influence the various orientations of the labor organizations they encountered. They reported the existence of several kinds of labor organizations.[24] There were those organized and directed by the KMT. Closely related were unions with leaderships sympathetic to the KMT, many of them having been appointed by that party, but that maintained a generally independent style of operation. These unions reportedly enjoyed a sizable membership following. Another kind of union was described as self-organized bodies of laborers with only economic goals, primarily those of protect-

Figure 9 Organizational Structure of a
Communist Labor Union

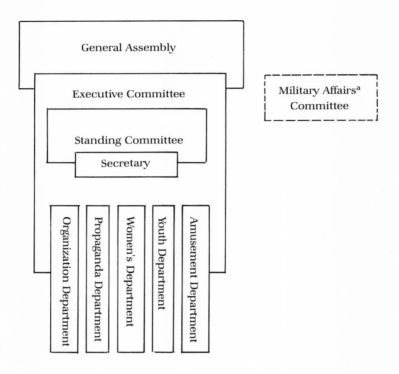

Source: Based on "Regulations Governing the Labor Unions" contained in the *Zhejiang Collection.* Shanghai Municipal Police Document no. 4772. Shanghai Municipal Police Files. 3:3–4.

[a] These Military Affairs committees, for security reasons, form a separate system with organs servicing the various levels of the labor union structure.

ing or enhancing their financial interests. If these had any shared political allegiances at all, presumably they would have been to side with the ruling party, the KMT. Finally, certain unions were mentioned as organized under the direction of the "wealthy capitalist classes" and were described as being of "the Fascist Form." Little additional information in the materials concerns those unions. The point is made, however, that they were close politically to the KMT and extremely anti-Communist.

The Communist labor organizers were to respond to the diverse conditions of the labor movement by attempting to consolidate the broadest possible support: "The fundamental idea of our strategy to unify the battle line is to unify the movement of the various cliques of laboring masses, and to obtain the support of the masses during struggle."[25] The strategy of unifying the battle line meant that Communist organizers in their relations with union leaders not rigidly controlled by very hostile forces such as the KMT, or industrialists closely allied with the KMT, should attempt to negotiate with the directing committees of these unions, especially if a movement existed with some momentum among the union's membership for demands that the Communists favored and could support. If these negotiations happened to fail, Party and League organizers then were expected to take best advantage of the existing worker sentiments and point out to union members the resistance of their leaders to the popular demands. The objective was to redirect the popular movement against the union leaders in order ultimately either to gain control of the union or at least to bring about substantial changes in the existing leadership in directions that would allow for increased Communist influence in the union.

Negotiations were one part of a two-part strategy that placed heavy emphasis on conducting extensive mass work among the membership of the unions in order to build pressure from within the broad membership. This mass work was considered the most important side of the policy. To carry it out, Party and League organizers were instructed to draw up general outlines of the principal demands that were practical and essential to workers in a certain locality, to serve as the basis for propaganda and organizational work. Operating under the slogan "union with the 'lower' masses," this side of the strategy was aimed at forcing the more right-leaning leaders of a union to a more moderate stance by bringing to bear on them popular mass pressure from below.

The most interesting aspect of the Communist urban strategy involved the approach to unions that were rigidly controlled by the KMT or rightist forces. One might speculate that what was developed to deal with these groups in 1928 became a basic aspect of Communists' urban work at least until the Second United Front beginning in 1937. The Communists envisioned opening up hostile urban organizations by expounding among their membership the immediate need for increased democratic freedoms. These included demands for freedom of speech, the press, and assembly, the organization of labor unions by the workers themselves, and the election of union committee members by union members.[26] The Communists reasoned that any headway gained in diffusing power through the implementation of democratic freedoms would help create an atmosphere that would offer more potential for a Communist reorganization of the directing urban labor organ in their favor and possible elimination of its most "reactionary" or anti-Communist leaders. The goal was to make the situation more fluid so that Communist organizers might have an opportunity to seize the initiative away from the union's current leadership.

One innovation in the field of urban labor work that came about as the Communists attempted to devise ways to cope with their perilous situation in the cities came in the form of a new organization. In February 1928 labor leader and Provisional Politburo member Su Zhaozheng introduced at a secret conference of the All-China Labor Federation a system of factory committees.[27] Based on the united-front concept, these bodies might "be formed at any time if there are workers, regardless of party differences."[28] Whereas the Red labor unions had to be organized secretly, the Factory Committee offered the advantage of being able to operate openly and thus reach a wide worker population. Unlike the labor union, this was to be a representative body: "In a factory, the labour union resembles an official organ or *Tangpu*, while the factory committee may be likened unto a legislative assembly."[29]

Members serving on a Factory Committee were to do so voluntarily and were not required to pay any regular union fees. The apparent objective was to use this representative body to extend Communist influence, educate the workers, and unify the broadest possible support behind programs that were compatible with or sometimes even shared by the Communists. Finally, it was stipulated that once a soviet was established in the factory district, the Factory Committee was to become the administrative body of that factory.

Unfortunately, the available information on factory committees does not allow for further clarification regarding the specific relationships among them, the labor unions, and the soviets. It appears, however, that the Factory Committee was a concept adopted as experimental by the Party because Red labor unions were proving almost impossible to establish. The committee was envisaged as a means to establish at least an urban revolutionary foothold in preparation for establishing a Red labor union.

Still, in spite of the difficult conditions, labor unions were to be the centerpiece of the Communist organizational efforts in the cities. Through them and affiliated mass organizations of youth and women, their memberships were to be exposed to Communist thinking and trained in military skills, organizational and propaganda techniques, and other skills essential to the Communists' urban program. Ultimately this urban constituency was to be mobilized and coordinated with its rural counterparts, with the establishment of a soviet government.

Organizing a Rural Movement

The overall strategy for penetrating the rural peasant population resembled the Communist labor movement policies in that the major thrust was toward consolidating the broadest possible base under Party and League organizational influence.[30] According to the policies: "During the present revolutionary period, the most important tactic of the Communist party is to form a united battle front of the largest possible numbers of farmer masses who are suffering under the evils of feudal influence."[31]

Communist organizational efforts were to be aimed initially at poor peasants, farm employees, and handicraft workers, including any existing organizations that represented these groups. In setting up new bodies, these elements were to provide the leadership for the new organizations. Small landowners or independent farmers (collectively referred to as middle peasants) were to be admitted as members but were not to fill any positions of influence in the organizations. As for rich peasants, policy dictated that admitting none at all was preferable to the risks of including too many.

While the middle peasants were to be excluded from important leadership roles in the peasant associations, the Party's united-front approach did ascribe to them an essential role: "The struggle of poor peasants and proletarians of the farming village under the leadership of the laboring class is the motive power of land revolution. It is also the main necessity to secure victory of land revolution to join with middle-class farmers."[32]

There is even some evidence, though not developed at length, that the Party was beginning to understand that a hard-and-fast implementation of the policy of total confiscation and equal division of land could jeopardize their chances for winning support from a sizable segment of the rural population. As the following passage indicates, even the interests of the rich peasants were discussed: "With regard to the equal division of land in places where middle-class farmers and small farmers are preponderant, this cannot be put into effect by compulsory means, as such action will result in the benefits of the middle class and large farmers being endangered."[33]

The peasant association was to be organized secretly and was to prepare the peasants in its area to redistribute land (land revolution), seize political power, and eventually establish a soviet organization. Initially a strong following in the area had to be organized and thoroughly educated and propagandized concerning the main points of the Communist revolutionary program. The association was to direct struggle campaigns aimed at improving the peasants' economic lot and making them aware of their potential political role in the village system. In addition, village work had to be coordinated with work in the urban centers so that the peasants understood that labor unions in the cities were really supporting arms of the larger movement and were working toward revolutionary goals beneficial to all. Finally, the association had to find ways to arm the peasants so that uprisings and the actual seizure of political power could be realized.

Rural organizations already under strong Communist direction were instructed to select certain activists to serve in secret armed fighting organizations. Members were to receive special training in field attack and night fighting, under the direction of military affairs committees. These armed groups were envisaged as constituting a major force for the eventual implementation of the agrarian revolution. The designation and structural nature of these groups were to be developed according to local conditions in different areas.

In places where a peasant association already existed independent of Communist influence, Party and League organizers were instructed to join it and work among its membership for the purpose of gradually bringing it under Communist direction. Where this goal seemed unattainable, Communists were to prod and motivate members to withdraw from the organization and to organize a new peasant committee or association, under Communist direction, which would better serve rural interests and demands. In areas of minimal Party or League strength, early efforts at organization had to be carried out in secret. Rather than attempting to organize an active peasant association under these conditions, other so-called "gray" organizations were put forth as the most practical means of making inroads in an area. One possibility was the formation of a "Locust Elimination Society." Or, as was done in the cities, athletic societies or amusement groups could be introduced.

Peasant associations were to be organized according to principles very similar to those that guided the formation of the urban labor structures.[34] The rural system, beginning with the village unit, functioned under the same kind of hierarchical command structure, with the basic levels totally subordinate to the higher levels. Also, like the urban system, the Party and the League peasant organs or peasant representatives were to exercise policy direction and guide only the levels in the system to which they were attached and not directly to command peasant associations at other levels. As was true within the urban system, however, the major policies developed at the presiding levels in the rural system were to serve as the basis for subordinate level policy.

Figure 10 illustrates the organization of the peasant associations at the various levels, including village, district, and *xian*.[35] At the *xian* level the Standing Committee was to consist of seven members and the executive committee of thirteen. Like the system of organization for rural soviets, the *xian* level took on special responsibilities because of its long-standing role as a key point in local administration. At the basic village level there were to be seven on the Executive Committee and three on the Standing Committee. The district level was to have five on the Standing Committee and nine on the Executive Committee. The principal leadership at each level included the secretary, the chairman of the Standing Committee, and the chiefs of each of the four departments functioning under the direction of the Executive Committee.

Figure 10 Organizational Structure of a
Communist Peasant Association

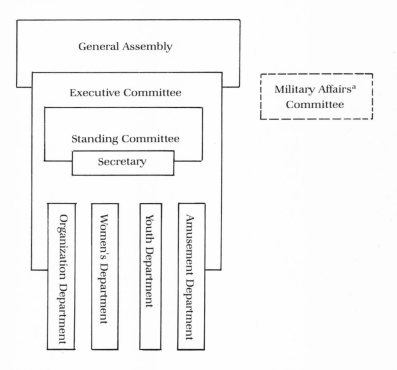

Source: *Zhejiang Collection.* Shanghai Municipal Police Document no. 4772. Shanghai Municipal Police Files. 3:6–8. These documents contain county-level peasant association regulations. Like those for the labor unions, their authoritative tone suggests they were issued at senior Party levels. They include the comment that their contents "may be amended by the General Assembly" of the peasant association.
[a] Like the Military Affairs committees attached to urban labor unions, these committees formed a separate system that had organs servicing the various levels of the peasant association structure.

No guidance is provided concerning the structure of a provincial-level peasant association. Earlier peasant charters instructed that five county-level peasant associations must precede formation of a provincial-level body.[36] Under the policy of building rural soviets in early 1928, however, the previous existence of such extensive organized rural support probably would have been channeled at building soviets rather than at establishing a provincial-level peasant association.

Once a soviet government was established, the peasant association was to be abolished and replaced by a Union of Farm Employees. If successful preliminary struggle campaigns were carried out by the peasant association, it was to function as the representative body of the peasants until a soviet government could be formed.

In essence, the role of the peasant association was to prepare the groundwork for soviets. It was to familiarize the peasants with principles of organization and discipline so as to make up an effective rural social movement. This was the relatively simple part, because rural inhabitants had taken part in collective action for centuries through secret societies, rural militia, bandit patrols, and crop-watching societies. The real challenge to the peasant association was in instilling in participants a clear and precise understanding of local politics or the power relationships defining their village or *xian* communities. The sociopolitical concepts of class and class interests, so alien to the peasants, were supposed to supplant the old passionate motivation of peasant revenge in bringing about local change. Even Peng Pai struggled under this burden, and eventually gave way to participating in extremely violent Red Terror campaigns.[37] But at least in the Party guidance there was a general recognition that without careful and thorough instruction and indoctrination, any rural soviets established by the peasant associations would be short-lived and fail in their primary work of consolidating the political and economic gains of an uprising.

Work Among Military and Police Groups

In addition to organizing formal military bodies such as Red armies, the Communists emphasized doing external organizational work among KMT troops and other opposing forces.[38] The rationale, of course, was that without any influence whatsoever among bodies such as the Provincial Defense Corps and local police forces, Communist activities among peasant and worker groups could be easily crushed.[39] One of the most direct means for carrying on subversion was to designate certain trusted cadres to join one of the hostile military or police bodies. Once in, they were to attempt to win support or sympathy from others and generally attempt to stir up resentments and create problems within the organization. Special training was to be given to cadres undertaking these dangerous assignments. Rather than joining an organization, cadres sometimes might work at becoming close friends with important members of the opposition forces. This might be done directly or by working through family members or other friends, offering them services such as composing letters for friends and relatives who could not write or conveying messages to the front.[40]

Reportedly, a common problem among units of militarist forces and even those of the KMT was the dissatisfaction among the troops brought on because of arrears in payment of wages, poor equipment, or the uncertainties that often accompanied service. Frequently, units became separated from the main force or were judged as no longer essential to the organization. These units were disbanded, and members often faced a period of prolonged unemployment. The Communists were to use such vulnerabilities to stir up trouble in opposition forces and win over support among the enemy troops. Peng Dehuai was very successful at carrying out political education work among the KMT soldier ranks in Pingjiang by organizing study societies and dramatic events, using key local issues as the subject matter.[41]

Soldiers wounded in battle were to receive special Communist attention, mainly because they were relatively accessible, having sometimes a lengthy recuperation period, and because they did seem to have real grievances. Communists were to focus their propaganda efforts on pointing out the poor medical treatment available through the government authorities and push soldiers to demand compensation for their condition. Obviously, the Communists were interested in these soldiers because eventually many of them would return to regular service with their units. Thus they represented a means to penetrate main troop units in an area.[42]

Occasionally there was some overlap between the Communists' work among peasants and workers and their success at penetrating the oppositions' military ranks. As might be expected, the KMT drew many of its regular troops from conscription drives amid the poor rural classes. The Communists often noted this potential opportunity for gaining access to the enemy military forces, and they pushed organizers to work hardest in areas frequently used by the KMT for replenishing its military forces. One common propaganda theme directed at soldier-recruits emphasized that fighting against workers and peasants was like fighting against themselves.

At least in Zhejiang, both the police and Merchant Volunteers were special targets for Communist organizers. The police reportedly were badly underpaid and often the victims of extortion from officers on the force. Usually, their employment was seasonal, coming only three or four months during the winter, after which they remained largely unemployed and without roots.[43] The Merchant Volunteers, who acted as a kind of private army or police force for the wealthy or landowners, reportedly were paid even less than soldiers and police, although supposedly their opportunities for public extortion more than compensated. Communists were to approach these groups in much the same way they approached the other groups mentioned above.

Work among bandit groups and secret societies also came under Communist external organizational work. For the most part, the leadership of secret societies was in the hands of local gentry, landlords, and rich peasants.[44] Having an extensive following in the countryside, these militaristic societies were regarded as another promising area for external organizational work. Communist rural organizers were to work among the broad membership of the influential secret societies in order to gain a basic foothold in the organizations, from which gradually to secure control over them or at least to be in a position to exert substantial influence over their operation.[45] Indicating an approach to bandit leaders clearly at variance with that followed by Mao Zedong in the Jinggang Mountains, Party guidance prohibited cadres from negotiating with bandit leaders or trying to buy them over in order to gain their considerable military power in support of Communist rural campaigns.[46] The following summarizes the prescribed approach: "The movement of bandits is by no means a major work, but it is not necessary to abandon it. Our work among bandits is similar to that among soldiers, that is, it is necessary to destroy their feudal organization, seize control of their lower masses, and introduce a proper organization."[47]

Characteristics of the Transition

In the planned internal and external functioning of the Party and League organizations, at least three characteristics or themes are notable. One was a serious concern with expanding military strength and the militarization of the movement that accompanied this. Another was the more clearly mass-styled organization that was emerging. Third was the tendency among Party and League members to move away from abstract theories concerning China's future and to concentrate on the immediate questions of survival. Each one of these is evident in organizational developments within the Communist system.

In addition to building support among groups with clear military potential, the Communists in their organizational style and goals displayed strong military overtones, even with their predominantly civilian organizations. A good example is the Communist Boys' Corps.[48] This organization for both urban and rural male youth eight to sixteen years of age worked directly under the youth departments of the various ranks of the labor unions and peasant associations and received substantive guidance and policy direction from the League. The youths' motto was "Rush Forward," and they wore red neck scarves to identify their membership affiliation.

The principal work of the Boys' Corps included political training, mainly teaching the concept of struggle and illustrating how it might be used to serve the boys' interests. Further, corps organs were to supply amusement, education, and cultural training through evening schools, clubs, and so forth to both urban and rural youth. Rural corps members were to encourage their parents and siblings to join the peasant association, the corps, and other Communist organizations. They were also to serve as village activists working to wipe out superstitions, ancestor worship, and any evidence of local observance of other rites and ceremonies. The youth and vitality of the rural corps caused Communist youth leaders to view them as untainted by the old rites and traditions of rural Chinese society and thus as willing participants in the movement to bring about a new culture in the countryside: "Their instinct is active, they are imitative and constructive. They will act according to our propaganda and carry out what they are taught. Furthermore, they do not fear death. They have no family worries so that they can bravely struggle for their own principles."[49]

During urban armed struggle campaigns, members of the urban Boys' Corps were expected to serve as spies, propagandists, rescue workers, couriers, and so on. All corps members were to be trained and practiced in military skills and drill. Figure 11 illustrates the basic structure of the Boys' Corps and indicates the relationship of the

Figure 11 The Boys' Corps:
Basic Structure and Relationships

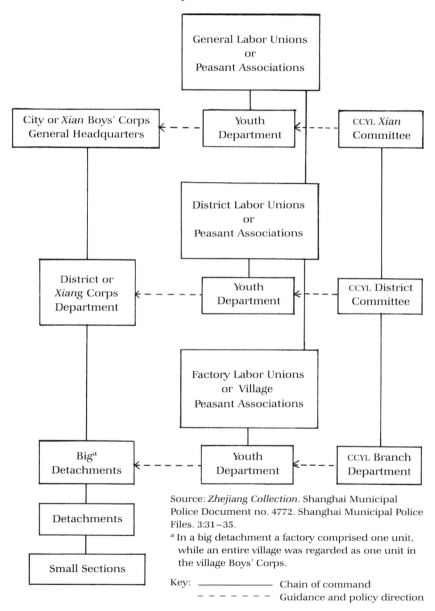

Source: *Zhejiang Collection*. Shanghai Municipal
Police Document no. 4772. Shanghai Municipal Police
Files. 3:31–35.

[a] In a big detachment a factory comprised one unit,
while an entire village was regarded as one unit in
the village Boys' Corps.

Key: ——————— Chain of command
– – – – – – – Guidance and policy direction

League and the labor and peasant unions to the corps. Further, it suggests the militaristic style of the organization.

Children were similarly organized in the Hailufeng Soviet under the name Children's Brigade. Under the direction of the League, the brigades focused on instilling in members revolutionary fervor and devotion to the soviet government. Some reports tell of members identifying their mothers as antirevolutionary if they displayed old-fashioned attitudes.[50]

In contrast to urban organizational work, rural work by its very nature seemed to have the potential for producing a more broadly based organization of a more heterogeneous mass character. This difference is ascribed to the fundamental nature of the two organizational systems, as dictated by their design. With the labor unions, the basic unit was the trade union branch attached to a factory. The branch and its subordinate departments of youth, women, and children drew their membership from individuals employed in that particular factory. In the rural system, on the other hand, a village formed the basic unit.

The importance of this fact and how it accounted for the different overall character of rural organizations and their urban counterparts can be seen by considering the membership of the Boys' Corps, which was both urban and rural. While membership in the urban Boys' Corps (supervised by the trade union's youth department) was limited to sons of workers in a particular factory, the rural Boys' Corps (supervised by the peasant association's youth department) might well be composed of sons of peasants, village handicraft workers, local intellectuals or teachers, hired hands, small landowners, and so forth. In fact, all boys of the village except, of course, those with "reactionary" connections with big landlords, gentry, or the KMT, were to be organized into the rural Boys' Corps. This inherent diversity in member backgrounds had the effect of making the corps and other rural organs more broadly based or more clearly mass-styled than their urban counterparts. Certainly the rural organizational style was comprehensive in that every "revolutionary" segment of society, whether identified by vocation (handicraft worker, farm laborer, peasant), by sex, or age grouping, fell under the organizational auspices ultimately of the Communist-led peasant association. This characteristic of rural organization provided Communist organizers with a more inclusive and potentially responsive constituency compared to the fragmented nature of the vertically defined urban organizational system.

The Communist organization serving older youth was even more unusual. The shift in the Communist focus from a strong earlier interest in the educated, petit bourgeois, or intellectual groups to an absorption with establishing strength among rural and urban proletarian classes was particularly evident with regard to student associations, which throughout the 1920s had been receptive to radical and even revolutionary causes. Instructions explaining this shift revealed that: "It is an undesirable fact that since the rapid development of the revolution and up to the uprising of the laborers and peasants to seize political power, the students have shown a tendency to veer towards the small capitalists and their revolutionary spirit has been lowered. At present, the students can never entertain any longer the carrying on of the people's organization under our leadership, although certain poor and radical student elements can still be made use of."[51] What happened was that the severe KMT repression, especially in the cities, resulted in student hesitation and faltering enthusiasm for Communist work and also seriously limited opportunities for Communist organizers to reach these groups. Under these circumstances the Communists began to develop guidance for a major new organization of youth in rural areas, which embodied most of the new aspects of Communist external organizational work. This organization was the Youth Vanguards (*shaonian xianfengdui*) or Young Pioneers, which was rural in focus, mass-styled in composition, strongly militaristic in tone and purpose, and distinctively practical in its goals and approach.[52]

The Youth Vanguards included rural youths between sixteen and twenty-three years of age.[53] The practical thrust of the organization is apparent in all three of its basic categories of work: cultural, political, and military. Its cultural responsibilities, rather than focusing on sponsorship of literary research societies or political debating groups as had been the style of urban Communist student unions, stressed providing practical educational instruction to village youth. This included basic language instruction and courses in regional history and folklore —all of which would make the youth better candidates for eventually receiving the Communists' political message. In addition, Vanguards leaders were to organize music societies, which would collect and compile popular village songs and instruct youth in performing them. Music students would perform the songs at music parties sponsored by the Vanguards, and the whole village would be entertained under the auspices of the Vanguards. Sports training and sporting events were to be organized by the Vanguards. In addition to their popular entertainment value, these activities were considered important to the eventual successful introduction of basic military training.

The Youth Vanguards were to perform major political tasks and bear major responsibilities. A principal one was to provide instruction in the general principles of Communism, the meaning of the land revolution, and the broad benefits to be gained from bringing about a soviet government to members of the peasant associations and village youth. Those aims were to be accomplished largely by heavy Vanguards' involvement in Communist propaganda activities. In fact, the Youth Vanguards were to be "the central element in the Peasant Union to undertake propaganda work and spread it among the members of the Unions."[54] They were entrusted with disseminating various kinds of propaganda materials as well as actually setting up new peasant newspapers and pictorials containing material that would attract general rural interest and would develop a substantial following for Communist programs in the local areas.

Vanguards leaders were to serve as political activists, involving the village youth in propaganda campaigns and getting them accustomed to participating in organized struggle movements. Often this was done through mass demonstrations and processions on the occasion of the various revolutionary anniversary dates. At these events Vanguards members in "fancy dress" or colorful and stylish outfits were to deliver emotional speeches accompanied by the posting of appropriate wall posters and by active sloganeering by various members. The objective was to impress and motivate youth and raise their political consciousness to such an extent that, combined with the rudimentary practical experience gained from participation in these events, an effective youth struggle movement could be created, with a life of its own, which the participants could then carry on independently. These new movements were to develop alongside existing ones and add to the further growth of the village's potential for carrying out a successful uprising. In districts where no peasant unions or committees existed, Vanguards groups were to concentrate on instigating basic mass struggle campaigns that might lead to the successful formation of a peasant organization under Communist direction.[55]

In many ways the functions and responsibilities of Vanguards leaders resembled those of the Youth League: they were to be youth leaders, propagandists, and political activists. The most active and successful among the Vanguards leaders reportedly were often selected for simultaneous membership either in the Party or the League, particularly the League. The major differences were that the Youth Vanguards was a mass organization of all youth within a certain age grouping, which the League was not at this time, and the Vanguards operated only in the countryside.[56]

Another characteristic of the Youth Vanguards that set it apart from the League was its strong military tone: "The Youth Vanguard is an organization for the armed struggle of the young peasants for their rights."[57] In areas where the Red Army was active or where there was substantial Red Guard participation, Youth Vanguards were to establish close contacts with those forces and provide them with able members.[58] In all respects, the Vanguards were to be the most important providers of military training to youth. That training included military drill, detective work and spying on enemy positions, and preparation for service as sentinels and military couriers. Specially trained Vanguards squads were to be used on dangerous combat assignments such as attacking enemy police forces and units of the Peace Preservation Corps. Under the direction of the Hailufeng Soviet, some 10,700 youth were organized in Haifeng and 200 in Lufeng to serve in the Youth Vanguards. From these, an elite force of 300 was selected to serve as special units of the Red Army for intelligence work and related activities.[59]

Vanguards members also were to infiltrate local armed secret societies such as the populous Red Spears Society and the "Daggers Association" in order to win over the general membership of these bodies and recruit them for service in Communist military units. Working in rural militaristic societies was one important way in which the Vanguards were to build up their own forces and make them ready for carrying out their primary military mission: organizing and directing local guerrilla warfare campaigns. Their military training, combined with heavy exposure to political work, was to make them potentially a very effective force for stimulating local armed struggle campaigns.

Figure 12 The Youth Vanguards:
Basic Structure and Relationships

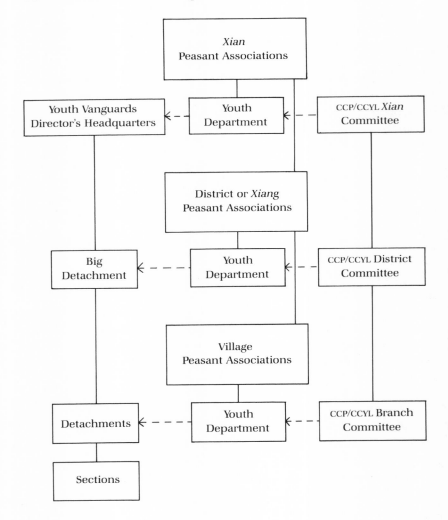

Key: ————————————— Chain of command
– – – – – – – – – – – Guidance and policy direction

Source: *Zhejiang Collection*. Shanghai Municipal Police Document no. 4772. Shanghai Municipal Police Files. 3:26–30.

After a successful uprising and the establishment of a soviet, Vanguards units were to serve as a defensive force, while at the same time continuing to extend the revolution to other areas. In time of armed uprising or war, the direction of the Vanguards was to be taken over by officials of the Red Army, who were to work closely with the top level, namely the general directors, of the Youth Vanguards.[60]

Party and League direction of Vanguards activities was plainly evident. The Vanguards functioned under the supervision of the youth department of the peasant association. The chairman of the association's youth department was usually a member of the Youth League. In addition, all key leadership positions at the various levels of the organization were to be held by Communist cadres. Further, the Vanguards were established as an independent organization, but the leadership at all levels was required to maintain close working relationships with the corresponding Party or League leadership levels for all basic policy guidance and direction.

The Village Detachment was designated as the basic unit of the Vanguards organizational structure. When this unit possessed more than ten members, it might be divided into subunits or sections. Once two or more detachments existed in the village, the next level, which was the Big Detachment, could be established. When three big detachments came into being, a Youth Vanguards Director's Headquarters could then be formed. The headquarters operated at the *xian* level and apparently was the senior level of the organization. Officials of the Vanguards headquarters were to communicate regularly with the *xian*-level youth leaders of the peasant association, which supplied the operational funds for the Vanguards. General policy direction came from their communications with the *xian* Party or League committees. Similar relationships between the Vanguards, the peasant association, and the CCP/CCYL were to exist at the district and village levels. An organizational chart showing the internal structure of the Youth Vanguards, as well as its organizational relationship to the youth departments of the peasant associations' structure and the corresponding Party and League leadership levels, is shown in figure 12.

To a large extent, the transitional features of the Communist organizational system discussed above emerged from the conditions confronting the Communists. Constantly pursued by mostly superior forces, the Communists were enjoined to give a high priority to military training and extend it to all age groups. This need spawned new and innovative bodies of omnicompetent rural youth. Forced to operate in the countryside, the Communists adapted their organizational approach to the rural setting, originating comprehensive and mass-styled organizational concepts, as inclusive and pervasive in their scope and potential as traditional rural lineage systems.[61] All ages and all vocations were candidates for Communist organization. As a female CCP leader reported to Nym Wales on Haifeng *xian*, the Chinese Communists extended their organizational work even to young children. She observed that the work there was spontaneous and not based on detailed knowledge of the Russian organizational models.[62] Finally, the concern with practical matters was dictated by circumstances. To produce supporters trained in military and political skills to participate in and lead the Communist movement, the basic cultural level of the mostly illiterate countryside had to be elevated.

From our examination of the nature and direction of organizational work in the emerging soviets, the affinity for the new style discussed above seems quite apparent in the work of Fang Zhimin.[63] Fang, in northeast Jiangxi, was attempting to give a comprehensive framework to rural work by studying, categorizing, and registering the local population for purposes of organization. No one was exempt from military training, and the goal for all to aspire to and train for was service in the Red Army. Fang, like Peng Pai, also was very adept at grasping the essence of rural traditions and working through them to gain the confidence and allegiance of rural supporters in order to mobilize them behind Communist goals and programs.

Chapter 9. The Revolutionary Process: Its Basic Components

The formal reconstitution of the National Government took place on October 10, 1927, and Chiang Kai-shek in January 1928 assumed all key military posts.[1] Subsequently a campaign against the northern militarist government was initiated, which ultimately delivered Peking to the KMT in June 1928. In a race to capture this prize, Chiang's forces invaded Shandong, only to be turned back by the Japanese armies at Jinan. The Guangxi Army under Li Zongren's command advanced north toward Peking along an alternate route, while the Shanxi warlord Yen Xishan and Feng Yuxiang advanced east, crossing the provinces of Hebei and Chahar.[2]

These campaigns diverted the forces of key militarists from their regular, anti-Communist, "village-purification" activities. The Communists regarded this development as an opportunity for expansion.[3] To support the military campaigns, local officials in charge of government administration were forced to exact higher taxes and carry out troop levies, which together increased the burden on the local, particularly the rural, population. The Communists regarded this, too, as creating opportunities for exploiting and mobilizing areas of rising discontent. The Party Central instructed, "During this period, we should strive to create independent bases in preparation for a general uprising."[4]

During the early months of 1928 the Party Central groped to formulate a revolutionary strategy for mobilizing broad support in both rural and urban areas, directed against the KMT and toward enhancing Communist strength and influence. Basically it still adhered to plans for concentrating Communist forces in what were regarded as the two "revolutionary centers" in the country: one in Guangdong directed at taking Guangzhou, and a second in Hunan, Hubei, Jiangxi, and southern Henan directed at taking Wuhan. Uprisings taking place in these areas were to precede a general uprising on a national scale, leading to power being seized in one or more provinces.

On April 30, 1928, this policy of general uprising was rescinded. The Party Central issued a Central Notice reporting the main contents of the ECCI's Ninth Plenum Resolution, which pointed out that no revolutionary high tide was developing throughout the country, even though some positive signs existed. It instructed that steps be taken as early as possible to end any activities aimed at implementing the policy of general uprisings.[5]

While terminating the policy of general uprisings, the Party Central continued, of course, to issue extensive instructions to Party cadres and to receive reports of their operations in the field. Together these came to define the various aspects of the Communist movement and produced the general revolutionary policies and strategy for its development. Instructional materials circulating within the system reveal the Party leadership's conception of the nature of the revolutionary process. As presented in the documentation, the revolutionary movement was a social and political process that was not constantly progressive—developing without interruption toward the goal of establishing soviets. That conception of the Chinese revolution as being constantly progressive had been rejected by the ECCI in early 1928, when it condemned the November plenum's descriptive term "permanent revolution," associated with Trotsky. The problem with using the term "permanent revolution" to describe the Chinese revolution was that "this permitted the possibility of interpreting the revolution as continuously ascending, and thus resulted in false tactics."[6]

The point was that, to those operating in the field, where conditions were in a constant state of flux and varied considerably from place to place, there could be no blind and rigid implementation of policies in order to fulfill expectations that the revolutionary process should be "continuously ascending." Rather, experience had shown that the circumstances actually confronted often required a temporary change of direction away from realizing the immediate goals. Under those conditions, cadres needed to stop attempting any forward development and concentrate on consolidating existing positions, while looking for more realistic and promising directions in which to shift their efforts. The crucial requirement was that in any situation encountered by the Communists, they were always to remain active and adaptive, whether this meant falling back temporarily to engage in basic, preparatory activities in order to regain lost or declining influence in an area, or moving ahead quickly to form the spearhead of a vigorous partisan mass movement and directing it toward an early realization of the soviet. The dynamics of this process can better be understood after examining in some detail the basic concepts that defined the revolutionary process. One of the most important was the concept of struggle.

The Concept of Struggle

"Struggle need not be extensive nor widely developed. It is only necessary that it should achieve its objective, securing the confidence of the masses and consolidating their political understanding and class conception."[7] A struggle campaign denoted a social movement begun in a specific locality, almost always on a limited scale, and based on actual concrete problems clearly recognized by the participants involved. With constant threats from KMT White Terror campaigns, large-scale social movements such as strikes became extremely dangerous to organize, especially in cities where the KMT's opposing forces were strongest. In the countryside peasant unrest was not as difficult to incite, especially if directed against urban centers where area landowners often lived, but it was difficult to keep it under control. Frequently the Communists were unable to channel peasant movements, which easily became violent, in directions that would develop and help unify the overall rural movement. What often occurred were excited and spontaneous peasant attacks on cities in which superior military forces were based. Those troops had no difficulty in destroying or dispersing the peasant attackers. Thus for purposes of maintaining control over incipient movements and in order to be able to operate successfully from their position of relative weakness, the Party and the Youth League emphasized in their instructions the immediate necessity for limiting struggle activities to a modest scale.[8]

The task for cadres was to take a close look at the social conditions in an area, whether that be a factory, school, or village, and to determine the problems and issues that most affected the daily lives of the people. This might be accomplished by visiting the teashops where the workers assembled to talk as Mao did.[9] Peng Pai and Yun Daiying learned early on that dressing like the peasants and meeting with them at their local family temples helped break down social barriers and open communication.[10] Brief "flying meetings" were recommended at factory sites when the workers changed shifts.[11] Or, on a grander scale, some, particularly the Guangdong CCP Committee, called for a systematic survey of rural conditions in order to gain a thorough understanding on which to base policies.[12] With a focus on what was learned by any of these means, a movement subsequently was to be organized, making full use of existing propaganda and organizational skills and concentrating on motivating all participants to struggle for the resolution of any disputed issues or the realization of popular demands.

The point repeatedly emphasized, however, was that actual struggle had to come about voluntarily.[13] It had to be independent of heavy Communist participation and control. As the following instructional passage indicates, this had not always been the procedure in previous struggle activities: "To compel laborers to declare strikes by force of arms and threaten peasants to carry out massacres and arson with 'Guerrilla Warfare Groups' in the past was not the proper way to stir up struggles of the masses."[14] Experience had shown that if Communist involvement in any public mass movement was very extensive, two undesirable trends often followed. First, the participants became too dependent on Communist leadership and direction, thus denying themselves the opportunity to discover their own potential and to play an important leadership role in social movements. This dependency also limited their ability to grasp fully the political and social issues involved in a struggle situation, thus inhibiting their growth and sophistication in these crucial matters. Full participation by the masses in struggle campaigns was recommended as the only way to politicize them and prepare them adequately for eventual action against the bigger and uniquely political targets—the local establishment, the imperialist powers, and, mainly, the KMT.

Second, a movement with extensive Communist involvement, although possibly effective in its early stages, eventually would begin to have less influence because it would take on the appearance to the community of being only a Communist movement, led by "heroes of the Communist Party."[15] In becoming isolated from essential community participation, it ran the additional risk of being more vulnerable to attack and destruction by its enemies and the local authorities. The following guidance was provided to cadres attempting to direct successful struggle activities in Zhejiang:

> Never prevent the masses if a struggle is fermenting (as in Yuyao), but let their fermentation develop. . . During struggles, the masses usually take a risk in carrying out their revenge due to their high spirit and without regard to their own ability. Their high spirit, however, will flag if we fail to secure a better way on their behalf. Consequently, we must study our circumstances and conditions from other points of view during our advance. As soon as we are unable to advance, we must try hard to expand our movement from other angles, in order to avoid the change of their viewpoint and to prevent their spirits from drooping. He is not a leader if he is unable to direct the masses. Rash advance without due care is liable to meet with unexpected rebuffs (as in Laiqi).[16]

In sum, carrying out successful struggle campaigns required a thorough understanding of the purpose and limits of struggle. Cadres had to be particularly sensitive to the receptiveness of the community to be influenced. If a locality was at all ripe for penetration, cadres then had to identify through careful investigations among the population those issues that would likely serve as a good basis for a struggle campaign. Around those issues, propaganda materials were to be developed and initial organization work done to give the aroused following some structural coherence. As the movement gained momentum, Party and League cadres were required to spot those participants who were the most politically advanced and aggressive and recruit them into their organizations. As the materials relate: "It is natural that we should do organization work before the outbreak of struggle, yet it is equally of importance for us to extend the organization in the course of the struggle (by recommending to the Group [League] able elements)."[17]

Clearly, one necessary component of successful struggle activity was the existence of quite exceptional cadres at every level of the organization. This was essential considering the Communists' designs concerning the mission to be accomplished. Cadres' qualifications needed to include a thorough understanding of the Party's basic internal political program, an acute sense of timing for initiating any movement activity, and a finely tuned awareness of the existing social conditions.

Leaders who excelled at these skills, like Fang Zhimin, Peng Pai, and Mao Zedong, did so because they were able to employ their urban educational experiences and previous Marxist exposure to best define and manipulate their operational settings.[18] Thus they could articulate the substance of local issues and concerns and organize around this usually explosive material a committed following. An equally important characteristic was their rural roots or native-place ties. These provided a solid and indigenous foundation on which to integrate the world of ideas with the world of practical reality.

Other requirements of the paradigmatic leader were the ability to lead without stifling the natural responses of the led, the capability to carry on without constant instruction and direction from the higher levels, and a fine judgment of the best among the participants who might be elevated into the ranks of Communist leadership. The Party's inability to fulfill these personnel requirements consistently was surely one important reason why frequent difficulties were encountered when attempting to put the theory of struggle into practice.

Urban Struggle Campaigns. Struggle activities in the dangerous urban environment necessarily focused on relatively minor issues. Thus any emerging points of dissension between the workers and factory management were to be given special attention by the Communists. These might include ill-treatment of a worker by the foreman, reductions in wages, wages in arrears, abrupt dismissals, or extensive layoffs.[19]

In building upon these issues the Communist objective was to spark a sympathetic response or gesture from others immediately involved in the matter or thoroughly familiar with the events. Once the issues were felt widely enough so that a body of united opinion was recognizable, then most of the Communists' efforts were to turn to giving organizational substance to this opinion. When new organizations could not be formed easily, workers were encouraged to join existing labor groups sympathetic or at least not wholly unfavorable to the Communists. Eventually, when enough minor issues were developed into effective struggle campaigns with some organized support, the Communists could attempt to unify these into a more forceful campaign, such as a strike, against factory management.[20] The point was, however, that the initial activities would need to center on minor daily occurrences and only gradually, as circumstances allowed, be expanded into large-scale struggle.

Two kinds of failure in approach were observed to occur with some frequency in Communist urban work. One was the tendency to compel workers in a factory or shop by force to initiate large struggles, such as strikes, in hopes of being able to realize some really significant gain for the Communist movement in the area. This was based on the assumption that small struggles over minor matters were not worthwhile. Apparently many cadres believed that, to be recognized as important, an action had to be large-scale and involve violence and major issues.[21] The other extreme in approach was almost no approach at all. It counted on bringing about peaceful negotiations between the disputants or else awaiting gradual change coming from quarters outside of Communist influence or control.[22] For example, new laws or regulations passed by the factory management or the KMT government might eventually loosen up conditions in a factory, which could result in some favorable circumstances and opportunities for the Communists.

The Communists labeled the first error as that of "blind obedience" and instructed that the result of this approach was inevitable failure. In place of force, cadres were told always to rely on "influencing by speech."[23] Struggle could be incited successfully only by developing effective propaganda around concrete popular issues, and then providing the organizational framework to turn opinion into a forceful social action or struggle movement. After extensive exposure to Communist propaganda and education, workers might be induced to engage in minor struggle activities that seemed to promise them a favorable outcome. A successful experience in these initial campaigns would give them confidence in their ability to get something they wanted, as well as instill in them faith in Communist leadership and programs. Then the path would be open to larger, even political, struggles.

The Communists denounced the second approach as "opportunism" and warned that neither the Party nor the League could develop, or perhaps even survive, without some form of active struggle campaign that was under their influence or direction: "The organization in a long period of peace (that is to say when no struggle has occurred) whereby its comrades receive no training, is just like a building on sand and will be easily destroyed when wind and rain come. It is far from being bolshevized."[24]

Among urban student groups, the struggle campaigns were to focus on such issues as improving the curriculum; the right of students to select teachers; self-study; freedom of speech, assembly, and publication; and public exposure of school finances.[25] From these relatively minor issues the struggle was planned to develop into massive student demonstrations against the presence of foreign powers in China and against their alleged KMT collaborators. Communist propagandists were to link the widespread nationalistic aspiration of opposing imperialistic powers with their own revolutionary aim of opposing the KMT, which they characterized as in cooperation with the imperialists.

Among merchant groups the main focus for Communist struggle campaigns was high taxes. Initially, cadres were to attempt to unify the general merchant attitude of dissent against the existing exorbitant tax rates. This was part of the groundwork for eventually escalating the campaign into one that concentrated on motivating merchant groups jointly to refuse to pay any taxes.[26]

Thus strategists of the Communist urban movement were planning a course that involved initiating separate struggle movements among different worker groups, students, merchants, and trading organizations. Once each of these achieved a substantial level of development, then the planning projected the coordination of these various movements in order to establish the basis for a strong urban Communist movement.[27] As will be shown below, similar methods and procedures were to be followed in developing the rural Communist movement.

According to policy, the ideal situation was for growth in both the urban and rural areas to remain in proportion. This meant that the Party and League were burdened with the enormous responsibility of having to coordinate the development of these two very separate movements.[28] The Communists reasoned that without close coordination, one movement or the other was in great danger of becoming isolated and thus vulnerable to attacks and eventual destruction at the hands of opposition forces.

Rural Struggle Campaigns. The Communists approached agrarian revolution and the establishment of rural soviets with as much caution and incremental planning as they did the work in urban areas. The issue that received primary attention was the high rent rate paid by peasants, often to absentee landlords living in urban areas. This was a long-standing issue among the rural population. The Communists planned to cultivate and use it to win the advantage in rural areas. They saw rural struggle campaigns unfolding in a two-stage process.

The first stage involved initiation of a rent-education movement as the basis for struggle in the countryside.[29] Party and League cadres were instructed to hold general meetings to discuss existing rent rates. Robert Marks describes how Peng Pai pioneered this activity as early as 1922, when he conversed with peasants at rural crossroads and local temples about rent and other issues.[30] In areas where rents had already been paid, cadres were to encourage peasants to demand that land-lords return a portion of the rent. In areas where rents were about to come due, peasants were to be provoked to pay only at the rate that they themselves agreed upon as fair and to deduct total back payments in accordance with the new rate. If a certain village had suffered a bad year, owing to weather or other influences, rent reduction might be calculated on the basis of the amount of losses sustained, or demands might be raised against estate owners for compensation for seed losses.[31]

The Kuomintang Bureau of Farm Affairs was a central target of the Communist rent-reduction movement.[32] It had been established in response to deep peasant unrest over high rent and initiated a policy to bring some relief to the countryside in the form of rent reductions. The Communists planned to counter this by inciting the peasants to insist that rent remission rates be decided by the peasants themselves, and not by KMT organs. Another tactic against the bureau was to encourage peasants to issue common demands that the bureau could not possibly meet, thus causing it to lose the confidence of the peasants. These demands were mainly excessive reductions in rent payment rates. If feelings ran strong enough among the peasants against the bureau, the Communists might incite the peasants to attack the local bureau and destroy its premises.

If the rent-reduction movement succeeded in taking hold in an area, then preparations could be made to embark on the second stage of the rural struggle campaign: refusal to pay any rent and taxes and cancellation of all outstanding debts.[33] These goals would already have been raised in a general way during the initial stage of rent reduction, but once that movement really got underway, these new issues could become the main concern. Also at this point the Communists could begin to disseminate, as widely as possible, anti-Kuomintang literature and material discussing the land revolution and the nature and benefits of a soviet administration in the countryside.

The introduction of political propaganda was considered an important factor in raising the struggle campaign from a level concerned only with daily economic matters to one that challenged and offered alternatives to the existing political power structure. Another factor was the Communists' ability to relate the actual experiences gained by the participants in the preliminary economic struggle campaigns so as to broaden their understanding of organized social action and make them better aware of their own political force as an organized group. The Communists were convinced that instilling political consciousness into struggle participants and coupling this with actual successes in gaining certain objectives of the struggle movement could win them a committed following and lead subsequently to larger and more politically focused struggle campaigns. Some of this is apparent in the following: "From these minor clashes, they will be led to political struggles through economic struggles such as refusing to pay rentals. While the small struggles are being extended and united into a major struggle, the masses besides benefiting by the enrichment of their struggle experience, will become more animated in spirit and their faith in us will be more firmly established, thereby stabilizing the foundation and strengthening the struggle force of our Group [League]."[34]

At this point it is useful to look at the two-stage process of struggle campaigns—the initial stage of demanding rent reductions, followed by the second stage of refusing to pay rents—in order to determine the immediate stakes involved. The first action was limited only to economic issues and posed no threat to the political fabric of the village or rural community. The second, however, severely threatened the economic position of the ruling group, in that it posited taking away the "major source of livelihood," thus undercutting their predominant role and status in the village, a development that became a political matter. It challenged the traditional landlord-peasant power relationship by turning over decisions concerning the rents to organized peasants.

To realize this second, advanced stage, the Communists were to play up political propaganda themes that already had some widespread support, like those emphasizing the dangers to China and its suffering at the hands of imperialists. Then the Communists were to make a connection between the KMT government and the imperialists by pointing out instances where both appeared to overlook or resist the best interests of the Chinese people. These broader political themes, usually much removed from local affairs, were next to be related gradually to the existing enmities developing locally between the peasants and the village ruling classes. Through this gradual process, the Communists envisioned building political opposition at local levels. To heighten this development, the Communists were to disseminate propaganda offering the peasants even greater economic gains through promises of peasant land ownership. Besides economic benefits, the Communists were to point out in propaganda that, once established, the soviets would allow the peasants a substantial political role in the villages.[35]

Thus international, national, and local themes, all with significant economic or political import, were to be used selectively by the Communists in different combinations or with varying emphasis, depending on the actual circumstances and conditions of the movement in a particular area. The one overriding goal was to infuse the basic economic struggle movement with political content in order to extend it toward eventually bringing about the establishment of soviets: "Should we lead labor and peasant masses in economic struggles without using any political propaganda, the laborers and peasants will become economists. On the contrary should we lead them in political struggles (anti-Imperialist and anti-Kuomintang) without any economic demands, they will not persevere in the struggles. So the most important thing in the struggles is to let them know the revolutionary route of the labor and peasant Soviet."[36]

Once the rural struggle movement reached the stage of rent refusals, and the various features of the Communist policy on land revolution were clear to the rural population, disputes were bound to arise among the different social strata of agrarian communities. The position to be taken by the Communists in these disputes is clearly reflected in the Party documents. When the movement developed and realization of its objectives seemed imminent, the rich peasants could be expected to turn reactionary and use their force against the movement.[37] At the other end of the scale, poor peasants and village proletarians (hired hands) were described by the Communists as "the motive power of land revolution."[38] Their potential could be best realized by organizing them into peasant associations and rural proletarian unions.

Groups in the lowest strata, however, could not operate alone successfully. Middle-class farmers and small landowners were very numerous in many parts of the country, and the Communists made it their goal to gain them as allies. For example, when it came to the question of whether or not to implement the equal distribution of lands at an advanced stage of the struggle movement, cadres were instructed to proceed only if the majority of the entire peasant population in an area supported this policy. This cautious approach resulted from the practical recognition by the Communists that the middle and small landowners would stand to lose much from this policy. In areas where landowners were numerically strong, application of this policy, if indeed it could be applied, would have the effect of converting a potentially substantial following into a massive opposition.[39]

Developments in the soldiers' movement were to be closely coordinated with growth in both the rural and urban struggle movements. A solid military movement, including military organizations of workers and peasants and Communist strength amid the opposition military forces, was essential to the progress and even survival of the other two movements. Peng Dehuai's work with the soldiers' committees reflected a carefully planned process, beginning with educating the soldiers about basic economic issues affecting their welfare, such as back pay; organizing them into successful struggle campaigns to rectify these heightened complaints; and then using any good results from these campaigns to convince soldiers that when united and organized, they were capable of realizing important gains. Peng saw the kind of gradual politicization involved as essential to leading the soldiers to take the major step of participating in a general uprising.[40] Party guidance also warned against devoting too much attention to military preparations and training and overlooking the development of the basic struggle campaigns. This was called following the "Military Route."[41] On the other hand, exclusive concern with daily struggle could preclude the struggle movements from reaching the more advanced stage—that of uprising.

As the overall Communist movement developed, all aspects including the urban, rural, and soldiers' movements were to be closely coordinated. This was essential for two reasons: to prevent one movement (usually the rural) from overwhelming and possibly damaging another (usually the urban) and to provide protection and armed force (the soldiers' movement) to the general movement. Heavy emphasis was placed on thorough preparations and controlled growth:

> The Central considers that [the present task] is to step up or commence the work among the workers, peasants, and soldiers. According to their urgent demands, we should lead them to unleash mass economic struggles openly, push forward the revolutionary high tide of the masses, build secret red labor unions among the workers, establish soldiers' committees, and develop the organization and struggle of the peasant association in the countryside, *after which* we should establish rural soviets and create independent rural bases.[42]

Guidance stressing cautious growth and careful preparations came out of hard experience. Fang Zhimin had to contend with mounting pressure from members of the Peasant Revolutionary Corps in destitute Hengfang *xian*. During the year-end, settlement-of-debts period in 1927, the organized peasants wanted to resist and stage an immediate uprising, claiming that "pressure from the gentry and landlords is killing us."[43] Fang found himself having to explain repeatedly to peasant gatherings that past costly failures had resulted from a lack of thorough preparatory work.

The Concept of Uprising

"Uprising is not child's play. It is not a thing that can be accomplished when we want it. If we want to stage an uprising, we hope it will be successful, and if we wish it to be successful, we must attain the following conditions. . . ."[44] Party Central enumerated six conditions for a successful uprising: (1) the public is organized into strong bodies, such as peasants' associations and labor unions, which are responsive to Communist direction; (2) vigorous Party and League branch organs are providing effective leadership and coordination of the area struggle movements among workers, peasants, and soldiers; and these cadres are well trained and experienced enough that in times of emergency they are able to operate effectively without constant supervision from superiors; (3) sufficient propaganda work has been done that the public is willing, even determined, to take action to realize the well-publicized goals; (4) important struggle movements, such as strikes or rent-refusal campaigns, are already in progress and can serve to light the fuse; (5) the public has some military training and many belong to secret military organizations; and (6) the ruling class is in a state of distraction brought on, for example, by internal power struggles, food shortages, natural disasters, or warlord battles. No matter what the circumstances, the strength of the opposition has to be carefully estimated so that no excessive risks are taken.

The aim of an uprising was the occupation of a village, district, *xian*, or province—depending on the extent of the uprising—and the establishment of a soviet.[45] It was to come about as the result of careful preparation: "Struggle need not necessarily be uprising. An uprising is the continuation of the struggle and is the development of the struggle to such a strong degree that political power is seized and the soviet established. Without daily training in struggle, you cannot expect to start an uprising nor can you start a sudden uprising without having maintained and developed the daily struggle. . . ."[46]

Fang Zhimin, Huang Dao, and Shao Shiping, in laying the groundwork for a successful uprising in the Yiheng districts in northeast Jiangxi, combined Communist organization and propaganda techniques with existing rural traditions to strengthen the local struggle campaigns. They joined with members of the Peasant Revolutionary Corps in ceremonies reminiscent of rural secret societies, burning incense and drinking toasts of chicken blood and wine. They took an oath to maintain strict secrecy about their operations and used their close village ties to build new units. For military strength they collected and seized weapons and began drill exercises under the guise of hunting expeditions.[47] In this way traditional methods of uniting the peasants were combined with Communist discipline and organizational know-how in the direction of producing a fully mobilized rural movement.

It is important to note that the Communists intended to make very careful plans and extensive preparations in the countryside before making any attempts to occupy urban centers. As noted above, peasant uprisings were often easier to start than they were to control. When a large number of organized peasants agreed to participate in rent-refusal struggles, the next step, fairly easily managed since many of the village landowners lived away in the cities, was direct occupation of the village land and assertion of political power in the village. The difficulty for the Communists was to contain the movement after this stage. They were sometimes unable to impress the peasants, and even some of their own cadres, with the fact that the uprising could not then immediately develop further to include attacks on the cities where the hated "reactionary" forces resided. The correct procedure was for cadres in the newly occupied areas to consolidate their recent gains, stabilize their areas, and work on extending their influence into neighboring villages, often with the assistance of guerrilla warfare units, which the Communists envisioned as emerging at this point. The message, repeatedly emphasized, was that construction of a solid rural base must precede any action against urban centers.[48]

What often happened was that peasants, once they tasted success in their rural uprising, immediately directed military attacks against the cities, often without considering that the cities were where the opposition strength, both political and military, was most firmly entrenched. Not only were they usually defeated, but often in the process of their raid they harassed and even killed workers and Communist cadres active in the urban struggle movement. This caused urban groups to look with disfavor on the new soviet governments being established in the countryside, which they viewed as mere peasant governments, having little to offer their own movement:

> As more than 80 to 90 percent of the population of China are peasants, the movement of the Party at present consequently tends to follow the peasant idea. As soon as an uprising is started, the peasants regard the city as their only enemy owing to the fact that the cruel taxation and oppression originates from these, and therefore instead of co-operating with the laborers to deal with the reactionary, attack the inhabitants of the city without exception. Arson and manslaughter occur time after time to such an extent that the small capitalists oppose us and the laborers, feeling that they do not benefit by the uprising, look upon the soviet as a Peasant's Government only.[49]

To remedy this recurring problem, Party and League organs were instructed to take certain measures. Urban cadres were to inform and educate workers concerning the real significance of what was taking place in the countryside. Rural cadres, on the other hand, were to focus strictly on building a strong, armed mass foundation in the occupied soviet areas and on extending activities into other rural areas. Emphatically, they were to refrain from attacking cities. In fact, it is clear that the cities were to be the last areas occupied: "When there is a sufficiently strong foundation in the peasant movement in these villages, the city will then be occupied, thus completing the uprising of this city. This applies to the provincial city which will only be attacked when the revolution in the whole province is nearing completion. No vain attempt should be made before the time is ripe."[50]

The Party provided specific guidelines on the conditions that must exist for occupying a city. In some important ways those guidelines are similar to the general preconditions for uprising given above. First, in a *xian*, for example, the rural Communist movement must develop to the point where there is a strong mass foundation in several villages, or certain villages have already been occupied and have established an adequate military defense system. Second, the workers within the *xian* city to be occupied must be well organized and have secret military organizations. Also some effective penetration of the opposition troops must have been realized. Merchants, shopkeepers, and other petit bourgeois elements must have begun to show some interest or support for the Communists. Third, the existing authorities in the city must be weak or in a state of disintegration. Finally, conditions favorable to successful uprisings and occupation must exist in the neighboring *xian*.[51]

Before the actual move could be made to occupy a city, very careful military plans had to be prepared. These were to exist, however, only as valuable tools that would be available at the time the uprising began: "In short the mass movement is to be responsible for the occupation of a city while the military force is only to assist."[52] Any other procedure carried with it the danger of the urban population seeing the Communists as much like bandit or warlord forces.

The Role of Red Terror

The Communists envisioned only a limited and carefully controlled use of Red Terror in the course of carrying out the uprising and establishing the soviet.[53] This was because it was recognized to be as dangerous a weapon for their cause as it was helpful, especially if improperly used. For example, the ill-timed injection of Red Terror activities such as arson, manslaughter, or assassination into an overheated peasant uprising could easily cause the situation to get out of control. Lacking a full understanding of the effective use of Red Terror, the excited participants would be most likely to apply it widely and rashly, with the result that very violent actions would follow. In the course of it, the Communists would find themselves at the tail rather than the head of a reckless revolt. To a large segment of the public, such violent actions might resemble the work of bandit groups. The Communists could not afford to be linked with that image when one of their proclaimed goals was eventually to become the respected and leading authority in the locality.

From the amount of reproval concerning the past use of Red Terror, it is clear that in actual practice the Communists had great difficulty controlling its use, keeping it focused, and making it at all effective in serving their ends. They expressed a certain ambivalence in their thinking concerning its role and value: "The Party, of course, should lead the struggle of the peasants in exterminating landowners and corrupt gentry and diminishing the influence of reactionaries, but a careful scheme must be laid out before taking the lead in incendiarism and homicide as these have no direct relation with the proper work and no real benefit to the revolution."[54]

It has already been noted how Peng Pai participated in the mass public executions in the Hailufeng Soviet. This served to escalate the level of reaction from regular KMT forces, which, once united, eventually destroyed the soviet. In this respect Peng's remarkable abilities for grasping and articulating peasant discontent under the conditions of rural oppression actually worked against the realization of his otherwise well-formed plans. He allowed what might be viewed as the "modern" aspects of his work—the careful surveys and evaluations of peasant needs and aspirations, and thorough organizational work—to become submerged in a tidal wave of violent and long-penned-up peasant desires for revenge. The crucial balance between the rational and voluntaristic components of rural work was lost.

The proper use of Red Terror required that the target always be clearly reactionary, in the view of both Communists and the public. Also, especially in the early stages, the application of terror was to be limited in scope and carefully focused. For example, in a village just undergoing revolutionary change, the Communists were not to condone the wholesale extermination of landlords and the burning of their property, which would create a reign of terror in the area. Communist forces were never to undertake that kind of action on their own. Instead the village leadership was to be encouraged to concentrate on eliminating only those whom the public masses had discussed in meetings and agreed upon as being the major obstruction to the further development of the agrarian revolution and establishment of the soviet.[55]

It was permissible to use a controlled amount of terror to combat KMT White Terror campaigns. In this case survival was involved, and there could be no doubt about the identity of the enemy. Also, because the issues and targets were more clear-cut, there was less danger that any accompanying violence would spill over and become directed against other social groups, which, as a result, would be turned against the Communists.

The Role of Guerrilla Warfare

The final concept included in the Party's strategy to form and expand a viable revolutionary movement involved the role of guerrilla warfare. This kind of warfare was not new to rural China, having been used for centuries by various bandit and rebel groups with inferior strength vis-à-vis an established enemy. What was innovative on the Communists' part was that they recognized the utility of this indigenous style of rural-based warfare and fully integrated it with their modern organizational concepts and emphasis on politicization, which, as discussed above, comprised the primary substance of their approach to the rural masses. This inclusion of the style and tactics of guerrilla warfare further attested to the ingenuity, flexibility, practicality, and omnicompetent character of Communist cadres. Guerrilla warfare was recognized as the final and necessary ingredient for producing a fully mobilized rural Chinese Communist movement. As the Party explained, "Guerrilla warfare is one of the forms of the struggle or new tactics in warfare. Although it is closely related to struggle and the masses, its main object is to extend the movement of the masses and establish a more extensive revolutionary area."[56]

In short, the role of guerrilla warfare was to provide needed military training and assistance to the masses in their concerted effort to implement the uprising and establish the soviet. In effect, it provided basic muscle that allowed the mass movement to set the spark to the uprising when conditions were ripe, contain and defeat the resistance of reactionary forces once the uprising began, and realize the goals of the slogans put forth in the peasant struggle (confiscating and dividing the lands, killing off oppressive landlords and gentry, and setting up peasant representative bodies in the process of establishing the soviets). In addition, local guerrilla warfare units were to be one of the principal suppliers of recruits for developing the Red Army.[57]

Guerrilla warfare was always to remain closely linked with the ongoing mass movement and never take the form of an independent military movement that might, in the public view, resemble bandit forces.[58] Party documents stated: "Guerrilla warfare is to be used to resist the armed forces of reactionaries in a mass struggle (volunteer troops and policemen) or to attack the reactionaries (disarming the landlords and gentry). It is to use a small number of armed men to support the mass struggle in order to make further progress. Consequently, it should not be separated from the mass struggle and particular attention must be paid to create armed organization among the masses."[59]

In order to extend the areas already occupied by Communist and partisan forces, Red Army forces, Red Guards, and Youth Vanguards were to expand and be strengthened. Units of the Red Guards and Vanguards forces were to infiltrate neighboring villages and incite villagers to begin struggle campaigns or, if conditions in the village were developed to the point that an uprising was imminent, reinforce the secret military bodies and begin the uprising.

Communist forces, in the course of consolidating rural soviets and base areas, acquired considerable experience in the use of Red Terror and guerrilla warfare. Regarding the military aspects of guerrilla warfare, Zhu De is credited with having developed by May 1928 the famous sixteen-character formula: "the enemy advances, we retreat; the enemy camps, we harass; the enemy tires, we attack; the enemy retreats, we pursue."[60] Zhu reportedly developed these revolutionary tactics based on his experience before and during the early 1920s in fighting bandit forces on the southwest border area in Yunnan province.

Fang Zhimin in June 1928 described principles of guerrilla warfare derived from his experience in northeast Jiangxi. He explained: "In the future when we fight, we must lure the enemy in deep, avoid his strength and hit his weaknesses, use many troops when the enemy forces are few, and fight a quick battle to force a quick decision."[61] One year later, with more experience, Fang added to this the necessity to strike the enemy by surprise and from unexpected directions. Battles should occur at the Communists' initiative, at their chosen time, and with no strategic openings or points of vulnerability to Communist forces. Battle plans should include ambushes and small skirmishes.[62] To carry this out, cadres had to remain flexible, selecting the most suitable guerrilla tactic to confront a given situation.

These military tactics were given an essential political dimension with the so-called "Three Main Rules of Discipline," developed by Mao Zedong prior to the march to the Jinggang Mountains, and the "Eight Points for Attention" formulated in January 1928 by him.[63] Mao intended his contributions to solidify the relationship of the Communist military forces with the populations they confronted and provide the military with essential mass support. In a letter to He Long dated June 15, 1929, the Party Central described the principles of guerrilla warfare being developed by Mao and Zhu. Mao and Zhu practiced tactics similar to those ascribed to Fang Zhimin, but in addition they reportedly emphasized a two-sided policy of dividing the Communist military forces in order to mobilize the masses, and concentrating the armed forces to confront an enemy. Fundamental to the successful implementation of this policy was the commander's flexibility and responsiveness to local conditions. The imagery used was that of opening a net to win over the masses, and then being able to close it to deal with the enemy. Mao and Zhu also advanced the tactic of using one area as a base and then advancing and retreating from it according to the recognized strength of the enemy. With a strong enemy, the goal was to make him chase the Communist forces, which would then initiate a circling maneuver against him.[64] The required dynamic relationship between the Communist military forces, partisan supporters, and the enemy is revealed in the following passage:

> What is guerrilla warfare? It is like this: At a place where our power is not strong enough and the peasant army is not well armed, and yet the struggle of the public has reached its zenith

and at the same time the reactionary party is still able to defeat us with an army, we cannot therefore occupy this area and are obliged to mobilize our followers in various villages who will be advised not to fight face to face with the reactionary soldiers but to evade them and start riots and uprisings in other villages. They should be advised to shift their activities from the original place to other places on the arrival of the reactionary soldiers. On the other hand, sudden attacks are to be made on these soldiers en route, disarm some of them, seize their rice and extend our influence from one place to another with a view to establishing the soviet. . . .[65]

The Party directed that guerrilla warfare was an integral part of the revolutionary process and was always to remain closely linked and responsive to the ongoing mass movement. Moreover military cadres were not to make the mistake of taking it upon themselves to replace the peasants in initiating uprisings.[66] Guerrilla forces were to provide only the necessary element of force, as needed, to carry the revolutionary mass movement to more advanced stages.

Overturning the rural power structure presupposed a great deal of previous planning and preparation on the part of Communist cadres. The goals of the revolutionary movement needed to be clearly understood and broadly supported within the community; a vital and efficient Communist organization was necessary to direct each stage of activity; and this body required assistance from the mass-based guerrilla organization that could provide the essential element of force as needed at the various stages of development. Peasant organizations had to be well established and enjoy widespread public participation and support. When all these factors existed or, in other words, "when conditions were ripe," events were to proceed as follows:

When the masses' struggle feelings are very excited, several tens of persons may disarm the Peace Preservation Corps and burn their houses as well as massacre rowdies and evil gentry and confiscate their properties, which would be distributed among poor peasants. A meeting of a large number of peasants and masses should then be immediately convened to promulgate the general regulations of land revolution and establish the Soviet. The land deeds should be burnt publicly and the wrongs of these rowdies denounced.

> Propaganda in favor of the extension of Soviet land revolution
> should be carried out by the peasants' committee if the commit-
> tee is well-organized and has the trust of the farming masses.[67]

In sum, prior to the departure of Chinese delegates for the Party's
Sixth Congress convening in Moscow June 18–July 11, 1928, issues
fundamental to the Chinese Communist movement were being extensively examined and resolved. These became part of the discussion
and formal documentation developed at that congress. The nature
and function of soviets had been treated extensively in Party directives.
Rural base areas existed, and leading cadres in the field were studying
the problems and opportunities afforded by local conditions and for-
mulating their specific policies and approaches accordingly. Their
findings and experiences contributed to comprehensive organizational
guidance concerning the development of the Red Army and supporting military bodies. Detailed instructions were circulating concerning
the external mobilization of a united front of support through labor
unions, peasant associations, and other mass organizations. The CCP
had formulated an overall revolutionary strategy for the movement's
survival and growth, which emphasized careful preparations and coordination of urban and rural developments and the effective use of
military support to protect and expand the movement.

All of these developments, apparent by the early months of 1928,
occurred outside the purview, in fact largely in the absence, of a principal Comintern adviser in China. Of course, many of the basic concepts
had been derived from Comintern-developed strategy and tactics for
leading revolutionary movements. What is significant, however, is that
in order to promote their survival, the Chinese Communists had to
apply and integrate these concepts to their immediate situation. Local
issues and conditions quickly became the critical element in the development of Communist policy. Out of the process, the Party developed
unique concepts and approaches, the most notable of which was to
locate the base of their movement in the countryside with the objective of eventually, when conditions were favorable, overwhelming the
urban political centers with a force of fully mobilized workers and
peasants.

Chapter 10. The Sixth Party Congress and Its Aftermath

The Chinese Communist leadership convened Party congresses almost annually after the first one in 1921. This trend ended with the Sixth Congress (June 18–July 11, 1928), for the seventh was not held until 1945. The convening of the Sixth Party Congress had been placed on the agenda at the CCP's November plenum in 1927. The subsequent long interval between the sixth and seventh congresses can be explained in part by a series of intervening events, including the immediate tumultuous state of the Communist movement, the arduous retreat to the Northwest during the famous Long March, and then the period of the Second United Front with the KMT, directed at confronting the overwhelming Japanese threat. Another important factor emerging in 1927–28 was the shift in the priorities of many key Chinese Communist leaders, away from seeking Comintern guidance and toward accommodating the Communist movement to the demanding and unique local Chinese conditions. Accompanying this shift was a growing independence from Moscow's direction concerning the development of policies and operational guidance for the Chinese Communist movement. Evidence of these changes was already apparent in the composition of those attending and in the proceedings of the Sixth Party Congress held in Moscow.

The Site and Participants

Moscow was selected as the site for the Sixth Congress for several reasons. Principal among them were the exceedingly dangerous operating conditions in China. At least eighteen key Communist leaders were executed by the KMT police during 1927–28, including luminaries

such as Li Dazhao, Zhang Tailei, and Luo Yinong. Then Party Secretary
Chen Duxiu lost two sons during Chiang's April 12 Shanghai coup.
Scores of lesser Party figures and followers were rounded up and shot
during police raids on Communist headquarters around the country.
The new Communist security procedures developed during the fall of
1927 discouraged holding executive meetings of more than seven Party
leaders. When the congress did convene, more than one hundred
Chinese delegates and observers attended. Such a gathering would
have involved unthinkable risk under the existing conditions in China.

A second reason for holding the congress in Moscow was that three
other major Communist conferences attended by Chinese delegates
were scheduled to meet in Moscow in 1928. The Fourth Profitern
(Labor International) Congress was scheduled to convene in Moscow
in the spring of 1928, while the Sixth Comintern Congress and the Fifth
Congress of the Young Communist Internationale were slated for the
summer months. With a number of key Chinese Communist leaders
already gathering in Moscow, it is not surprising that the Sixth CCP
Congress also convened in this center of orthodoxy and safety from
the KMT White Terror campaigns.

Key Leaders Are Absent

The congress was held in a village on the outskirts of Moscow.[1] Eighty-
four voting delegates attended the congress, along with thirty-four
alternates or nonvoting delegates, representing a total party membership of 40,000.[2] Orders to attend the congress were issued in April,
making it virtually impossible for those in the more inaccessible rural
areas to receive instructions and reach Moscow in time.[3] In fact, perhaps the most striking feature of the Sixth Party Congress is the list of
those who did not attend. To mention only the most prominent: Mao
Zedong, Peng Pai, Zhu De, He Long, Fang Zhimin, Peng Dehuai, Yun
Daiying, Ren Bishi, and Li Fuchun. Zhou Enlai explained that because
"it was felt that the work at home was more important," some key and
experienced cadres did not attend the congress.[4] The reasons for their
absence are obvious in that they were fully occupied with the heavy
responsibilities of carving out the independent armed areas in China
to sustain an ongoing Communist movement under the mostly unfavorable conditions. Ironically, while CCP leaders were meeting in Mos-

cow supposedly to determine the direction and substance of the Chinese Communist movement, those who remained in China were actually originating the policies and making the innovations that would characterize a successful Chinese Communist movement.

Both Zhang Guotao and Zhou Enlai, who left accounts based on their participation in the congress, emphasize that the Comintern played a decisive role in the proceedings of the Sixth CCP Congress.[5] Stalin himself met with the delegates just prior to the opening of the congress. Bukharin delivered the keynote speech that served as the basis for the "Political Resolution," the principal document produced at the congress. Pavel Mif, Stalin's leading China expert and at that time rector of Sun Yat-sen University in Moscow, handled the administrative arrangements for the congress.[6] He marshaled a considerable number of Chinese students attending Sun Yat-sen University to perform translation and secretarial tasks in support of the proceedings. In addition, a few student assistants were recruited from the Chinese department of the Communist University for the Toilers of the East.[7]

The New Party Leadership

There is no question about the revolutionary credentials of those attending the congress. They had participated in and directed major Communist activities for years. The fact remains, however, that most were not directly involved in building and developing the emerging revolutionary base areas. Having operated only within the mainstream of Communist activity, and with regular Comintern guidance, they were thus predisposed to receive and respond to Comintern direction and influence. As Zhou Enlai remarked from the vantage point of writing in 1944, "If more comrades engaged in the day-to-day work had gone, it would have been possible for the Congress to learn more about actual problems and to collect more opinions."[8] At the time of the congress the only really active daily work was taking place in the more protected rural areas, and certainly not in the cities. This was directly contradictory to Stalin's and the Comintern's renewed emphasis and commitment to reestablishing Party strength in the cities.

The new Party leadership elected at the congress reflected the persuasions of the Chinese delegates and the Comintern's preferences. Voting delegates at the congress elected a Central Committee com-

posed of twenty-three full members and thirteen alternates.[9] At its first
plenum, immediately following the congress, the new Central Committee elected a seven-member Politburo that included Qu Qiubai, Li
Lisan, Zhou Enlai, Cai Hesen, Zhang Guotao, Xiang Ying, and was
presided over by Xiang Zhongfa, the new general secretary.[10] Although
removed from the presiding post, Qu did not become the subject of
personal attacks as had former secretary Chen Duxiu, who had been
charged with having personally misapplied correct Comintern policy
in China.[11] However, the problems and disasters of the past year, particularly those related to the interpretation of events as being in a state of
uninterrupted revolution, which led to charges at the ECCI's February
Plenum of putschism, became associated with Qu's leadership. Thus
weakened, Qu could not continue in the leading post, but he did
retain a seat on the Politburo. He presented the opening speech to the
Sixth Congress and went on to present a major address and commentary at the Sixth Comintern Congress, which followed almost immediately after the CCP Congress. As for the key specialized departments
within the Central Committee, the crucial functions of the Organization Department eventually were assumed once again by Li Weihan.[12]
Li Lisan headed the Propaganda Department, Zhou Enlai the Military
and Security Affairs, Xiang Ying the Workers' Department, Peng Pai
(appointed in absentia) the Peasant Department, and Deng Yingchao
(wife of Zhou Enlai) the Party Women's Department.[13]

Xiang Zhongfa's election as Party general secretary mainly indicated
the growing concern primarily from within the Comintern that the CCP
was losing its vital connection with the urban proletariat. The crushing of urban Party organizations, especially trade union bodies, seemed
to threaten the Party's identity as a genuine Marxist-Leninist Party. In
February at the ECCI's Ninth Plenum, which Xiang attended, the
Comintern had instructed the CCP to recapture its urban proletarian
bases, and in this regard Xiang Zhongfa was one of the few Party
leaders with genuine proletarian origins.

As reward for his work within Wuhan labor circles, Xiang had been
sent to Moscow to study during 1925–27. On his return to China in
early 1927 Xiang became chairman of the key Hubei Provincial General
Trade Labor Union. He also had very recent Comintern ties, having
spent the past year in the Soviet Union as the CCP representative to the
Comintern following the break with Wuhan. Zhang Guotao, in his

colorful account of the congress proceedings, charged Xiang with excessive subservience to Comintern authority, particularly to Pavel Mif. Ridiculing Xiang's behavior, Zhang claimed that both he and Li Lisan resented Xiang's "Miffy airs" and penchant for invoking the phrase on numerous occasions, "This is the correct line of the Comintern."[14] Of course, Xiang's sojourn in Moscow also meant that he was not current concerning the important new developments of the past year in China. His absence did have one positive aspect, in that Xiang did not become embroiled in Party factional conflicts, such as that between Qu and Zhang Guotao, which had heated up during that period. This probably further enhanced his appeal within both Party and Comintern circles for the top Party post.

Although Xiang's abilities as a labor leader were readily recognized, his potential for playing a broader leadership role in the Chinese movement apparently was limited. During the next three years of his tenure he quickly lost power over the Party to the new propaganda chief, Li Lisan. Li, an articulate public speaker and prominent labor organizer, particularly in leading centers such as Shanghai, Wuhan, and Guangzhou, was a key participant in the celebrated May 30th Movement and the Nanchang and Guangzhou uprisings. Li's urban labor background and communication talents made him a logical selection for the key propaganda post at a time when the Party was directed to regain strength among the workers. It no doubt also helped him maintain Comintern backing when he took control of the CCP.

However, Li's urban frame of reference also estranged him from acquiring a quick grasp of the urgency and long-range significance of building base areas and military strength in the countryside. He worked from a different set of priorities, which were responsive mainly to the centralizing features of democratic centralism. He adhered to the Comintern's direction that the CCP-led urban proletariat provided the main impetus to revolution, with the vast peasantry serving as principal allies. This contrasted with those operating under great pressure in the countryside, whose priorities emphasized building a Communist movement from a rural base. This latter approach required a responsiveness to the key characteristics of the indigenous rural culture, local economic conditions, and the actual physical surroundings. It entailed having leaders skilled enough to mobilize a movement that was viable because it integrated these local characteristics.

Another up-and-coming group of young leaders also participated in the congress. These were the Chinese student associates of Pavel Mif who, according to Zhang Guotao, mainly "took pride in being extraordinary."[15] Purporting to be masters of Marxism-Leninism, the students criticized Qu Qiubai's interpretations, charged Zhang Guotao with opportunism, and generally subjected the veteran Party leaders attending the congress to ridicule and derision. Mif, who was preparing his charges for eventual Party leadership, reportedly did nothing to discourage this negative disposure to the prevailing CCP leadership.[16]

Qu and Bukharin Differ

Qu Qiubai clearly was a key transitional figure during this critical period. His grounding in Marxism-Leninism and work in the urban labor movement have already been noted. He had established his credentials as a major voice on rural questions with his writings and by lecturing at the Peasant Movement Training Institute at Wuzhang. When Peng Shuzhi denied publication in *Guide Weekly* of the second part of Mao Zedong's "Report on an Investigation into the Agrarian Movement in Hunan," Qu published it in book form and wrote a preface to it. He had enhanced his military experience by teaching at the Central Military Academy.[17] Most important, for the purposes of the congress, Qu attended as the party secretary who had directed the events of the past year.

Being headquartered in Shanghai, Qu was denied the direct experience of those operating in the field. Nevertheless, the evidence is clear that Qu received and coordinated field reporting, using its contents to develop guidance and regulations for the overall movement. With this background, Qu was able to function as an intermediary at the congress, relating information concerning the past year's developments. Not surprisingly, this led to misunderstanding and disagreement with the Comintern leadership. Stalin and Bukharin continued to view China as just one part of the overall world Communist movement. They had little comprehension or perhaps interest in the specific nature and recent course of events in China.

Qu Qiubai presented a lengthy and comprehensive report to the congress entitled "The Past and Future of the Chinese Communist Party."[18] He recounted the major events in Party history during the years 1925–27 and interpreted their significance for understanding the Chinese revolution. He commented on the tensions that resulted from Party leaders attempting to maintain Party discipline by adhering to increasingly infeasible Comintern directives while at the same time trying to shore up the slipping Communist influence in China.

Qu's discussion of events since mid-1927 not surprisingly indicated his enthusiasm for the course and direction of the events that occurred under his own provisional direction. Qu praised the redirection of Party organizational work toward building strong secret units at the basic level. He noted the difficulties experienced during the fall of 1927, when Party leaders attempted to avoid making compromises with "counterrevolutionary" elements, which would repeat the opportunistic behavior that he claimed had caused the Party serious damage since 1925.

Qu maintained that a revolutionary strategy to guide the successful development of a Chinese Communist movement had been developed during the early months of 1928. It focused on the establishment of soviets first in the countryside, which would extend to urban centers with the support and protection of organized military forces. He explained that eventually these developments would lead to the establishment of authoritative soviet governments in "one or more provinces" to serve as the basis for the future realization of a national soviet government, under the direction of the CCP. As described above, the basic concepts and instruction regarding this strategy were the subject of numerous Party resolutions and directives already circulating in China.

Speaking to the congress as Comintern head, Bukharin delivered a major address that reportedly lasted nine hours and was to provide the theoretical framework for the resolutions passed by the congress.[19] He repeated the theoretical findings of the ECCI's Ninth Plenum, which had defined the Chinese revolution as being at the bourgeois-democratic stage. Thus, the Party-led dictatorship of the workers and peasants was to carry out agrarian revolution and develop the largely urban anti-imperialist movement.

In contrast to Qu's emphasis on the rural basis for revolution in China, Bukharin left no doubt about the preeminence of the workers in this temporary partnership with the peasants, who served only as the workers' principal ally. He identified the workers as the advanced class that could be trusted to carry the revolution through its necessary stages on the way to bringing about a socialist society in the future. With the proletariat in charge, the tasks of the agrarian revolution aimed at eradicating feudalism and imperialism could be accomplished, and the revolution subsequently advanced to the next higher stage—that of establishing socialism and its concomitant destruction of capitalist social and productive relations.

Bukharin provided a critique of the CCP's past management of the Chinese revolution and identified three major shortcomings: (1) the CCP lost an independent critical nature by becoming too subservient to the KMT during their alliance; (2) the CCP leadership failed to recognize the transition from a stage of productive alliance to one of harmful associations, or, in other words, CCP leaders failed to foresee the counterrevolutionary turns by Chiang Kai-shek and the Wuhan leadership; and (3) the Party lost its position as the leading nucleus for mass movements. As might be expected, although Bukharin did mention the failings of Comintern representatives in China, he neglected to recognize that it was Moscow's directives dictating the course of CCP policy that were directly responsible for creating these "opportunistic" shortcomings reported in his critique.

Bukharin made explicit what was suggested in the Ninth Plenum Resolution—that the Chinese revolution currently was in a trough between "two crests of a revolutionary tide."[20] The heroic but failed Guangzhou Uprising was described during the proceedings as a "rearguard action," bringing to a close a major revolutionary tide and leading the revolution on to the new soviet stage. Using the wave imagery and no doubt needing to appear suitably optimistic about the prospective fortunes of the Chinese revolution under Comintern guidance and direction, Bukharin claimed that "the beginning of this new wave is now before us; we are on the verge of a resurgence; or we are near the verge of a resurgence. . . . We are now approaching the second upsurge; we are facing a great nationwide revolutionary upsurge."[21] Searching the Chinese horizons for concrete evidence of this impending upsurge, Bukharin could only muster the explanation that because the main tasks of the bourgeois-democratic stage—the unification of the country and the anti-imperialist and agrarian revolutions—had not yet been realized, and because the KMT was incapable of accomplishing this work, the Chinese revolution must inevitably take an upward turn.

Significantly, Bukharin refused to include the emerging Chinese soviet movement, on which Qu and others reported, as promising evidence of a resurgence. From his standpoint, he simply could not, for good reason. This Communist-led movement was taking place in remote rural regions, still far removed from the immediate leadership or even participation of the urban proletariat. His resistance and even ignorance of the significance of this activity is apparent in one part of his speech where, in responding to Qu's speech, Bukharin asked: "Is there really an army or merely a power for organizing military affairs" in China?[22] Zhou Enlai reported that Bukharin was so pessimistic about the prospects of the soviet and Red Army movements in China that he recommended at the congress that high-ranking cadres be transferred out of the military, presumably to more productive Party posts in the cities.[23]

In a major section of his address emphasizing work in major cities, Bukharin further downplayed the significance of the new soviet movement. He explained: "One cannot confuse the existence of soviet regimes in a few *hsien* [*xian*] with the victory of the Chinese revolution. Although there are now quite a few *hsien* soviet regimes, and although comrades there are doing excellent work, that the Chinese revolution has suffered defeat is an absolute fact. Revolutionary victory without victory in the industrial centers is wild nonsense."[24]

Bukharin also took issue with the land-distribution policies practiced with the emerging soviet movement, claiming that the ECCI "has never proposed the slogan of confiscating all land."[25] He castigated the notion that equal division of land could produce socialism, referring to it as mere "peasant socialism." Only the proletariat was capable of constructing socialism and the total social system, both rural and urban, that underpinned its existence. Although he recognized the peasants as having a key supporting role to play by the eradication of feudalism in the countryside—which would have a profound effect on the landlords' urban bourgeois counterpart—the peasantry, acting without the proletariat, could not bring about true socialism in China. Bukharin described the question of total confiscation and equal division of land as "the most radical slogan to those who aspire to reach socialist heaven in a single leap" and noted that "this is to commit the error of the theory of uninterrupted revolution."[26] It omitted the essential stage of the bourgeois-democratic revolution under which the proletariat mobilizes the peasantry to overthrow the landlord class.

At the conclusion of his speech, Bukharin stressed the Party's essential role in leading the anti-imperialist movement, particularly by dramatizing all concessions made by the KMT to foreign powers. The explosive issue of the moment concerned the Japanese encroachments in Manchuria and Shandong, the subject of several key instructions originated by the Party Central in Shanghai while the congress was in session.[27] The popular response surrounding this matter in the northeast was to be used to revive the flagging urban movement.

Key Resolutions Passed

The centerpiece of the documentation produced at the Party's Sixth Congress was the "Political Resolution."[28] Regarding the process of drafting the congress resolutions, Zhou Enlai said: "The resolutions of the Sixth Congress were drafted by Comrade Qu Qiubai. Mif and Bukharin revised the drafts, and then Comrade Qu Qiubai read them over and made further changes."[29] Whatever the extent of Qu's changes to the text of resolutions, it is certain that the key "Political Resolution" incorporated the interpretation and guidance of the Comintern leadership now fully consolidated under Stalin's administrative authority. It provided the theoretical framework defining the Chinese revolution, placed it in the historical context of world revolution, and provided authoritative guidance for its further development.

Key areas of Communist work, which could be touched upon only in the comprehensive "Political Resolution," became the subject of several separate resolutions developed at the congress. Commenting upon their development, Zhang Guotao said that the attending delegates "made grandiose resolutions, which resulted in the congress being publicized as the most successful of all CCP congresses. Scrutiny, however, reveals that the contents of the resolutions were vague and inconsistent on many points, even containing hidden rocks."[30] Certainly, one rocky area concerned policy regarding the soviets. The resolution on the soviets represented a major departure from writings circulating in China concerning the organization, purpose, and role of the soviets.[31]

This was a serious matter because the Ninth ECCI Plenum and the Sixth Congress "Political Resolution" both had laid down the political interpretation that the Chinese revolution had entered the key stage of soviets. Therefore, authoritative guidance developed at the congress regarding the establishment of soviets and their role in the Communist movement necessarily would be especially important.

The main exemplary material used in drafting the resolution on the soviets included quotations from Lenin on the Russian Bolshevik experience at establishing soviets, lessons provided by organizations connected with the Shanghai labor movements, and the experience gained during the short-lived Guangzhou Soviet. Commenting specifically on the congress's attempt to deal with the question of soviets, Zhou Enlai said: "the congress merely copied the experience of the Soviet Union, stressing the establishment of soviets in the cities. . . ."[32] The preoccupation with urban soviets is conveyed clearly in the guidance that the leadership role in the new soviets was to be held exclusively by the urban proletariat: "It [the soviet] should guarantee the leadership function of the industrial workers."[33] In other materials generated by the congress the workers were more loosely defined, to include at least the poorest or hired elements in countryside, but in this document it is the industrial workers who are given the presiding role in the new political form, the soviet. In addition, the offices to be established under the soviets were geared toward urban needs. Besides a Department of Military Affairs, one concerned with finance, and something called "the people's economics department," only two other departments were identified: (1) Department of Municipal Administration, concerned with schools, waterworks, medical needs, etc., and (2) Department of Social Security, concerned with the correct implementation of labor laws and housing, "and the work of the workers and peasants."[34]

Even regarding Party organizational work aimed at establishing rural soviets, the workers were to play the predominant role. The resolution instructed the Revolutionary Committee to absorb the most resolute revolutionary leaders of the peasant movement, particularly the industrial workers living in the villages and the workers who were originally from the cities or had returned from the cities. It identified the industrial workers as being the mainstay of Party work in rural areas.[35]

Another main difference between this document and the earlier ones concerning soviets was in the discussion of the military. In this resolution the overriding concern was with building a regular military force, patterned after the Soviet Union's experience in organizing a Red Army, complete with a Political Department and its emissaries sent to oversee the Red Army officers and troops, the political commissars. Most important, rather than acting as a protective force for the further consolidation of already established soviets, as had been the goal stated in materials circulating in China, the Red Army was to act as an aggressive force for territorial expansion. In fact, the resolution stated that if the workers and peasants showed concern only with the protection of their local soviet regime, the Party should use every means to smash such local prejudice. The only legitimate goal was to strive forward, not merely to act in self-defense, because expansion was recognized as the only guarantee of the existence of soviet political power.[36]

With the "Political Resolution" having predicted the inevitability of a new revolutionary wave that would permit the CCP to recapture its urban proletarian bases, combined with this conception of an aggressive role for the Red armies, the path was cleared for the subsequent development of policies calling for Red Army attacks to gain control over industrial centers. Such tactics became the basis of the so-called "Li Lisan line," the failure of which caused Li's downfall by November 1930 and brought further setbacks to the Chinese Communist movement.

At the time of the congress, however, neither Bukharin nor Stalin actually put much stock in the rural soviet and Red Army movements in China, separated as they were from close urban contacts. Zhang Guotao reported Stalin's remarks just prior to the opening of the congress that, in his view, perhaps the most significant feature of the rural soviet movement was that it provided temporary refuge and protection for Party cadres during this period of White Terror, presumably until they could resume the important urban work. Stalin's ignorance of the soviet movement in China is again suggested when, referring to an example of its existence, rather than singling out the Jinggang Mountains or another key base, he picked out what Zhang called "the most separatist regime of Liu Ts'un-hou in the farthest outpost" in Sichuan.[37]

Stalin was similarly pessimistic in his evaluation of the existing Red armies in China, located only in remote areas. Zhou Enlai claimed that "it was not in 1928 but on the eve of the Red Army's attack on Changsha in 1930 that he [Stalin] came to regard the Red Army as of prime importance to the Chinese revolution."[38] It appears that in 1928 Stalin viewed the Chinese Red Army as a potential tool, but one that needed considerable work and strengthening, since he saw as its only purpose the recapturing of urban bases. This skepticism is further reflected in the "Resolution for Work in Military Affairs," which unlike other resolutions was presented to the congress only in draft form.[39] Why this was so is not certain, but it is likely that the Chinese experience in military work, especially in guerrilla warfare, was difficult to reconcile with Comintern experience and understanding.

It is clear that the Comintern leaders did not grasp the intimate connection between regular Red Army units and partisan forces for implementing the strategy of guerrilla warfare. This connection was a key insight gained from the Chinese experience. Comintern leaders may not even have considered the two related, or the guerrilla struggle as a bona fide military activity. The "Military Resolution" conveyed the Comintern's conviction that military work had great importance to the prospects of the Communist movement, in view of their prediction that the Chinese revolution was headed "for the upsurge of a new revolutionary wave." In order to be ready for and take best advantage of the inevitable "high tide," a strong Red Army had to be built.[40] A feeling of haste or at least pressure to reach this stage comes through: "In regions where the workers and peasants have succeeded in their revolts and in the establishment of soviet governments, our Party should quickly convert the organization of its own guerrilla–style armed forces into a regular Red Army."[41] This is different from CCP guidance circulating in China, which envisioned the Red Guards and Youth Vanguards as essential forces for infiltrating adjacent areas and expanding the movement. According to the overall Chinese military strategy, partisan forces coexisted with and complemented the Red Army, which served mainly to conserve and protect existing soviets. In China both kinds of military force were regarded as essential for different but consecutive and ongoing tasks.

The "Military Resolution" contained the usual Comintern guidance recommending secret work within the KMT military ranks and warlord troops and laid out principles for establishing a Red Army. What is striking, however, in light of what was happening in China at the time of the congress, is that the whole complicated subject of guerrilla warfare was largely omitted from this resolution and covered instead in the congress's "Resolution on the Peasant Movement."[42] It was a subject that required reliance on Chinese experience and knowledge for guidance and probably entailed substantial contributions from Qu Qiubai. In the major section of this resolution entitled "Guerrilla Warfare," the lessons of revolt learned over the past year are evident. They included the mobilization of rural support beginning with the villages and based on issues of local concern; the direction of that support toward local armed revolt and the establishment of rural and eventually urban soviets; and, finally, the implied necessary replacement, at least at the early stages of this process, of "the leadership of the proletariat" with Communist Party leaders, whether worker or peasant by background, who were attuned to and flexible in the face of local conditions.[43]

Qu Qiubai had grasped the basic points of this strategy as early as December 1927. He then attributed much of guerrilla warfare strategy and tactics to the lengthy indigenous traditions of battling secret societies. But Qu added that what the guerrilla struggle required was the Party's centralizing leadership and skillful articulation of demands for change. Done effectively, this could produce a fully mobilized populace, capable of powerful military action.[44]

The Peasant Movement Resolution reinforced earlier guidance that emphasized gearing the extent of agrarian revolution to the particular conditions in a local area. Under conditions that were unfavorable to the Communists, their agrarian program had to be tempered, allowing the full disclosure of the basic internal political program only among those at the bottom of the rural social structure. Total confiscation of all lands (leading to the eradication of feudalism) could appeal only to those landless and desperate. Such would be correct tactics when these have-nots were in the majority in an area. If middle peasants or small landholders were in the majority, however, then the internal demands would have to be softened in a way that would make them appeal to this majority group, thus allowing the Communists some chance of building a rural base of mass support. In some localities even rich peasants (landholders who hired labor) might be courted in order to build a base of support against the never-tolerated, inevitable enemy, the big landlord or local power holder. To whatever degree the internal demands might have to be tailored or diluted, however, the welfare of the poorest class had to be considered and could not be sacrificed to hold the coalition together.

The difficulty that the CCP leadership had had in coming to grips with agrarian questions in China had already been apparent at the November plenum, when only a draft resolution, to be sent out for discussion and comment prior to the convening of the Sixth Congress, could be produced. Continuing difficulty in unraveling the complexities in the Chinese countryside is reflected in the rambling, repetitive, and contradictory "Resolution on the Land Question."[45] This lengthy document was an amateur but perhaps hopeless attempt to use the available Marxist-Leninist categories and definitions to make sense of rural conditions in China and to provide the basic economic and social policies of the agrarian program to be enacted in newly established soviets. The analysis produced results like the following: "The Chinese peasant classes can be divided into rich peasants, hired farmhands, the smallest peasants, small peasants, and middle peasants."[46] Although poorly organized and peculiar in its use of Marxist terminology, this resolution did tackle questions and issues that had not been handled before. In so doing, its authors may have performed some of the necessary spadework for producing the much more cogent and authoritative "Resolution on the Peasant Movement."

The Sixth Congress passed an "Outline of the Resolution on the Question of Organization," which repeated many of the points contained in Party directives circulated during the spring concerning the organization of workers, peasants, youth, women, military, and bandit groups.[47] But overall this document reflected the Comintern's emphasis on regaining strength within the urban trade union movement: "We should adjust the Party membership. We should absorb a large number of worker-activists into the Party."[48]

In addition, a fifteen-chapter, fifty-three-article Party Constitution was included to clarify organizational matters. It defined mainly the membership rules, organizational structure, and financial system for the CCP.[49] It contained basically the same material as that describing the Chinese Communist Youth League and available during the fall of 1927 to Chinese cadres.[50] Stress was placed on the role of Comintern and key Party supervisory organs in the development of the basic internal Communist political line. The bulk of the materials, however, concerned rules and regulations for building and rebuilding an organization and membership in China beginning with and emphasizing the importance of basic branch levels. In this respect it reinforced the Chinese experience after the end of the First United Front of having to start over, this time from the bottom upward.

In support of organizational work, the congress produced a "Resolution on Propaganda Work" "to prepare for the arrival of a new and broad revolutionary tide."[51] It repeated many of the points elaborated on in Party correspondence during the preceding months. The congress also produced a "Resolution on the Trade Union Movement" to support the Comintern's insistence on a resurgence of Communist work in the cities.[52]

The Aftermath of the Congress

Zhang Guotao reported that about half the delegates to the Sixth Congress remained in Moscow to attend the Sixth Comintern Congress, which met from July 17 to September 1, 1928. Key leaders who returned to China included Xiang Zhongfa, Li Lisan, and Cai Hesen.[53] Qu Qiubai's continued high status within Communist circles gained him membership on the ECCI's Presidium and appointment as chief of the official Chinese delegation to the congress,[54] which included four other members: Zhang Guotao, Deng Zhongxia, Huang Ping, and Yu Fei.

During the fall of 1928 the Shanghai Party Central conveyed the general policy guidance produced at the Sixth Party Congress to the subordinate Party levels and existing base areas to guide work in the Communist movement. It also relayed examples of successful experiences and findings developed in different base areas. This produced some interesting results. For example, the Party Central informed He Long in the early months of 1929 about the effective guerrilla methods being practiced by the Fourth Army under Mao Zedong and Zhu De. He Long responded by acclaiming the value of their contributions but also reported that the same procedures and other successful ones were already being followed in the western Hunan-Hubei Base in response to conditions there.[55] In other words, local pressures for survival compelled a practical approach, and He, Mao, and Zhu in the course of bitter rural struggle were learning and implementing strategic concepts and tactics that took into consideration the unique conditions and challenges of each base area.

What was emerging in the Chinese Communist movement was a distinct separation between those whose outlook and approach was shaped by exposure to the mainstream orthodox Marxist-Leninist tradition and those for whom the actual experience of building a viable Communist movement taught the added importance of responding to the existing Chinese realities. This separation widened into a debilitating division as Li Lisan's hold over the Party apparatus tightened. Li operated from a frame of reference heavily influenced by Comintern direction, which extolled the seminal role of the urban proletariat. Operating from this perspective, Li attempted to reverse the direction of the Communist movement to make the villages once again serve the cities.

To carry this out, Li initiated a process to centralize the power of the Party apparatus, which he headed, by establishing action committees starting in March 1930. The action committees absorbed the memberships of disbanded mass organizations, including even the Youth League, and centralized them into one organizational system presided over by the General Action Committee.[56] This policy completely reversed the previous one of providing diverse organizations matched to serve all segments of the masses. With this powerful tool under his command, Li intended to execute his bold military strategy of using the Red armies to attack and occupy key cities in the Wuhan area, with the goal of establishing an urban soviet government under genuine proletarian leadership.

Dispersing the Red armies and dispensing them against the well-armed and protected major cities ended in disaster, just as had happened in 1927. It also stepped up KMT mobilization efforts against the Communist bases. After a second attempt to seize Changsha and establish an urban soviet in September 1931, the Li Lisan line came under heavy attack and finally was formally discredited by the Party in January 1932. Li was replaced by leaders from the Russian-Returned Students, notably Chen Shaoyu, Qin Bangxian, and Zhang Wentian. The new leadership set about abolishing Li's action committees and purging the Party ranks of his supporters. But as KMT police and military pressure mounted in the wake of Li's adventurist policies, the Shanghai Party Central was forced to move in stages from the Shanghai headquarters to the Jiangxi Soviet Government Headquarters in Ruijin, a move that was completed by early 1933.

Ilpyong J. Kim has explained how in this new operational setting and with continued KMT pressure in the form of the encirclement campaigns, Party leader Qin Bangxian (Bo Gu) and other returned students found it expedient to make certain compromises with the experienced soviet government leadership under Mao Zedong. On November 27, 1931, Mao had become chairman of the Chinese Soviet Republic.[57] The source of the differences between the returned students and the experienced leaders centered on their disparate opinions regarding the contemporary revolutionary situation. The returned students followed a class-line approach characterized by its grounding in orthodox Marxism-Leninism. It emphasized the centralization of authority through the Party structure, viewed society in rigid class terms, and followed the Comintern's anti-imperialist and urban proletarian priorities. In contrast, the experienced leaders followed a mass-line approach, which stressed a decentralized approach to organizing support rooted in local economic and social issues and directed at involving the broadest measure of organized armed support. Kim explains factionalism within the Jiangxi Soviet period in terms of leaders being committed to one or the other of these approaches.[58]

The findings of this book indicate that Kim's analysis needs refinement, in that the situation was not as much an either-or situation as his work seems to imply. Rather, the mass-line approach needs to be understood as an adding-on to the contents of the class-line approach of the crucial findings developed by practicing revolutionaries in China. It also involved reordering the priorities of revolution to make them realistic under Chinese conditions. Further, this book documents that the resulting mass-line policies and organizations, which Kim has ascribed solely to Mao and the activities of the Jiangxi Soviet period, already had taken substantial form. They emerged out of the firsthand experiences of those, including Mao, who had participated in building and directing the several independent armed base areas since 1927.

The modus vivendi between the returned students and soviet government leadership produced remarkable expansion and growth during the Jiangxi Soviet period. Its curtailment came about as a result of overwhelming KMT military power, which was challenged when the Party leadership initiated a positional military strategy, recommended by the Comintern's military representative, to combat the KMT's massive 5th Encirclement campaign. The outcome is well known. It precipitated the famous Long March beginning in October 1934, in the course of which those opposed to the Party's disastrous military strategy, especially Mao, quickly gained substantial strategic and leadership credibility. Mao made immediate use of this new stature to assume military leadership and a place on the Standing Committee of the Party's Political Bureau at the Zunyi Conference meeting in Guizhou January 15–18, 1935.[59]

After reaching the Northwest and during the Yan'an Period, the proven concepts and techniques for mass mobilization once again were applied, practiced, and further refined. After nationwide power was seized in 1949, these concepts supplied the foundation and framework for the Chinese Communists' Party-governmental system.

Conclusions

Before mid-1927 the mainstream of Chinese Communist activity was located in the cities, close to Party headquarters and to Comintern guidance, funds, and channels. Increasingly this position was undermined by the KMT or KMT-allied military superiority. The importance of military pressure as an instigating factor of basic change in the policies and direction of the Chinese Communist Party cannot be overstated. Eventually, it forced the urban-based CCP out of its narrow intellectual and territorial perimeters. To survive military challenges, the Party leadership had to discover its own resources and recognize its local opportunities. The solution that emerged was a political style stressing the importance of mass organization and the mass line.

Operating in a rural setting, Party activists became the principal actors in the revolutionary movement, attempting to shape its development sometimes according to orthodoxy, sometimes in response to the best alternatives of the moment. They had to supplement heavily the organizational and ideological concepts and skills inherited from orthodox Marxism-Leninism. They confronted a populace that was illiterate and for whom concepts such as class and class interests were totally alien. It was a predicament that demanded of cadres extra resourcefulness and suggested their having to become practitioners of revolution as an art. In essence, their task was to work out a synthesis between the pervasive rural folk culture and their Marxist-Leninist revolutionary program. In retrospect, this can be seen as the only possible way for them to involve, motivate, and mobilize a Communist-led following under the rural conditions in China.

Communists' success, and ultimately their survival, depended on Party cadres becoming intimately familiar with the full scope of local conditions. They gained competence through experience, study, and observation. Peng Pai, Fang Zhimin, Peng Dehuai, Mao Zedong, and others used familiar local cultural forms (plays, poems, songs, and rituals) as media for introducing the new ideas contained in the Communists' rural mass political program. With frequent exposure, peasant participants gained a better understanding of the political and social dynamics of their local situation. Their previously vague and diffused aspirations for change began to coalesce into the generalized principles, terms, and slogans of the Party's mass program. And introduced through these indigenous channels, the otherwise foreign concepts inherent in the Party's mass program acquired a quality of authenticity for the local population. They were incorporated into a common outlook. Thus by a process of adaptation and integration, Peng and others fashioned a new and rational frame of reference that was transferable and became the basis for linking peasant organizations across rural borders.

The Party's articulation of local issues required the addition of a disciplined organization. The aroused mass following had to be consolidated into a group in order that the initial, always economic, motivations could continue to be elevated and sustained at the political level. Through the organization, Party cadres could further clarify their program and educate the mass membership in political affairs. The mass organization was also essential to keep a growing movement from boiling out of control and being destroyed by superior military force.

Military pressure forced the scope of organizational activity to include every segment of the population in horizontally defined mass organizations, as was demonstrated in Fang Zhimin's seminal work. These mass bodies, linked, guided, and politicized by the centralized Party structure, made up the mobilized support of the Chinese Communist movement. But again, to survive, Party cadres had to experiment and find an effective response to local conditions. Experience proved the efficacy of establishing armed base areas in relatively secure mountainous regions, from which Communist forces could advance or retreat according to the relative strength of Communist and enemy forces. Following guerrilla practices used by Chinese bandit heroes for centuries, Mao Zedong, Zhu De, He Long, and Fang Zhimin all contributed to developing strategies and tactics to successfully confront superior armed forces.

Through their practice of revolution as an art, the able and resourceful Chinese Communist Party leaders thus initiated a process of integrating the principles and concepts of Marxism-Leninism with indigenous Chinese traditions, cultural patterns, and geographical conditions. Demanded of them was a creative and flexible responsiveness to the obstacles and the potentialities afforded by local rural conditions. The result of their efforts was the mass-line system of comprehensive mobilized and armed support, located in base areas in the countryside. Of course, in the process of integrating traditional cultural elements, some ideas that clearly were feudal in Marxist-Leninist terms became part of the new political culture in the countryside. The residual influence of these ideas was said to create a lag in revolutionary development, and over time Party cadres had to expunge them by means of Party-directed education and propaganda campaigns. Thus the revolutionary process aimed at rural transformation became an ongoing and prolonged experience. It required repeated Party campaigns carried out within the mass organizations, and even the Party itself, to raise the level of political consciousness and keep it at least in tune with the Party's own internal Marxist-Leninist political program, decided at the highest Party levels.

In Jiangxi and later in the Northwest, this mass-line system became refined, expanded, and codified, and represented a permanent addition to the concepts and organizational forms introduced with orthodox Marxism-Leninism. It provided the basis for a politically unified and culturally integrated nation when the Communists came to power in 1949.

When military pressures ended in 1949, the demands on the Chinese leaders for practicing the art of revolution became secondary to requirements for practicing what might be described as the art of government. The task of leadership became managing the tensions inherent in a system bifurcated in nature, or having two fundamental spheres. The highly centralized features of the Party system existed alongside the horizontally defined and comprehensive mass organizations. Together they seemed to offer significant creative potential for interaction and growth. The inclusiveness of the umbrella mass-organizations-people's-congresses theoretically meant that all members of society had quasi-governmental bodies to identify and represent common issues or needs. The system also allowed for these findings to be transmitted through the existing connections to the vertically defined Party structure, for passage ultimately to the highest Party decisionmaking levels.

While the system had the potential structurally for keeping policies in tune with real conditions and mass aspirations, the burden fell on the Party leaders themselves to keep the centralizing and consultative aspects in a stable and creative relationship. A listing of policy in one direction, upsetting the equilibrium, might produce a rigid stagnation into formalistic approaches seriously divorced and unresponsive to real conditions. The reverse imbalance toward mass pressure could result in a situation like that underlying the Cultural Revolution era, in which the consultative forces, once mobilized directly, were able to overwhelm the Party's decisionmaking and disciplinary authority, producing chaos. To redress the balance, the other centralized, armed authority—the military—had to be brought in. Maintaining this balance is still a key challenge to China's leadership, although China again seems to be in the thick of experimentation and momentous change. In any case, as this book shows, the definition of the Chinese Communist system as bipolar began in 1927 and 1928.

Finally, these early years also revealed that change in China became a product of influences from both the centralized Party and the mass organizations of the bifurcated Communist system, so that the process of change occurred in an irregular or evolutionary rather than constantly progressive manner. One sphere had to interact constantly with the other in order to sustain a process of development. As shown in this book, such was the conception of revolutionary change arrived at by Party leaders in the course of their revolutionary activities as early as 1928.

Notes

Chapter 1

1. Maurice Meisner, in his intellectual biography of Li Dazhao, one of the earliest and most influential Chinese Marxists, explains how Li's voluntaristic interpretation of Marxism led him to conceive of precapitalist China as a proletarian nation formed from the intrusion of outside forces. See Meisner, *Li Ta-chao and the Origins of Chinese Marxism* (Cambridge, Mass.: Harvard University Press, 1967), 144–45.
2. Arif Dirlik, *Revolution and History: Origins of Marxist Historiography in China, 1919–1937* (Berkeley: University of California Press, 1978), 263.
3. Hélène Carrère d'Encausse and Stuart R. Schram, *Marxism and Asia: An Introduction with Readings* (London: Allen Lane, The Penguin Press, 1969), 24.
4. Vladimir Ilyich Lenin, "Theses on the National and Colonial Questions," in Jane Degras, *The Communist International: 1919–1943, Documents* (London: Frank Cass, 1960), 1:139–44.
5. Lee Feigon, *Chen Duxiu: Founder of the Chinese Communist Party* (Princeton: Princeton University Press, 1983), 60.
6. Ibid., 180–81. Feigon explains that because Chen was unsure of himself concerning Marxist doctrine, he was deferential to his Soviet advisers on these matters. See also Dirlik, *Revolution and History*, 44.
7. Dirlik, *Revolution and History*, 264.
8. Harold R. Isaacs, *The Tragedy of the Chinese Revolution* (Stanford: Stanford University Press, 1961), 133, 137, 140–41.
9. Elizabeth J. Perry, *Rebels and Revolutionaries in North China, 1845–1945* (Stanford: Stanford University Press, 1980), 257.
10. Ibid., 255.
11. Ibid., 115. For discussion of traditional rebels' use of guerrilla warfare tactics, see Teng Ssu-yu, *The Nien Army and Their Guerrilla Warfare, 1851–1868* (Paris, 1961).
12. Robert Marks, *Rural Revolution in South China: Peasants and the Making of History in Haifeng County, 1570–1930* (Madison: University of Wisconsin Press, 1984), xx–xxi.
13. Ibid., 228–29.
14. Ibid., 215, 218. Fernando Galbiati relates that the Peasant Department was decided upon only in 1925. It actually started operation in November 1926 under Mao Zedong's

direction. See Fernando Galbiati, *P'eng P'ai and the Hai-lu-feng Soviet* (Stanford: Stanford University Press, 1985), 406 n. 35.

15. This was later defined as a coalition of four classes—bourgeoisie, petite bourgeoisie, peasantry, and proletariat.

16. Bukharin's key role in policy development is well documented in Stephen F. Cohen, *Bukharin and the Bolshevik Revolution: A Political Biography, 1888–1938* (New York: Alfred A. Knopf, 1973).

17. Allen S. Whiting, *Soviet Policies in China, 1917–1924* (Stanford: Stanford University Press, 1968), 251–52.

18. For a summary of Dai Jitao's views, see C. Martin Wilbur and Julie Lien-ying How, eds., *Documents on Communism, Nationalism, and Soviet Advisers in China, 1918–1927* (New York: Columbia University Press, 1956; reprint ed., New York: Octagon Books, 1972), 206–7.

19. Isaacs, *Tragedy*, 175–85; for the Soviet response, see Xenia J. Eudin and Robert C. North, *Soviet Russia and the East, 1920–1927: A Documentary Survey* (Stanford: Stanford University Press, 1957), 364–65.

20. In May 1927 peasant association members in Hunan numbered 4,517,140; in Hubei, 2,502,000. Roy M. Hofheinz, Jr., *The Broken Wave: The Chinese Communist Peasant Movement, 1922–1928* (Cambridge, Mass.: Harvard University Press, 1977), 104.

21. For an account of events in Changsha (Horse Day Incident of May 21, 1927), see Li Jiu, *The Early Revolutionary Activities of Comrade Mao Tse-tung* (White Plains, N.Y.: M. E. Sharpe, 1977), 313–17; see also Wang Chien-min, *Zhongguo gongchandang shigao* (Draft history of the Chinese Communist Party) (Taipei, 1965), 1:444–49; Isaacs, *Tragedy*, 234–36; and Hofheinz, *The Broken Wave*, 46.

22. For a summary discussion of Trotsky's "permanent revolution," see Baruch Knei-paz, *The Social and Political Thought of Leon Trotsky* (Oxford: Oxford University Press, 1978), 144–52.

23. Les Evans and Russell Block, eds., *Leon Trotsky on China: Introduction by P'eng Shu-tse* (New York: Monad Press, 1976), 170.

24. This position is explained in a key theoretical document, denied publication by the CPSU Politburo, entitled "The Chinese Revolution and the Theses of Comrade Stalin" (May 7, 1927), which was Trotsky's rebuttal to Stalin's "Questions of the Chinese Revolution," published in *Pravda*, April 21, 1927. See Evans and Block, *Trotsky*, especially pp. 180–84. Trotsky developed the theory of permanent revolution based on his observations of the processes underlying the Bolshevik Revolution. See Knei-paz, *The Social and Political Thought of Leon Trotsky*, chaps. 3–4; and Germaine A. Hoston, "State and Revolution in China and Japan: Marxist Perspectives on Nationalism and Revolution in Asia" (Ph.D. dissertation, Harvard University, 1981).

25. This plenum devoted five sessions to China between May 18 and 20, 1927. See "Extracts from the Resolution of the Eighth ECCI Plenum on the Chinese Question," in Degras, *The Communist International*, 2:382–90, 365–67; Eudin and North, *Soviet Russia and the East*, 370, 373, 374.

26. Trotsky at the plenum claimed that "the Hankow government will have to adapt itself to the soviets in some way or other or else—disappear." In his second speech to the plenum, Trotsky took his argument even further. Addressing himself to the

Chinese peasantry, he warned that the Left KMT, under Wang's leadership, would inevitably betray them. Further, he emphasized that the *"Chinese bourgeois-democratic revolution will go forward and be victorious either in the soviet form or not at all."* See Evans and Block, *Trotsky*, 232, 235.

27. For opposing arguments by Borodin and Roy, see Robert C. North and Xenia J. Eudin, *M. N. Roy's Mission to China: The Communist Kuomintang Split of 1927* (Berkeley: University of California Press, 1963), 105.

28. Ibid., 106–7.

29. See "Why Have We Not Called for Withdrawal from the Kuomintang Until Now?" in Evans and Block, *Trotsky*, 249–50. Trotsky had temporized on demanding a complete break with the KMT because of resistance to this stance from within the Trotsky Opposition.

30. "Is It Not Time to Understand?," in Evans and Block, *Trotsky*, 245.

31. Degras, *The Communist International*, 2:394.

32. See "Extracts from an ECCI Resolution on the Present Stage of the Chinese Revolution" (July 14, 1927), in Degras, *The Communist International*, 2:395–96.

Chapter 2

1. When the CCP came to power in 1949 the two Chinese characters for August 1, *bayi* and a five-pointed star, both on a red field, were designated to make up the official Red Army flag. Feng Jianhui and Sun Xiangzhu, "From here on, wind and thunder spread to all parts of the world—in commemoration of the 50th anniversary of the Nanchang Uprising" (Congci fengleibian jiugai—jinian Nanchang qiyi wushizhounian), reprinted from *Lishi yanjiu* (Historical research), no. 4 (1977), in Zhu Chengjia, ed., *Zhonggong dangshi yanjiu lunwenxuan* (Changsha: Hunan renmin chubanshe, 1983), 2:15.

2. Nie Rongzhen, "The Nanchang Uprising: Memoirs," *Renmin Ribao* (Beijing) (July 27, 1983), 5. This is abridged from a chapter of "Nie Rongzhen's Memoirs," originally carried in *Zhonggeng* (CRISSCROSS), no. 1, translated in JPRS *China Report*, no. 451 (August 25, 1983), 75–85.

3. For detailed discussion of the political and military conditions in Jiangxi at this time, see Stephen C. Averill, "Revolution in the Highlands: The Rise of the Communist Movement in Jiangxi Province" (Ph.D. dissertation, Cornell University, 1982), 137–50.

4. Chang Kuo-t'ao, *The Rise of the Chinese Communist Party, 1921–1927: An Autobiography of Chang Kuo-t'ao* (Lawrence: The University Press of Kansas), 1:662.

5. A table showing the military commands and key posts held by Communists in the Second Front Army is found in Wu T'ien-wei, "Review of the Wuhan Debacle: The Kuomintang-Communist Split of 1927," *Journal of Asian Studies* (November 1969), 139. See also Jacques Guillermaz, "The Nanchang Uprising," *The China Quarterly*, no. 11 (July–September 1962) 165–66; Wang Chien-min, *Draft History of the Chinese Communist Party* (Taipei, 1965), 1:534–35.

6. Because of the nature of the KMT/CCP relationship, the Communists could not develop or command any independent troops, but during the course of the Northern

Expedition, Communists did rise to high positions in the National Revolutionary Army.

7. Feng and Sun, "Nanchang Uprising," 2:2; Guillermaz, "The Nanchang Uprising," 163.
8. Ch'ü Ch'iu-pai (Qu Qiubai), "The Past and Future of the Chinese Communist Party," *Chinese Studies in History*, no. 1 (Fall 1971), 42.
9. C. Martin Wilbur, "The Ashes of Defeat," *The China Quarterly*, no. 18 (April–June 1964), 9–10. This article contains translations from *Zhongyang tongxin* (Central newsletter), an official Party publication, of four accounts from three participants, Li Lisan, Zhang Guotao, and Zhou Yiqun, in the Nanchang Uprising.
10. "He Long," in Hu Hua, ed., *Zhonggong dangshi renwu zhuan* (Chinese Communist Party biographies) (Xi'an: Shaanxi renmin chubanshe, 1982), 2:140.
11. Ren Wuxiang et al., "Yun Daiying," in Hu Hua, *Zhonggong dangshi renwu zhuan*, 5:35–36.
12. Nie Rongzhen, "Memoirs," 76–77. Borodin, romanized, became Bao Luoding.
13. Branko Lazitch and Milorad M. Drachkovitch, *Biographical Dictionary of the Comintern* (Stanford: Hoover Institution Press, 1973), 234–35.
14. Chang Kuo-t'ao, *Autobiography*, 1:671.
15. Ibid., 1:672; Wilbur, "Ashes," 45 (Zhang Guotao's account).
16. Chang Kuo-t'ao, *Autobiography*, 1:673; Wilbur, "Ashes," 46 (Zhang Guotao's account).
17. Conrad Brandt, *Stalin's Failure in China, 1924–1927* (Cambridge, Mass.: Harvard University Press, 1958), 142–43.
18. Chang Kuo-t'ao, *Autobiography*, 1:671–73; Wilbur, "Ashes," 46 (Zhang Guotao's account).
19. Chang Kuo-t'ao, *Autobiography*, 2:4–5.
20. Wilbur, "Ashes," 11 (Li Lisan's account); Nieh Jung-chen (Nie Rongzhen), "The Nanchang Uprising: Its Historical Significance," *China Reconstructs*, no. 8 (August 1977), 21; Hsiao Tso-liang, *Chinese Communism in 1927: City vs. Countryside* (Hong Kong: Chinese University of Hong Kong, 1970), 86.
21. Feng and Sun, "Nanchang Uprising," 2:9.
22. Chang Kuo-t'ao, *Autobiography*, 2:5–8.
23. Wilbur, "Ashes," 25 (Zhou Yiqun's account); Feng and Sun, "Nanchang Uprising," 2:9.
24. Chang Kuo-t'ao, *Autobiography*, 2:6.
25. Ren, "Yun Daiying," 5:36.
26. Zhu De, "From the Nanchang Uprising to Going Up the Jinggang Mountain" (conversation with Zhu De in July 1962), *Xinhua* (July 31, 1982), translated in FBIS *Daily Report* (August 3, 1982), K1–6.
27. Nieh Jung-chen, "The Nanchang Uprising," 21.
28. Wilbur, "Ashes," 25 (Zhou Yiqun's account); "He Long," in Hu Hua, *Zhonggong dangshi renwu zhuan*, 2:143; Nie Rongzhen, *Memoirs*, 79.
29. Guillermaz, "The Nanchang Uprising," 164; Gong Chu, *Wo yu hongjun* (I and the Red Army) (Hong Kong, 1954), 55–56.
30. Chang Kuo-t'ao, *Autobiography*, 2:12.
31. Guillermaz, "The Nanchang Uprising," 165; Chang Kuo-t'ao, *Autobiography*, 2:12.
32. Wilbur, "Ashes," 15 (Li Lisan's account).
33. Guillermaz, "The Nanchang Uprising," 165.

34. Feng and Sun, "Nanchang Uprising," 2:2–3.
35. Ibid., 2:2; Wilbur, "Ashes," 40; Warren Kuo, *Analytical History of the Chinese Communist Party* (Taipei: Institute of International Relations, 1966), 1:429; "He Long," 2:144; Nie Rongzhen, *Memoirs*, 79.
36. Averill, "Revolution in the Highlands," 149–50.
37. Wilbur, "Ashes," 12 (Li Lisan's account).
38. Li Lisan reported Communist casualties totaling 1,400 in these campaigns; ibid., 13. See also Zhou Yiqun's account, ibid., 28–29, and Zhang Guotao's account, ibid., 33.
39. Chang Kuo-t'ao, *Autobiography*, 2:15; Wilbur, "Ashes," 33 (Zhang Guotao's account).
40. Wilbur, "Ashes," 33 (Zhang Guotao's account).
41. Ibid., 16 (Li Lisan's account); Feng and Sun, "Nanchang Uprising," 2:16.
42. Wilbur, "Ashes," 16–17 (Li Lisan's account).
43. Ibid., 17. The Guangdong program actually set land expropriation limits at 35–50 *mu*. Ibid., 50–51 (Zhang Guotao's account).
44. Ibid., 19 (Li Lisan's account).
45. Ibid., 21.
46. Ibid., 22; "Party Central's Announcement (Number 13): On the Matter of the Defeat of Yeh and Ho," 41.
47. Zhang Tailei had attended the August 7 (1927) conference and had been appointed secretary of the Guangdong CCP Committee and head of the Party's South China Bureau. Zhang left Shantou to assume these new posts in early October. Chang Kuo-t'ao, *Autobiography*, 2:28–31; Donald W. Klein and Anne B. Clark, *Biographic Dictionary of Chinese Communism, 1921–1965* (Cambridge, Mass.: Harvard University Press, 1971), 1:51.
48. Party Central refers to leaders in charge of Party decisionmaking and overseeing policy implementation. It can be considered interchangeable with the term Politburo. The years 1927 and 1928 are confusing, because the Politburo elected at the CCP Fifth Congress soon was replaced by an "interim" Politburo following Chen Duxiu's July resignation. This body was then replaced by the Provisional Politburo selected at the August 7 (1927) Emergency Conference. The Provisional Politburo served with some changes in personnel until a fully constituted Politburo was produced by the CCP Sixth Congress in the summer of 1928.
49. Chang Kuo-t'ao, *Autobiography*, 2:28.
50. Tan's errors, going back to his term as minister of agriculture in the Nationalist Government from the spring of 1927 through the Nanchang Revolt, are reported in portions of the "Resolution on Political Discipline," developed at the CCP Enlarged Plenum, November 9–10, in Shanghai, in Wilbur, "Ashes," 53–54. Zhang Guotao's errors are also dealt with in this document.
51. Chang Kuo-t'ao, *Autobiography*, 2:30.
52. Wilbur, "Ashes," 29–30 (Zhou Yiqun's Report). Zhang Guotao recalls the Tangkeng battle defeat as occurring on October 3 in Chang Kuo-t'ao, *Autobiography*, 2:30.
53. Nie Rongzhen, *Memoirs*, 83.
54. Ibid., 84; Feng and Sun, "Nanchang Uprising," 2:3.
55. Kuo, *Analytical History*, 1:467–73.

56. A comprehensive review of the Nanchang Uprising and the Southern Expedition are found in the CCP Notice no. 13, "On the Failure of Yeh Ting and Ho Lung," October 24, 1927, in Kuo, *Analytical History*, 1:425–37.

57. C. Martin Wilbur demonstrated that of the CCP leadership (by April 1927), most were young (under thirty-five), from central China (provinces bordering the Chang Jiang) and educated (47 percent studied abroad). See Wilbur, "The Influence of the Past: How the Early Years Helped to Shape the Future of the Chinese Communist Party," *The China Quarterly*, no. 36 (October–November 1968), 29–30.

58. See "Central's Letter of Reply (to Zhang Guotao)" in Wilbur, "Ashes," 52–53.

59. Brandt, *Stalin's Failure in China*, 145.

60. Feng and Sun, "Nanchang Uprising," 2:3; Wilbur, "Ashes," 31 (Zhou Yiqun's account).

Chapter 3

1. Pi Mingxiu, "Guanyu 'Baqi' huiyide jigewenti" (Several questions concerning the August 7 Meeting), reprinted from *Jindaishi yanjiu*, no. 4 (1980), in Zhu Chengjia, ed., *Zhonggong dangshi yanjiu lunwenxuan* (Changsha: Hunan renmin chubanshe, 1983), 2:24.

2. "Resolution of the ECCI on the Present Situation of the Chinese Revolution," *International Press Correspondence* (July 28, 1927), 984; Jane Degras, *Communist International, 1919–1943: Documents* (London: Frank Cass, 1956–1971), 2:395.

3. James P. Harrison, *The Long March to Power* (New York: Praeger Publishers, 1972), 123–24.

4. Pi, "August 7," 2:26.

5. Ibid., 30. This source relies on Li Weihan's recollections of the meeting participants and the document "Yijiu erqinian bayue qiri zhongyang jinjihuiyi xiaoyin" (foreword to the August 7 Emergency Conference) issued by the Provisional Politburo on August 21, 1927. Both of these sources report Deng Xiaoping in attendance. While Communist historians sometimes yield to political considerations to provide a current Chinese leader with a role in a key historical event, it is known that Deng had been expelled from Feng Yuxiang's forces in mid-1927 and went to work for the Party Central. Thus he might well have done organizational and preparatory work for this conference. See Donald W. Klein and Anne B. Clark, *Biographic Dictionary of Chinese Communism, 1921–1965* (Cambridge, Mass.: Harvard University Press, 1971), 2:820.

6. *Zhongyang tongxin* (Central newsletter), no. 2 (August 23, 1927), 8.

7. Harrison, *The Long March to Power*. For an accounting of other membership listings, see ibid., 547, fn. 17. Pi Mingxiu lists Provisional Politburo members as Su Zhaozheng, Xiang Zhongfa, Qu Qiubai, Luo Yinong, Gu Shunzhang, Wang Hebo, Li Weihan, Peng Pai, and Ren Bishi; alternate members were Deng Zhongxia, Zhou Enlai, Mao Zedong, Peng Gongda, Zhang Tailei, Zhang Guotao (or Luo Zhanglong) and Li Lisan. Pi, "August 7," 2:33. Another recent source, Liao Gailong, in *Renmin Ribao* (December 3, 1981), 5, lists "Su Zhaozheng, Qu Qiubai, Luo Yinong, Peng Pai, and others as members, and Mao Zedong, Zhou Enlai, and Deng Zhongxia as alternate members."

8. Li Weihan, "A Retrospective Study of Qu Qiubai's 'Left' Adventurism," *Social Sci-*

ences in China, no. 3 (September 1983), 21–27. For the Chinese language original, see *Zhongguo shehui kexue*, no. 3 (May 1983), 47–51.

9. *Zhou Yongxiang, ed., Qu Qiubai nianpu (1899–1935)* (Chronical of Qu Qiubai's life) (Guangdong: Guangdong renmin chubanshe, 1983), 18–69. See also Bernadette Yu-ning Li, "A Biography of Ch'ü Ch'iu-pai: From Youth to Party Leadership (1899–1928)" (Ph.D. dissertation, Columbia University, 1967); Donald W. Klein and Anne B. Clark, *Biographic Dictionary of Chinese Communism, 1921–1965* (Cambridge, Mass.: Harvard University Press, 1971), 240–42.

10. *Xinhua* (Beijing), May 11, 1983, in FBIS *Daily Report* (May 13, 1983), K5.

11. Pi, "August 7," 2:32.

12. Xenia J. Eudin and Robert C. North, *Soviet Russia and the East, 1920–1927: A Documentary Survey* (Stanford: Stanford University Press, 1957), 359.

13. Ibid., 369.

14. Robert C. North, *Moscow and Chinese Communists* (Stanford: Stanford University Press, 1953), 109.

15. Eudin and North, *Soviet Russia and the East*, 383; *International Press Correspondence*, no. 48 (August 18, 1927), 1076.

16. Li Weihan's recollection was that after the discussion and the decision to pass this "Circular Letter," a group consisting of Qu Qiubai, Li Weihan, and Su Zhaocheng was appointed to revise its language. Pi, "August 7," 2:32.

17. Extensive extracts from this document are contained in Conrad Brandt, Benjamin Schwartz, and John K. Fairbank, eds., *A Documentary History of Chinese Communism* (Cambridge, Mass.: Harvard University Press, 1952), 102–18; see also Wang Chien-min, *Draft History of the Chinese Communist Party*, (Taipei, 1965), 1:504–23.

18. Pi, "August 7," 2:37.

19. Brandt, *Documentary History*, 112–13; Wang, *Draft History*, 1:513–14.

20. Pi, "August 7," 2:36–37.

21. Brandt, *Documentary History*, 114; Wang, *Draft History*, 1:514.

22. Trotsky as quoted in Degras, *Communist International*, 2:392.

23. Zhou Enlai, *Selected Works of Zhou Enlai* (Beijing: Foreign Languages Press, 1981), 1:193.

24. Brandt, *Documentary History*, 116; Wang, *Draft History*, 1:522.

25. Pi, "August 7," 2:32–33.

26. Described as "Excerpts from CCPCC's mimeographed secret material Circular no. 2, August 23, 1927," this document is contained in Warren Kuo, *Analytical History of the Chinese Communist Party* (Taipei: Institute of International Relations, 1966), 1:437–51. For an abridged version from *Zhongyang tongxin*, no. 2, August 23, 1927, see Wang Chien-min, *Draft History*, 1:524–25.

27. Kuo, *Analytical History*, 1:438. At the beginning of this document, the authors identify "all bourgeoisie" as targets for the workers and peasants, while further on it becomes clear that the petite bourgeoisie are potential allies of the Communists, who intend to win them away from the "counterrevolutionary KMT right faction."

28. Ibid., 1:441. Lominadze was rebuked for using this interpretation at the ECCI Ninth Plenum in February 1928.

29. Pi, "August 7," 2:34–35.

30. Han Taihua, "Guanyu dageming shibaihou wo dang fangqi Goumindang qizhi wenti" (Concerning the question of our Party's abandoning the KMT banner after the failure of the Great Revolution), in Zhu Chengjia, ed., *Zhonggong dangshi yanjiu lunwenxuan* (Changsha: Hunan renmin chubanshe, 1983), 2:54–55.

31. Kuo, *Analytical History*, 1:447.

32. Ibid., 1:448–49.

33. Ibid., 1:444.

34. These resolutions on Party organization, published in *Zhongyang tongxin*, no. 2 (August 23, 1927), are found in Kuo, *Analytical History*, 1:451–55.

35. Brandt, *Documentary History*, 122; Wang Chien-min, *Draft History*, 526–28; Pi, "August 7," 2:40.

36. Brandt, *Documentary History*, 122; Pi, "August 7," 2:39–40.

37. Brandt, *Documentary History*, 122.

38. Pi, "August 7," 2:35.

39. Brandt, *Documentary History*, 123.

40. Pi, "August 7," 2:35.

41. Zhou Enlai, *Selected Works*, 1:196.

Chapter 4

1. For a discussion of the evolution of various uprising plans, see Roy M. Hofheinz, Jr., "The Autumn Harvest Insurrection," *The China Quarterly*, no. 32 (October–December 1967), 40–45.

2. Conrad Brandt, Benjamin Schwartz, and John K. Fairbank, eds., "Resolutions of the August 7 Emergency Conference," *A Documentary History of Chinese Communism* (Cambridge, Mass.: Harvard University Press, 1952), 122.

3. Warren Kuo, "Resolution on the Political Task and Policy of the CCP," *Analytical History of the Chinese Communist Party* (Taipei: Institute of International Relations, 1966), 1:444.

4. Hsiao Tso-liang, *Chinese Communism in 1927: City vs. Countryside* (Hong Kong: Chinese University of Hong Kong, 1970), 45.

5. Kuo, *Analytical History*, 1:444.

6. *This letter is quoted and discussed at length by Stuart R. Schram, "On the Nature of Mao Tse-tung's Deviation in 1927," The China Quarterly, no. 18 (April–June 1964), 55–59. A translation of this letter from Zhongyang tongxin, no. 3 (August 30, 1927) is found in Hyobom Pak, ed. and trans., Documents of the Chinese Communist Party, 1927–1930 (Hong Kong: Union Research Institute, 1971), 87–89. Parts of the letter are quoted and ascribed to Mao in Han Taihua, "Guanyu dageming shibaihou wo dang fangqi Goumindang qizhi wenti" (Concerning the question of our Party's abandoning the KMT banner after the failure of the Great Revolution), in Zhu Chengjia, ed., Zhonggong dangshi yanjiu lunwenxuan (Changsha: Hunan renmin chubanshe, 1983), 2:55.*

7. Pak, *Documents*, 88.

8. Ibid., 87.

9. Ibid., 88; Han Taihua, "Abandoning the KMT banner," 2:55.

10. Pak, *Documents*, 94. The Party Central's reply to Mao's letter is found on pp. 91–95.
11. Ibid., 91.
12. This August 30 letter is translated in Pak, *Documents*, 97–98.
13. Ibid., 97.
14. Liu Yitao, "Mao Zedong tongzhi yu Xiang-Gan bian qiushou qiyi" (Mao Zedong and the Autumn Harvest Uprisings on the Hunan-Jiangxi Border) in Zhu Chengjia, *Zhonggong danshi yanjiu lunwenxuan*, 2:60.
15. This September 5 reply is translated in Pak, *Documents*, 99–101.
16. This plan is translated in ibid., 60–66; the Chinese text from *Zhongyang tongxin*, no. 4 (September 12, 1927), with omissions concerning very specific details on operational planning, is found in Wang Chien-min, *Draft History of the Chinese Communist Party* (Taipei, 1965), 1:553–55; for an abridged translation, see Kuo, *Analytical History*, 1:455–59.
17. Pak, *Documents*, 60; Wang, *Draft History*, 1:553.
18. Pak, *Documents*, 65; Wang, *Draft History*, 1:554.
19. Pak, *Documents*, 61; Wang, *Draft History*, 1:553.
20. Pak, *Documents*, 66; Wang, *Draft History*, 1:555.
21. Pak, *Documents*, 61.
22. Ibid., 63.
23. Ibid.
24. Ibid.
25. A special committee was an ad hoc body established to facilitate supervision and communication between a particularly sensitive area and the higher authorities. For a discussion of the nature and function of the special committees, see *Zhejiang Collection*, Shanghai Municipal Police Document no. 4772, Shanghai Municipal Police Files, 1:10–11.
26. Hofheinz, "Autumn Harvest," 49–50.
27. Ibid., 56.
28. For documentation on the damage done to Hunan Party organizations and memberships during and after the May 21 Horse Day Incident, see Pak, *Documents*, 31–35. Reportedly, Party ties to Changsha mass organizations were practically nonexistent (pp. 34–35).
29. Hsiao Tso-liang, *Chinese Communism*, 68–69; Hofheinz, "Autumn Harvest," 67–70. Miners in the Anyuan-Pingxiang region had long been the target of Party organizers and propagandists. In 1921 Mao himself reportedly organized a workers' club among the Anyuan miners. When the mines were closed in 1925, the unemployed workers became recruitment targets for Communist military commanders, including Ye Ting, who employed them in the Nanchang Uprising. Because of this lengthy exposure to Party discipline, instruction, and propaganda, the miners' unit performed the best of the four regiments in the Autumn Harvest action.
30. Hofheinz, "Autumn Harvest," 70–71.
31. Liu Yitao, "Mao Zedong and the Hunan-Jiangxi Autumn Harvest Uprising," 2:61.
32. For Mao's account of this incident, see Edgar Snow, *Red Star Over China* (New York: Random House, 1938), 150. See also Jerome Ch'en, *Mao and the Chinese Revolution* (London: Oxford University Press, 1965), 132; Lo Jungshan, "Early Days of the Chi-

nese Red Army," *Peking Review* 5, no. 31 (August 3, 1962), 10; Hofheinz, "Autumn Harvest," 75.

33. Liu Yitao, "Mao Zedong and the Hunan-Jiangxi Autumn Harvest Uprising," 2:61. Ye Ting made a similar observation earlier during his troops' retreat after the failed Nanchang Uprising. He said his forces needed a "stopping off place" (*zhanjiaode difang*) that was safe from warlord or imperialist attack. Feng Jianhui and Sun Xiangzhu, "From Here on, Wind and Thunder Spread to All Parts of the World—in Commemoration of the 50th Anniversary of the Nanchang Uprising," reprinted from *Lishi yanjiu*, no. 4 (1977), in Zhu Chengjia, *Zhonggong dangshi yanjiu lunwenxuan*, 17.

34. Liu Yitao, "Mao Zedong and the Hunan-Jiangxi Autumn Harvest Uprising," 61.

35. Xenia J. Eudin and Robert C. North, "Resolution of the Joint Plenum on Bukharin's Report," *Soviet Russia and the East, 1920–1927: A Documentary Survey* (Stanford: Stanford University Press, 1957), 383.

36. Robert C. North, *Moscow and the Chinese Communists* (Stanford: Stanford University Press, 1953), 115.

37. "Resolution on the Questions of the 'Left KMT' and the Soviet Slogan," is translated in Pak, *Documents*, 129–31.

38. Pak, *Documents*, 103–8; Hofheinz, "Autumn Harvest," 76–79.

39. Pak, *Documents*, 109. Both letters appear on pp. 109–11.

40. Ibid., 113.

41. Hsiao Tso-liang, *Chinese Communism*, 74.

42. This key resolution is contained in Kuo, *Analytical History*, 467–73. Both Li Weihan and Zhou Enlai claim this resolution was "proposed" by Lominadze. See Li Weihan, "A Retrospective Study of Qu Qiubai's 'Left' Adventurism," *Social Sciences in China*, no. 3 (September 1983), 47; Zhou Enlai, *Selected Works of Zhou Enlai* (Beijing: Foreign Languages Press, 1981), 1:194.

43. Kuo, *Analytical History*, 1:470–71.

44. Ibid., 473. Also, Peng, Mao, Yi Lirong, and Xia Minghan lost their status as Hunan CCP Provincial Committee members. See Li Weihan, "A Retrospective Study," 50.

45. Ch'ü Ch'iu-pai, "The Past and Future of the Chinese Communist Party," *Chinese Studies in History* 5, no. 1 (Fall 1971), 51.

46. For complaints from Hunan and Hubei, see Pak, *Documents*, 34, 215.

47. Ibid., 212.

48. Hsiao Tso-liang, *Chinese Communism*, 48.

49. Li T'ien-min, *Chou En-lai* (Taipei: Institute of International Relations, 1970), 115.

50. Pak, *Documents*, 204.

51. These hopes are reflected in the "Report on the Current Political Situation," published in *Zhonggong tongxin*, no. 7 (October 30, 1927), quoted in Pak, *Documents*, 143.

Chapter 5

1. This list is provided by Li Weihan, then Organization Bureau Head, in Li Weihan, "A Retrospective Study of Qu Qiubai's 'Left' Adventurism," *Social Sciences in China*, no. 3 (September 1983), 33–34.

2. Ibid., 33; Chang Kuo-t'ao, *The Rise of the Chinese Communist Party, 1921–1927: An*

Autobiography of Chang Kuo-t'ao, vol. 2 (Lawrence: The University Press of Kansas, 1971), 43, 46.

3. Li Weihan, "A Retrospective Study," 47. Li provides a listing of the leadership and membership of the "Labor Movement Committee" headed by Su Zhaozheng and the editorial board of *Bolshevik*. The latter had twenty-six members, including Mao Zedong.

4. Trotsky, "New Opportunities for the Chinese Revolution, New Tasks, and New Mistakes" (September 1927), in Les Evans and Russell Block, eds., *Leon Trotsky on China* (New York: Monad Press, 1976), 268.

5. Ibid., 269. Here Trotsky first suggests that the dictatorship of the proletariat and peasantry and call for establishing soviets would have been appropriate back at the start of the Northern Expedition. But in the fall of 1927 he claimed that such a call was dangerous as a "historically overdue slogan." See pp. 265–66.

6. "Zhongguo xianzhuang yu gongchandangde renwu jueyian" (Resolution on the present situation and tasks of the Communist Party) is found in a special issue, devoted to the November plenum, of the Party organ *Bu-er-se-wei-ke* (Bolshevik) (Shanghai), no. 6 (November 28, 1927), 140–153; see also Li Weihan, "A Retrospective Study," 34.

7. "Resolution on the Present Situation and Tasks of the Communist Party," 144.

8. Qu Qiubai, "What Kind of Revolution is the Chinese Revolution?" *Bu-er-se-wei-ke*, no. 5 (November 21, 1927), 130.

9. "Resolution on the Present Situation and Tasks of the Communist Party," 144.

10. Ibid., 145. Although the Chinese have ascribed permanent revolution to Marx, it was, of course, Trotsky's concept, based on his observations of the Russian experience.

11. Ibid.

12. Qu Qiubai, "What Kind of Revolution," 131.

13. "Tudi wenti jueyian caoyi" (Draft resolution on the land question) *Bu-er-se-wei-ke*, no. 6 (November 28, 1927), 165. A lengthy introduction to this resolution (pp. 154–65) analyzes conditions in the Chinese countryside, including existing social divisions and the impact of imperialism, and is followed by fifteen points that discuss the scope and purpose of the Communist land revolution program. The same fifteen points are included in Wang Chien-min, *Draft History of the Chinese Communist Party* (Taipei, 1965), 1:532–33.

14. Zhou Enlai states that Chinese leaders did not know that the concept of "permanent revolution" had originated with Lominadze until the Party's Sixth Congress. See Zhou Enlai, *Selected Works of Zhou Enlai* (Beijing: Foreign Languages Press, 1981), 1:194. Qu Qiubai carefully avoided the term "permanent revolution" except as it was used by Marx—not Trotsky—and used instead the phrase "uninterrupted revolution." See Qu Qiubai, "What Kind of Revolution," 127–30.

15. "Resolution on the Present Situation and Tasks of the Communist Party," 145.

16. Ibid., 146.

17. Ibid., 148.

18. Ibid., 147.

19. "Resolution on the Questions of the 'Left KMT' and the Soviet Slogan" (September 19, 1927), in Hyobom Pak, ed. and trans., *Documents of the Chinese Communist Party, 1927–30* (Hong Kong: Union Research Institute, 1971), 131.

20. "Resolution on the Political Tasks and Tactics of the CCP" (August 7, 1927), in Pak, *Documents*, 55–56.

21. Rural arrangements at the district (*qu*) and administrative village (*xiang*) level are discussed in a Guangdong Provincial CCP Resolution (September 30, 1927) contained in Pak, *Documents*, 117–18.

22. "Resolution on the Present Situation and Tasks of the Communist Party," 147. See also Qu Qiubai, "The Question of Armed Insurrection," *Bu-er-se-wei-ke*, no. 10 (December 19, 1927), 298.

23. "Resolution on the Present Situation and Tasks of the Communist Party," 147.

24. Warren Kuo, *Analytical History of the Chinese Communist Party* (Taipei: Institute of International Relations, 1966), 1:391. Provincial Party reporting of the period conveyed detailed plans for building the labor movement, while reporting on rural activities was criticized for being "very general and simple"; compare Pak, *Documents*, 175–81, 233–36.

25. Kuo, *Analytical History*, 466.

26. "Resolution on the Present Situation and Tasks of the Communist Party," 147.

27. "Letter from the (Shantung) Provincial Committee to the Kaomi (*Hsien* Committee) Concerning Revolts" (November 9, 1927), in Pak, *Documents*, 292.

28. "Comrade (Ts'ai) Ho-sen's Letter to the Central" (January 28, 1928), in Pak, *Documents*, 471.

29. Kuo, *Analytical History*, 390.

30. Ibid., 474–75. In this letter, Chen criticized Wang Ruofei (Standing Committee member of the Jiangsu Provincial CCP Committee) for stressing the seizure of political power in the cities, in particular Nanjing and Shanghai, and claimed he might have been influenced by Mao Runzhi, an alias of Mao Zedong.

31. Qu Qiubai, "The Past and Future of the Chinese Communist Party," *Chinese Studies in History* 5, no. 1 (Fall 1971) 59; Jin Zaiji, "Shilun baqi huiyidao 'liuda' de gongzuo zhuanbian" (My View of the Changes in Work from the August Seventh Meeting in 1927 to the Sixth National Congress of the CCP in 1928), *Lishi yanjiu* (Historical research), no. 1 (1983), 177–78.

32. Roy M. Hofheinz, Jr., "The Autumn Harvest Insurrection," *The China Quarterly*, no. 32 (October–December 1967), 81.

33. Hsiao Tso-liang, *Chinese Communism in 1927: City vs. Countryside* (Hong Kong: Chinese University of Hong Kong, 1970), 110.

34. "Resolution on the Present Situation and Tasks of the Communist Party," 146.

35. This passage is contained in the Party Central's instructions to the Shandong Provincial Party Committee on December 16, 1927, in Pak, *Documents*, 310.

36. Qu Qiubai, "The Question of Armed Insurrection," *Bolshevik*, no. 10 (December 19, 1927), 297. Section 1 of this article discusses "The Future of Rural Guerrilla Warfare," 294–97.

37. "Resolution on the Present Situation and Tasks of the Communist Party," 149.

38. A lengthy and illuminating report to the Party Central from the Jiangxi Provincial Party Committee (December 12, 1927) divided Party work in Jiangxi into three stages: August–September, "no Party work at all"; September–November, Party reorganization began but mass struggle was self-initiated and led; and November–December,

the Party began to lead, but was still weak. See Pak, *Documents*, 170.

39. "Resolutions on Recent Important Organizational Tasks" produced at the plenum is found in Kuo, *Analytical History*, 1:459–67; 464.

40. Ibid., 464.

41. These notices are mentioned in the Party Central's "Letter to the Shunchih (Hebei) Provincial Committee and (Comrade Ts'ai) Ho-sen" (December 25, 1927) in Pak, *Documents*, 343. Li Weihan mentions central notices nos. 17 and 20, issued respectively on December 1 and 10, which provided amplification of the November plenum's "Resolution on Organization." See Li Weihan, "A Retrospective Study," 46–47.

42. "Resolutions on Recent Important Organizational Tasks," Kuo, *Analytical History*, 1:463.

43. The *Zhejiang Collection* is included in the larger body of research materials known as the Shanghai Municipal Police Files, under Shanghai Municipal Police Document (SMPD) no. 4772. The collection, entitled "Important Excerpts from Communist Evidence," was compiled in three volumes by the Procurator's Office of the Zhejiang High Court. It contains key Chinese documents seized in police raids on important Communist headquarters and bases. The materials included are excerpted instructions, resolutions, regulations, criticisms, lists of slogans, charts, and security procedures. They describe the organizational structure, strategies, working methods, and support organizations of the Communists from August 1927 until at least August 1928. For extensive treatment of the *Zhejiang Collection*, see Marcia R. Ristaino, "The Chinese Communist Movement, 1927–1928: Organizations, Strategies, and Tactics for Making Revolution" (Ph.D. dissertation, Georgetown University, 1977).

44. The League's relationship to the Party is described in the *Zhejiang Collection*, 1:1–4. The Youth League during the period under study was an influential body that, during the Northern Expedition, pioneered in the organization of trade unions and peasant unions. By 1927 it was recognized as the preponderant Communist force in the countryside. See Ristaino, "Chinese Communist Movement," 30–56; Conrad Brandt, *Stalin's Failure in China, 1924–1927* (Cambridge, Mass.: Harvard University Press, 1958), 126–28.

45. The membership composition of the leading bodies at each level of the Party organizational structure, as determined at the November plenum, is provided in Wang Chien-min, *Draft History*, 1:530–31.

46. *Zhejiang Collection*, 1:5–6.

47. The specialized departments and committees under the Party Central Committee, noted on the organizational chart of figure 2, are identified as part of the provisional Political Bureau Central Committee in Wang Chien-min, *Draft History*, 1:530.

48. See work reports from Anhui, Manchuria, Shandong, and Jiangxi provinces in Pak, *Documents*, 223–24, 349–50, 305–7, 169–71.

49. "Resolutions on Recent Important Organizational Tasks," in Kuo, *Analytical History*, 1:462–63. Actually, the Sixth Congress could not be convened until June 1928.

50. Kuo, *Analytical History*, 452–55, 467.

51. Security procedures for each of these areas is included under "Secret Methods of the Communist Party and the Communist Youth League," in *Zhejiang Collection*, 1:13–22.

52. *Zhejiang Collection*, 1:15.

53. Ibid., 1:18.

Chapter 6

1. Feng Jianhui, "Wo dang kaichuang nongcun baowei chengshi daolude lishi kaocha" (A historical review: How the Communist Party of China found the road of encircling the cities from the rural areas), *Zhongguo shehui kexue*, no. 2 (March 1980), 137.

2. Jin Zaiji, "Shilun baqi huiyi dao 'liuda' de gongzuo zhuanbian" (My view on the changes in work from the August Seventh Meeting in 1927 to the Sixth National Congress of the Chinese Communist Party in 1928), *Lishi yanjiu* (Historical research), no. 1 (1983), 177.

3. Qu Qiubai, "The Past and Future of the Chinese Communist Party," *Chinese Studies in History* 5, no. 1 (Fall 1971), 58–59.

4. Ibid., 58.

5. Hsiao Tso-liang, "The Dispute Over a Wuhan Insurrection in 1927," *The China Quarterly*, no. 33 (January–March 1968), 108.

6. Ibid., 108–9.

7. Qu Qiubai, "The Past and Future," 59.

8. Jin Zaiji, "Shilun baqi huiyi dao 'liuda' de gongzuo zhuanbian," 179–80.

9. Ibid., 180.

10. Hsiao Tso-liang, *Chinese Communism in 1927: City vs. Countryside* (Hong Kong: Chinese University of Hong Kong, 1970), 122–23.

11. Ibid., 125.

12. The Party Central's resolution on the Hubei case is found in ibid., 130–33.

13. Jin Zaiji, "Shilun baqi huiyi dao 'liuda' de gongzuo zhuanbian," 180.

14. Qu Qiubai, "The Past and Future," 60.

15. Ibid., 60–61; "Zhang Tailei," in Hu Hua, ed., *Zhonggong dangshi renwu zhuan* (Biographies of leading figures in the Chinese Communist Party history) (Xi'an: Shaanxi renmin chubanshe, 1980), 4:100.

16. M. N. Roy, *Revolution and Counter-Revolution in China*, (Westport, Conn.: Hyperion Press, 1973), 557–58. See also Hsiao Tso-liang, "Chinese Communism and the Canton Soviet of 1927," *The China Quarterly*, no. 30 (April–June 1967), 66.

17. Hsiao Tso-liang, "Chinese Communism and the Canton Soviet," 73.

18. Jerome Ch'en, *Mao and the Chinese Revolution* (London: Oxford University Press, 1965), 136. Zhang Fakui in July 1927 dissolved the Central Military and Political Academy in Wuhan. Its cadets were reorganized into the Officers' Training Regiment. See Zhou Enlai, *Selected Works of Zhou Enlai* (Beijing: Foreign Languages Press, 1981) 1:448.

19. A. Neuberg, *Armed Insurrection* (New York: St. Martin's Press, 1971), 117–18; Zhou Enlai, *Selected Works*, 1:448.

20. Neuberg, *Armed Insurrection*, 113–14; See also Harold R. Isaacs, *The Tragedy of the Chinese Revolution* (Stanford: Stanford University Press, 1961), 283–84.

21. Jin Zaiji, "Shilun baqi huiyi dao 'liuda' de gongzuo zhuanbian," 179. This suggests

that Neumann was unaware that the cpsu Congress (December 2–19) had already begun.

22. J. C. Huston, American consul in charge at Canton, *Huston Report*, enclosure no. 2, "Soviet Administration's Message to the People," in Huston Collection, Hoover Institution Archives, Stanford University.

23. Warren Kuo, *Analytical History of the Chinese Communist Party* (Taipei: Institute of International Relations, 1966), 1:394; *Huston Report*, 16. The latter source notes that with Peng Pai chairing the Hailufeng Soviet, Zhao Zixuan was to act for him.

24. Neuberg, *Armed Insurrection*, 118.

25. Ibid., 127.

26. Ibid., 126–27, 118.

27. Feng Jianhui, "Wo dang kaichuang nongcun baowei chengshi daolude lishi kaocha," 136.

28. Hsiao Tso-liang, "Chinese Communism and the Canton Soviet," 69–70.

29. Those Russians killed in the course of the uprising included Vice-Consul Hassis, "Director of Affairs in the CCP" Mackinoff, and others identified as Antonoff, Gogol, Tzegeloff, Kornivaloff, Zawicki, Kroval, Lyboff, and Tzeplitzsky. See *Huston Report*, 24, 36–38.

30. Pavel Mif, *Heroic China: Fifteen Years of the Communist Party of China* (New York: Workers Library Publishers, 1937), 60.

31. Neuberg, *Armed Insurrection*, 127–28.

32. This Central Notice no. 23 is quoted in Jin Zaiji, "Shilun baqi huiyi dao 'liuda' de gongzuo zhuanbian," 180.

33. Isaacs cites Trotsky in this regard in *Tragedy*, 282. Other evidence supporting this position is cited in Benjamin Schwartz, *Chinese Communism and the Rise of Mao* (New York: Harper and Row, 1967), 105–6.

34. Isaac Deutscher, *The Prophet Unarmed: Trotsky: 1921–1929* (London: Oxford University Press, 1959), 379.

35. Ibid., 389.

36. This is based on a January 4, 1928, work report by Zeng Ganding concerning the Guangzhou Uprising, cited in Jin Zaiji, "Shilun baqi huiyi dao 'liuda' de gongzuo zhuanbian," 179.

37. Qu Qiubai, "The Past and Future," 61–62.

38. Hyobom Pak, ed. and trans., *Documents of the Chinese Communist Party, 1927–30* (Hong Kong: Union Research Institute, 1971), 297.

39. Kuo, *Analytical History*, 1:395; Wang Chien-min, *Draft History of the Chinese Communist Party* (Taipei, 1965), 1:571.

40. Jin Zaiji, "Shilun baqi huiyi dao 'liuda' de gongzuo zhuanbian," 180–81.

41. Ibid., 182.

42. Wang Chien-min, *Draft History*, 1:571.

43. Qu Qiubai, "The Past and Future," 62.

44. Ibid., 63–64.

45. B. Lominadze, "Historical Significance of the Canton Rising," *Communist International* (January 15, 1928), 31–34.

46. Qu Qiubai, "The Past and Future," 63; Jin Zaiji, "Shilun baqi huiyi dao 'liuda' de gongzuo zhuanbian," 183.
47. Qu Qiubai, "The Past and Future," 64.
48. *Zhejiang Collection*, Shanghai Municipal Police Document no. 4772, Shanghai Municipal Police Files, 2:50.
49. Included in excerpts from Trotsky's "On the New Stage" (December 1927), in Les Evans and Russell Block, eds., *Leon Trotsky on China: Introduction by P'eng Shu-tse* (New York: Monad Press, 1976), 274.
50. The entire resolution is contained in Xenia J. Eudin and Robert Slusser, eds., *Soviet Foreign Policy, 1928–1934: Documents and Materials* (University Park: Pennsylvania State University Press, 1966), 83–87; see also Jane Degras, *The Communist International, 1919–1943: Documents* (London: Frank Cass, 1956–1971), 2:437–40.
51. Eudin and Slusser, *Soviet Foreign Policy*, 83.
52. Ibid.
53. "ECCI Resolution on the Present Stage of the Chinese Revolution," (July 14, 1927) in Degras, *The Communist International*, 2:393.
54. Eudin and Slusser, *Soviet Foreign Policy*, 84.
55. Degras, *The Communist International*, 2:438.
56. Ibid.
57. Eudin and Slusser, *Soviet Foreign Policy*, 85–86.
58. "The Soviet System and Socialism in China," *Bu-er-se-wei-ke* (Bolshevik), no. 14 (January 16, 1928), 427–29.
59. Ibid., 431.
60. Ye Jianying, "Dageming shibai yu Guangzhou qiyi," *Xinghuo liaoyuan* (Beijing: Zhongguo renmin jiefangjun zhanshi chubanshe, 1979), 1:316–17.

Chapter 7

1. Qu Qiubai, "The Past and Future of the Chinese Communist Party," *Chinese Studies in History* 5, no. 1 (Fall 1971), 61–62. Qu mentions the circular, "On Armed Uprisings," but does not explain its contents.
2. *Zhejiang Collection*, Shanghai Municipal Police Document no. 4772, Shanghai Municipal Police Files, 3:45–55; Fernando Galbiati, *P'eng P'ai and the Hai-lu-feng Soviet* (Stanford: Stanford University Press, 1985), 293.
3. In a "Letter from the Central to the Shansi Provincial Committee on the New Work Policy in Shansi," dated March 26, 1928, the extent of policy development regarding Chinese soviets is reflected in the statement that: "As for the [land] confiscation and the establishing of the soviet political power, the Central has already issued a notice with detailed provisions." See Hyobom Pak, ed. and trans., *Documents of the Chinese Communist Party, 1927–30* (Hong Kong: Union Research Institute, 1971), 500.
4. *Zhongyang geming genjudi shiliao xuanbian* (Selected historical materials on the central revolutionary base area) (Nanchang: Jiangxi renmin chubanshe, 1982), 1:4–5.
5. Galbiati, *P'eng P'ai*, 286–87.
6. *Zhejiang Collection*, 3:45.
7. *Zhongyang geming genjudi shiliao xuanbian*, 1:5.

8. This organizational guidance, like that of November 1927 concerning the construction of primary Communist organizations, equates the level of county (*xian*) and
   municipal bodies.
9. *Zhejiang Collection*, 3:45.
10. Ibid., 3:44.
11. These charts are based on copies included in the *Zhejiang Collection*, 3:52–55.
12. Hsiao Tso-liang, *Chinese Communism in 1927: City vs. Countryside* (Hong Kong: Chi-
    nese University Press of Hong Kong, 1970), 139; Warren Kuo, *Analytical History of the
    Chinese Communist Party* (Taipei: Institute of International Relations, 1966), 1:394;
    Huston Report, Huston Collection, Hoover Institution Archives, Stanford University,
    16. As early as the Nanchang Uprising, the Communists had expected to gain foreign
    support, particularly from the Soviet Union, for their government, thus the reason for
    forming a Diplomatic Committee.
13. Pak, *Documents*, 117.
14. *Zhejiang Collection*, 3:44. The portions of this collection from which the above tables
    and figures were developed are not limited in scope or purpose to Zhejiang Province,
    but were to apply to all areas where Communists were active.
15. The key points of these land regulations are contained in the *Zhejiang Collection*,
    3:44–45.
16. Peng's criteria included consideration of the capacity for work of family members
    and any additional nonagricultural sources of income. See Robert B. Marks, *Rural
    Revolution in South China* (Madison: University of Wisconsin Press, 1984), 256.
17. *Zhejiang Collection*, 3:45.
18. The Central Soviet Government eventually was established on November 7, 1931, at
    Ruijin, Jiangxi Province.
19. Marks, *Rural Revolution*, 198.
20. Ibid., 208.
21. From its beginnings until its closing in Wuhan in May 1927, the Institute included
    seven classes. For information concerning the classes, principals, and student pro-
    vincial origins, see Roy M. Hofheinz, Jr., *The Broken Wave: The Chinese Communist
    Peasant Movement, 1922–28* (Cambridge, Mass.: Harvard University Press, 1977), 79.
22. Shinkichi Eto, "Hai-lu-feng–The First Chinese Soviet Government," Part 2, *The China
    Quarterly*, no. 9 (January–March 1962), 165–66; Marks, *Rural Revolution*, 236.
23. Eto, "Hai-lu-feng," Part 2, 169; Marks, *Rural Revolution*, 243–44.
24. Galbiati, *P'eng P'ai*, 277; Marks, *Rural Revolution*, 250. The backgrounds of representa-
    tives attending these conferences were similar to those required in the guidance
    contained in the *Zhejiang Collection* and shown in table 1. For the county soviet,
    peasants were to compose 60 percent of the representatives; workers 30 percent;
    and soldiers 10 percent. At a municipal soviet conference, workers 60 percent;
    peasants 30 percent; and soldiers 10 percent.
25. For Peng Pai's account of his activities in Hailufeng, see "Seeds of Peasant Revolt:
    Report on the Haifeng County Peasant Movement," translated by D. Holoch, *East Asia
    Papers*, no. 1 (Ithaca, N.Y.: Cornell University, 1973).
26. Eto, "Hai-lu-feng," Part 2, 173–74. The 4th Division was composed of forces that had
    participated in the Guangzhou Uprising.

27. Peng continued clandestine rural organization work until ordered by Party Central to Shanghai. While working in the Shanghai underground, he was betrayed by a Party member and on August 30, 1929, died after torture by Shanghai police. *Peng Pai zhuanlue* (Short biography of Peng Pai) (Guangzhou, 1980), 70–72.
28. Zhu De, "From the Nanchang Uprising to Going Up the Jinggang Mountain," an oral account provided by Zhu in June 1962, to *Xinhua* (Beijing) (July 31, 1982) in FBIS *Daily Report* (August 3, 1982), K1–6; K3.
29. Su Yu, "Memories of Zhu De and Chen Yi," Part 1, *China Reconstructs* (August 1979), 36.
30. "Brother [Chu] Te and All Comrades" (December 27, 1927), in Pak, *Documents*, 193–94.
31. "Brother [Chu] Te and All Comrades of the Army" (December 21, 1927) in Pak, *Documents*, 187.
32. Su Yu, "Memories of Zhu De and Chen Yi," Part 2, *China Reconstructs* (September 1979), 47–48.
33. Zhu De, "From the Nanchang Uprising," K5.
34. Estimates of the strength of the Fourth Red Army range from 3,000 in Kuo, *Analytical History*, 2:12, to 10,000 in "The Founding of the Chinese Red Army," translated by Hsüeh Chün-tu and Robert C. North, in *Contemporary China* (Hong Kong: Hong Kong University Press, 1968), 6:62. The Hsüeh and North source defines the Political Department as responsible for "indoctrination . . . and organizing the masses," 70. The political commissar was to ensure that Party policies were strictly followed by the military.
35. By mid-November Mao's forces succeeded in capturing the county seat city of Chaling, Hunan, and in January, Suichuan. Soviet governments were initiated, but stiffening local resistance rendered them inactive. Stephen C. Averill, "Revolution in the Highlands: The Rise of the Communist Movement in Jiangxi Province," (Ph.D. dissertation, Cornell University, 1982), 287.
36. Ibid., 282–86.
37. Mao Zedong, "The Struggle in the Chingkang Mountains," in *Selected Works* (Peking: Foreign Languages Press, 1975), 1:99.
38. Hsüeh and North, "The Founding of the Chinese Red Army," 63.
39. Mao Zedong, "The Struggle in the Chingkang Mountains," 78.
40. Ibid., 1:73.
41. Donald W. Klein and Anne B. Clark, *Biographic Dictionary of Chinese Communism, 1921–1965* (Cambridge, Mass.: Harvard University Press, 1971), 728.
42. Li Peicheng and Liu Menghua, "Pingjiang qiyi" (Pingjiang Uprising), in Zhu Chengjia, ed., *Zhonggong dangshi yanjiu lunwenxuan* (Changsha: Hunan renmin chubanshe, 1983), 138–40.
43. Klein and Clark, *Biographic Dictionary*, 728; Li and Liu, "Pingjiang qiyi," 141. In his autobiography written largely during the Cultural Revolution, Peng said he joined the CCP in February or March 1928. *Peng Dehuai zishu* (Peng Dehuai's memoirs) (Beijing: Renmin chubanshe, 1981), 67.
44. *Peng Dehuai zishu*, 46; Li and Liu, "Pingjiang qiyi," 142.
45. Li and Liu, "Pingjiang qiyi," 145.
46. Ibid., 146.

47. Ibid., 147.
48. *Peng Dehuai zishu*, 101.
49. Li and Liu, "Pingjiang qiyi," 151–52.
50. Ibid., 155–56.
51. *Peng Dehuai zishu*, 103–4.
52. There is no biography of Fang Zhimin in English except for a translation of the account of Miao Min (Fang's wife). Some excerpted memoirs appear in *Hongqi piaopiao*, vol. 9 (Beijing: Zhongguo qingnian chubanshe, 1958). A recent account is *Fang Zhimincuan* (Nanchang: Jiangxi renmin chubanshe, 1982).
53. Miao Min, *Fang Chih-min: Revolutionary Fighter* (Peking: Foreign Languages Press, 1962), 57. Miao says Fang joined the CCP in Nanchang in March 1923 (p. 37).
54. Li Qun, "Cong Yiheng baodong kan Fang Zhiminshi gongnong wuzhuang geju daolude xingcheng" (Based on the Yiheng Uprising, examination of the emergence of the process of establishing an armed independent regime of workers and peasants in the style of Fang Zhimin), in Zhu Chengjia, *Zhonggong dangshi yanjiu lunwenxuan*, 2:128. For information on Fang's early life and reform activities, see Averill, "Revolution in the Highlands," 158–202.
55. Fang's alias was Wang Zuhai; Huang Dao was Chen Songshou; and Shao Shiping was Yu Yanwang. Li Qun, "Cong Yiheng baodong," 129.
56. Miao Min, *Fang Chih-min*, 56.
57. Li Qun, "Cong Yiheng baodong," 130.
58. Miao Min, *Fang Chih-min*, 63.
59. Ibid., 73–74; "Huang Dao," in Hu Hua, ed., *Zhonggong dangshi renwu zhuan* (Biographies of leading figures in Chinese Communist Party history) (Xi'an: Shaanxi renmin chubanshe, 1980), 7:131.
60. Li Qun, "Cong Yiheng baodong," 131–32.
61. Ibid., 134; Huang Dao, *Zhongguo renmin jiefangjun di sanshi nian* (Thirty years of the Chinese People's Liberation Army) (Beijing: Renmin chubanshe, 1958), 2:589–590.
62. In January 1935 Fang's forces were surrounded near Yiyang, and Fang was captured. He was taken to Nanchang and paraded through the streets, fettered in an iron cage. On July 6, 1935, he was executed at age thirty-five. See Klein and Clark, *Biographic Dictionary*, 271.
63. Cai Kangzhi and Zhao Qingqu, "E-Yu-Wan suqu gongnong wuzhuang geju wenti chutan" (Preliminary exploration of the question of the Hubei, Henan, Anhui Soviet Armed Independent Area) in Zhu Chengjian, *Zhonggong dangshi yanjiu lunwenxuan*, 2:104.
64. Ibid., 105.
65. Ibid., 107.
66. Robert W. McColl, "The Oyüwan Soviet Area, 1927–1932," *The Journal of Asian Studies* 27, no. 1 (November 1967), 49–50.
67. Liang Qin, "Jinggangshan douzheng jingyan" (The Jinggang Mountains Struggle), in Zhu Chengjia, *Zhonggong dangshi yanjiu lunwenxuan*, 2:115–16.
68. Edgar Snow, *Red Star Over China* (New York: Random House, 1938), 153.
69. A brief discussion of soviet bases established from late 1927 to 1930 is found in He Ganzhi, *Zhongguo xiandai geming shi* (A history of the modern Chinese revolution)

(Beijing, 1959), 138–39. See also Guo Dehong, "The Development of the Land Policy of the Chinese Communist Party During the Second Revolutionary Civil War Period (1927–1937)," *Social Sciences in China*, no. 1 (1981), 24–27. The latter source emphasizes the experimental and formative stages of land policy development in the emerging soviets.

70. Kuo, *Analytical History*, 2:16.

71. *Zhejiang Collection*, 3:15; compare Pak, *Documents*, 431. Military subjects are discussed in the section "Secret Bodies: The Red Defense Corp and the Red Army," *Zhejiang Collection*, 15–21. The document cited from Pak's collection indicates that this Central Notice no. 51, "On the Military Work" (May 25, 1928), 431–46, was a reprint of a resolution on military questions adopted at an enlarged conference (n.d.) of the Guangdong Provincial Committee.

72. Under the subheading "The Question of Establishing a Red Army," in *Zhejiang Collection*, 3:18; compare Central Notice no. 51, in Pak, *Documents*, 442.

73. *Zhejiang Collection*, 3:18; Pak, *Documents*, 442.

74. Pak, *Documents*, 445; *Zhejiang Collection*, 3:18–19.

75. In late September 1927 Mao carried out the famous "Sanwan reorganization" at Sanwan, Jiangxi, in order to assert greater Party control and discipline over his troops. See James P. Harrison, *The Long March to Power* (New York: Praeger Publishers, 1972), 133; Song Shilun, "Mao Zedong's Military Thinking Is the Guide to Our Army's Victories," *Hongqi*, no. 16 (August 16, 1981) in FBIS *Daily Report* (September 17, 1981), K13. Under conditions similar to those confronting Mao's fleeing troops, Zhu De carried out an ideological reorganization of his forces in October 1927 at Tianxinxu, Jiangxi. According to Su Yu, Zhu told his troops: "Those who want to continue the revolution should come with us. Those who don't go home—we won't force you to stay." Continuing on with an all-volunteer force, in late October Zhu reorganized the Party and League organizations in the units to strengthen their influence at the grass-roots level. See Su Yu, "Memories," Part 1, 35.

76. Pak, *Documents*, 439; compare under the subheading, "The Problem for the Enlargement of Armed Labor and Peasant Masses," in *Zhejiang Collection*, 3:17.

77. Pak, *Documents*, 440.

78. *Zhejiang Collection*, 1:18; compare Pak, *Documents*, 444.

79. The Party Central specified that League organs were not to function in the Red Army or Red Guards. Instead, League members were to assist Party organs in their work of supervising military organizations. See *Zhejiang Collection*, 2:16.

80. Ibid., 3:20–21.

81. Ibid., 3:20; compare Pak, *Documents*, 444.

82. The relationship of the Party's military committees to the regular Party structure is illustrated in figure 2.

83. In December 1928 the Party Central denied the formation of a Hubei-Anhui Special Committee, where a strong Seventh Army had developed, calling such a request evidence of "mountain strongholdism" (*Zhaizi zhuyi*) on the part of the local military leaders. One suspects that the Party Central's real concern was that the concentration of military-political power might make these leaders too independent and

difficult to control. Cai and Zhao, "E-Yu-Wan suqu gongnong geju wenti chutan," 105–6.

84. *Zhejiang Collection*, 2:15.

85. Discussion of the soldiers' committees is contained under the subheading "Organizations Dealing with Soldiers," in *Zhejiang Collection*, 2:15–17.

Chapter 8

1. This discussion of the Communist system is based largely on the extensive materials concerning organizational matters in the *Zhejiang Collection*, Shanghai Municipal Police Document no. 4772, Shanghai Municipal Police Files. These materials, save one, lack dates. However, an approximate time period can be derived from references to important Party and League conferences, major historical events, and important developments within the movement, the dates for which are well known. Using this approach, we can say that the collection spans a period beginning at least as early as August 1927 and continuing until at least August 1928.

2. The distinctions between internal and external work are discussed under the heading "Organization," in *Zhejiang Collection*, 2:6.

3. "Resolutions on Recent Important Organizational Tasks" (November 9, 1927), in Warren Kuo, *Analytical History of the Chinese Communist Party* (Taipei: Institute of International Relations, 1966), 1:460. This shift in Communist recruitment preferences is indicated by the fact that factory youth and rural hired hands required only a general introduction and the approval of their affiliate factory or rural organ to be considered for membership in the League. Another group including "peasants, postal workers, manual workers, soldiers, shop assistants, junior coolies" needed a full recommendation from one member of the League or Party. A third category, including students and intellectuals, required the recommendation of two members of the Party or League. Final membership approval was to be granted by the district-level organ. See *Zhejiang Collection*, 2:3.

4. *Zhejiang Collection*, 2:10–11.

5. Ibid., 2:9.

6. Ibid., 2:8. The Party or League sponsor of a new member took responsibility for this training. They also were held personally accountable for the new member's performance and reliability.

7. Ibid., 2:7.

8. Ibid., 2:19, 21.

9. Ibid., 2:19.

10. Ibid., 2:8.

11. Ibid., 2:25.

12. The following data on propaganda mechanisms and methods are based on the *Zhejiang Collection*, 2:18–24.

13. The same point concerning altering the Party's external policy line according to local conditions is contained in Central Notice no. 54, entitled "On the Current Situation," issued on June 21, 1928. See Hyobom Pak, ed. and trans., *Documents of the Chinese*

Communist Party, 1927–30 (Hong Kong: Union Research Institute, 1971), 455–56.

14. Ibid., 2:18. Apparently, one such periodical did develop in Zhejiang. In another section, mention is made of the need to arrange for the widespread sale of "the periodical of the Provincial Committee, 'Hu Pu' [Lake Wave]," as well as the "'Cloth Paper' of the Central." See ibid., 2:19.

15. Fernando Galbiati, *P'eng P'ai and the Hai-lu-feng Soviet* (Stanford: Stanford University Press, 1985), 125.

16. The following data on external organization work are based on the *Zhejiang Collection*, 2:11–45; 3:1–14, 22–25.

17. Ibid., 2:33.

18. C. Martin Wilbur and Julie Lien-ying How, eds., *Documents on Communism, Nationalism, and Soviet Advisors in China, 1918–1927* (New York: Columbia University Press, 1956; reprint ed., New York: Octagon Books, 1976), 285.

19. Groups identified as the Brothers Groups, Sisters Groups, and the Anti-Japanese Society were to be secretly organized from among young workers and might precede the establishment of a Communist labor union in factories where unions were difficult to establish. See *Zhejiang Collection*, 3:12.

20. See the Party Central's instructions to the Shanxi Provincial Committee dated March 26, 1928, in Pak, *Documents*, 499. These referred cadres to the pamphlet "Guidelines for the Working Class of China," adopted by the 1927 Enlarged Conference of the All-China Labor Union Federation for additional specific guidance.

21. *Zhejiang Collection*, 2:15.

22. Ibid., 3:1. See also "The Shunchih [Hebei] Provincial Committee Plan of the Labor Movement," October 24, 1927, in Pak, *Documents*, 333.

23. These general regulations are contained in the *Zhejiang Collection*, 3:2–4. They are of Party origin and include the comment that their contents "may be amended by the General Assembly of the labor union."

24. The description of the various kinds of labor unions is presented under the heading "Movement of the Laborers," *Zhejiang Collection*, 2:30.

25. Ibid., 2:30.

26. Ibid., 2:43. A resolution adopted at a Henan Provincial Congress in February 1928 included in its list of demands for the labor movement the four freedoms of speech, press, assembly, and strike. See Pak, *Documents*, 389.

27. Donald W. Klein and Anne B. Clark, *Biographic Dictionary of Chinese Communism, 1921–1965* (Cambridge, Mass.: Harvard University Press, 1971), 2:772–73.

28. *Zhejiang Collection*, 3:11.

29. Ibid., 3:11.

30. Guidance and regulations concerning the peasant associations appear in the *Zhejiang Collection*, 3:4–8. Peng Pai, as early as July 7, 1923, had provided a constitution for peasant organizational work that included ten chapters and thirty-three sections. When he became secretary of the KMT Peasant Department in March 1924, a constitution for the peasant association was drafted under his direction with fifteen chapters and eighty-three articles. Thus policies concerning peasant organizational work developed subsequently had as reference

an extensive body of existing guidance and regulations. See Galbiati, *P'eng P'ai*, 139, 174–76.

31. *Zhejiang Collection*, 2:36.

32. This rural approach is described under the heading "Movement of the Peasants," ibid., 2:49.

33. Ibid., 2:36. Initial efforts to describe the rural population by identifying groups is evident in Mao Zedong's Hunan Peasant Report. Mao used the broad categories of poor, middle, and rich peasants, in *Selected Works* (Peking: Foreign Languages Press, 1975), 1:30. In his November 1928 Jinggang Mountains Report, Mao also reported the difficulties that the Party's land policy had produced for the "intermediate classes." See *Selected Works*, 1:87–89. See also Philip C. Huang, "Mao Tse-tung and the Middle Peasants, 1925–1928," *Modern China*, no. 3 (July 1975), 271–96.

34. By May 1927, before widespread serious reaction set in, the Communists claimed to have organized over nine million peasants; however, these figures are believed to have been seriously inflated. See Roy M. Hofheinz, Jr., *The Broken Wave: The Chinese Communist Peasant Movement, 1922–28* (Cambridge, Mass.: Harvard University Press, 1977), 103–5.

35. The full term for these rural organizations was *nongmin xiehui*. It was commonly abbreviated by the Communists to *nongxie*. See *Zhejiang Collection*, 3:56. The description of the organizational system of the peasant association is based on regulations contained in the *Zhejiang Collection*, 3:6–8. Although not specifically described as such, the village level very likely concerned the *xiang* or administrative village. In addition to serving as a distinct level of government, the district (*qu*) or other subcounty (*xian*) level may also have functioned occasionally as an authority delegated by the *xian* level to supervise administrative villages. In the soviet system, the *xiang* soviet generally functioned as the basic unit. See A. Doak Barnett, *Cadres, Bureaucracy, and Political Power in Communist China* (New York: Columbia University Press, 1967), 453; and Ilpyong J. Kim, "Mass Mobilization Policies and Techniques Developed in the Period of the Chinese Soviet Republic," in A. Doak Barnett, ed., *Chinese Communist Politics in Action* (Seattle: University of Washington Press, 1969), 88.

36. Hofheinz, *The Broken Wave*, 96.

37. Peng Pai participated in public executions in Hailufeng, equating the ethics of class struggle with peasant justice in his explanations of the public butchery. Galbiati, *P'eng P'ai*, 336.

38. For guidance concerning organizational work directed at subverting military and police organization, see *Zhejiang Collection*, 2:37–39, 44–45, 60. Most of the same points are contained in the Party Central's Notice no. 51 entitled "On the Military Work," issued on May 25, 1928. See Pak, *Documents*, 435–39.

39. The Provincial Defense Forces stationed in Zhejiang were noted as generally a difficult target for Communist infiltration programs. A reported mutiny by troops in the port city of Haimen over extensive back wages brought a hasty response from Zhejiang authorities to begin paying wages regularly. This and the fact that Zhejiang forces had not been involved in extensive fighting made them a difficult subject for the

Communists, who focused their efforts on playing upon economic hardship and personal suffering. See *Zhejiang Collection*, 2:39.

40. Ibid., 3:16.

41. Li Peicheng and Liu Menghua, "Pingjiang qiyi" (Pingjiang Uprising), in Zhu Chengjia, ed., *Zhonggong danshi yanjiu lunwenxuan* (Changsha: Hunan renmin chubanshe, 1983), 144–45.

42. *Zhejiang Collection*, 2:44–45.

43. Ibid., 2:38–39.

44. In 1928 the Red Spears Society in North China resisted efforts by the KMT military to integrate their forces into the National Revolutionary Army. See Donald A. Jordan, *The Northern Expedition: China's National Revolution of 1926–1928* (Honolulu: The University Press of Hawaii, 1976), 255–56.

45. *Zhejiang Collection*, 2:18.

46. In a section entitled "Organization Dealing with Bandits," ibid., 2:17–18.

47. In a section entitled "Movement of Bandits," ibid., 2:40.

48. The purpose and organization of the Boys' Corps is discussed in the *Zhejiang Collection*, 3:31–35.

49. Ibid., 3:32.

50. Galbiati, *P'eng P'ai*, 225, 308.

51. *Zhejiang Collection*, 2:12.

52. The term *shaonian xianfengdui* often is translated young pioneer. See Central Notice no. 51, "On Military Work," May 25, 1928, in Pak, *Documents*, 441. Data on the Youth Vanguards are taken from regulations explaining the organization and mission of this body, contained in the *Zhejiang Collection*, 3:22–31.

53. Under dangerous conditions, Youth Vanguards were to be organized secretly using different so-called "gray colored names": Brothers Association, Chivalry Learning Association, Youth Amusement Association, Youth Athletic Association, and so forth. In internal correspondence, however, Vanguards leaders were to refer consistently to the organization by its official title. See *Zhejiang Collection*, 3:24, 31.

54. Ibid., 3:25.

55. Ibid., 3:25–26.

56. In November 1935 the Party Central changed the League into a mass organization that included all "anti-Japanese youths," Communist or non-Communist. Subsequently several youth organizations came into being and focused their work on uniting the population and working toward a united front against Japan. The Youth Vanguards discussed here were the predecessor to the Anti-Japanese Youth Vanguards formed in the late 1930s and charged with both military and production duties in the countryside. See Klaus H. Pringsheim, "The Functions of the Chinese Communist Youth Leagues (1920–1949)," *The China Quarterly*, no. 12 (October–December 1962), 82–85.

57. *Zhejiang Collection*, 3:24.

58. Providing recruits for the Red Army is also noted in the Central Notice no. 51, "On Military Work." See Pak, *Documents*, 441–42.

59. Galbiati, *P'eng P'ai*, 308.

60. *Zhejiang Collection*, 3:27; see also Pak, *Documents*, 441.

61. One rural lineage member, unable to distinguish traditional clan organizations from the new soviet governments, referred to Fang Zhimin's soviet as the new "soviet clan." See Stephen C. Averill, "Revolution in the Highlands: The Rise of the Communist Movement in Jiangxi Province" (Ph.D. dissertation, Cornell University, 1982), 237–240.

62. Nym Wales, *Red Dust: Autobiographies of Chinese Communists* (Stanford: Stanford University Press, 1952), 202.

63. Li Qun, "Cong Yiheng baodong xingcheng," in Zhu Chengjia, ed., *Zhonggong dangshi yanjiu lunwenxuan* (Changsha: Hunan renmin chubanshe, 1983), 2:126–35.

Chapter 9

1. Chiang resumed the positions of commander in chief of the Nationalist armies and chairman of the National Military Council. He became chairman of the National Government and in March 1928 was elected chairman of the Central Political Council. See Howard L. Boorman and Richard C. Howard, eds., *Biographical Dictionary of Republican China* (New York: Columbia University Press, 1967), 1:326–27.

2. Donald G. Gillin, *Warlord: Yen Hsi-shan in Shansi Province, 1911–1949* (Princeton: Princeton University Press, 1967), 108–9. Chahar was part of what today is Nei Monggol Autonomous Region.

3. The rural opportunities afforded by diversions from "village-purification" work to competing for seizing cities is explained in a Party Central letter to the Hunan, Hubei, and Jiangxi provincial committees (March 10, 1928) in Hyobom Pak, ed. and trans., *Documents of the Chinese Communist Party, 1927–30* (Hong Kong: Union Research Institute, 1971), 370–71.

4. Ibid., 371.

5. This Central Notice no. 44, entitled "Concerning the Question of the Comintern's February Resolution on the Chinese Question," is noted in Jin Zaiji, "My View of the Changes in Work from the August Seventh Meeting in 1927 to the Sixth Chinese Communist Party Congress in 1928," *Lishi yanjiu* (Historical research), no. 1, 184. See also, Li Weihan, "A Retrospective Study of Qu Qiubai's 'Left' Adventurism," *Social Sciences in China*, no. 3 (September 1983), 78. Li claimed (p. 80) that this notice, when published, included the ECCI's "Resolution" as an appendix.

6. "Political Resolution" of the Sixth Party Congress (June 18–July 11, 1928), in Conrad Brandt, Benjamin Schwartz, and John K. Fairbank, eds., *A Documentary History of Chinese Communism* (Cambridge, Mass.: Harvard University Press, 1952), 137–38.

7. *Zhejiang Collection*, Shanghai Municipal Police Document no. 4772, Shanghai Municipal Police Files, 2:47. The middle volume of this collection contains numerous excerpts organized under the heading "Struggle." Each one is concluded by a tag and number, such as in this case "Great 42."

8. Ibid., 2:46–48, 50–51, 62. These instructions reportedly were based on the experience and observations of past struggle campaigns.

9. Li Jui, *The Early Revolutionary Activities of Comrade Mao Tse-tung* (White Plains, N.Y.: M. E. Sharpe, 1977), 183.

10. Fernando Galbiati, *P'eng P'ai and the Hai-lu-feng Soviet* (Stanford: Stanford University Press, 1985), 93; *Zhejiang Collection*, 2:23.
11. *Zhejiang Collection*, 2:24.
12. Robert B. Marks, *Rural Revolution in South China* (Madison: University of Wisconsin Press, 1984), 216.
13. *Zhejiang Collection*, 2:55.
14. Ibid., 2:47.
15. Ibid., 2:55.
16. Ibid., 2:46. One available report entitled "Report of One Comrade on Chekiang" tells of actual operating conditions there in the movement. The picture drawn is one of weakness and chaos, with mass resignations by Party leaders, arrests, documents lost, factionalism, and so on. It is dated September 17, 1927, but probably conditions were similar in 1928. See Pak, *Documents*, 273–83.
17. *Zhejiang Collection*, 2:61.
18. Fang attended the First Senior Industrial School in Nanchang, where he studied mechanical engineering. Expelled from this school for strike activities, he entered William Nast College, an American missionary college. His wife relates that Fang, with good English language skills, read extensively in Marxist and other radical literature at this school, even while the sermon was being delivered in required church services. See Miao Min, *Fang Chih-min: Revolutionary Fighter* (Peking: Foreign Languages Press, 1962), 13, 19, 24–26. Peng Pai's education included the study of political economy at Japan's Waseda University, a center of Japanese socialist thought. After graduating in 1921, Peng returned to China. See Donald W. Klein and Anne B. Clark, *Biographic Dictionary of Chinese Communism, 1921–1965* (Cambridge, Mass.: Harvard University Press, 1971), 2:720. Mao's graduation from the Hunan First Normal School is well known.
19. *Zhejiang Collection*, 2:49.
20. Ibid., 2:46, 61. The guidance repeated in these passages was that labor struggle is not limited to strikes only.
21. Ibid., 2:48. Some cadres reportedly did not consider any struggle activity less than a strike as worthwhile.
22. Ibid., 2:48, 52.
23. Ibid., 2:32.
24. Ibid., 2:51.
25. Ibid., 2:49, 59.
26. Ibid., 2:59.
27. Ibid., 2:50–51, 59, 60, 63.
28. Ibid., 2:40. This same requirement for coordinating the rural and urban movements is found in the "Political Resolution" of the Party's Sixth Congress. See Brandt, Schwartz, and Fairbank, *Documentary History*, 151.
29. *Zhejiang Collection*, 2:57–58.
30. Marks, *Rural Revolution*, 153. In 1926 the rent-reduction movement, backed by the peasant association, netted Haifeng peasants a 64 percent rent reduction. Part of the rate was to compensate for typhoon damage to crops (p. 209).
31. *Zhejiang Collection*, 2:60, 62.

32. Ibid., 2:56, 60, 63.
33. Ibid., 2:56–58.
34. Ibid., 2:50. The need to begin with economic struggle campaigns before advancing to political struggles had been emphasized in a report by the Hubei provincial secretary to the Party Central on September 10, 1927. See Pak, *Documents*, 214.
35. *Zhejiang Collection*, 2:50, 55–56. External propaganda efforts were to emphasize three themes: (1) anti-Japanese, anti-British, and anti-American imperialism; (2) anti-Kuomintang; and (3) issues appropriate to local struggle campaigns. Most important, the three were to be connected and interrelated.
36. Ibid., 2:54.
37. Ibid., 2:59.
38. Ibid., 2:49.
39. *Zhejiang Collection*, 2:36, 42, 49; The Party Central's position vis-à-vis rural social strata is reflected in the "Resolution of the Sixth National Congress (of the CCP) on the Peasant Movement," in Brandt, Schwartz, and Fairbank, *Documentary History*, 158.
40. Li Peicheng and Liu Menghua, "Pingjiang qiyi (Pingjiang Uprising), in Zhu Chengjia, ed., *Zhonggong dangshi yanjiu lunwenxuan* (Changsha: Hunan renmin chubanshe, 1983)," 142.
41. *Zhejiang Collection*, 2:54.
42. Ibid., 498. The Party Central, in late March 1928, provided a "new work policy" to the Shanxi Provincial CCP Committee, emphasizing that if "organized strength" is not widespread, then "the main basic condition for uprising is lacking." See Pak, *Documents*, 498.
43. Miao Min, *Fang Chih-min*, 64–65.
44. *Zhejiang Collection*, 2:65. The concept of uprising is dealt with at 2:65–67.
45. *Zhejiang Collection*, 2:74.
46. Ibid., 2:75. Central instructions (May 11, 1928) to the Shunzhi (Hebei) Provincial Committee emphasized similar points concerning the uprising: the importance of preparatory work leading to uprising, the need for a good foundation in mass work, the importance of daily struggle activities, and the need to persuade rather than compel worker participation. See Pak, *Documents*, 489–94.
47. Li Qun, "Cong Yiheng baodong kan Fangzhiminshi gongnong wuzhuang geju," in Zhu Chengjia, *Zhonggong dangshi yanjiu lunwenxuan*, 2:129; Miao Min, *Fang Chih-min*, 56.
48. *Zhejiang Collection*, 2:58, 66–67, 69–70, 74, 76, 78–79. Examples from the text are "the non-payment of rent movement should be extended and should penetrate into the masses. In its course of development, the occupation of cities must be avoided . . ." 2:58. "You must not attempt the movement until you feel sure of your success nor when the mass is not in a position to receive our direction in full. We have carefully considered matters and think that at present no cities should be occupied in Chekiang pending further developments in the work . . ." 2:74. Restraint concerning the cities was included in decisions concerning Party work in Shaanxi Province. See Document 60, dated 18 March 1928, in Pak, *Documents*, 417–18.
49. *Zhejiang Collection*, 2:67.
50. Ibid., 2:66.

51. Ibid., 2:74. These are basically the same preconditions for an urban uprising as those set forth at the November plenum. See Hsiao Tso-liang, *Chinese Communism in 1927: City vs. Countryside* (Hong Kong: Chinese University of Hong Kong, 1970), 162. Comparable instructions from Party Central to Shanxi cadres (March 26, 1928) said: "The direction in which the struggle is to develop is of course toward the center of the *hsiang* or county seat. Such a struggle as described above can also be called an agrarian uprising. When four important *hsiang* of a county have become a de facto independent base, it can link to the uprising force in the city to seize the county seat. But if there are not such conditions as an independent base of four important *hsiang* and a considerable foundation of the urban workers, it cannot be allowed to occupy the city." See Pak, *Documents*, 501.

52. *Zhejiang Collection*, 2:77.

53. A glossary entitled "Common Terms used by the Communist Party and the Communist Youth" is appended to vol. 3 of the *Zhejiang Collection*, 51. Red Terror is defined as the "massacre and incendiarism committed by Communists"; in the same list White Terror is explained as "suppression of Communism." Excerpts concerning Red Terror appear at 2:67–68.

54. Ibid., 2:68.

55. Ibid., 2:67.

56. Ibid., 2:69. Excerpts concerning guerrilla warfare appear at 2:69–73.

57. Ibid., 2:70. Zhou Enlai, in March 1929, defined the main tasks of guerrilla warfare as "to implement the slogans of the peasants' struggle, to wear down the strength of the reactionaries and to build the Red Army," *Selected Works of Zhou Enlai* (Beijing: Foreign Languages Press, 1981), 1:28.

58. Landowners and gentry often made this comparison for the peasantry in order to damage the Communists' position and reputation. See *Zhejiang Collection*, 2:76.

59. Ibid., 2:71.

60. Feng Jianhui, "Using the Countryside to Encircle the Cities," *Zhongguo shehui kexue*, no. 2 (1980) 177–78; Agnes Smedley, *The Great Road: The Life and Times of Chu Teh* (New York: Monthly Review Press, 1956), p. 229; Warren Kuo, *Analytical History of the Chinese Communist Party* (Taipei: Institute of International Relations, 1966), 2:22–23; Mao Zedong, *Selected Works* (Beijing: Foreign Languages Press, 1975), 1:213.

61. Li Qun, "Fang Zhiminshi," in Zhu Chengjia, *Zhonggong dangshi yanjiu lunwenxuan*, 2:133.

62. Ibid.

63. Edgar Snow, *Red Star Over China* (New York: Random House, 1938), 158; Smedley, *The Great Road*, 229. The three rules were (1) obey orders, (2) take nothing from the poor peasantry, (3) turn in all confiscated goods. The eight points were (1) put back the doors taken down for bed boards, (2) put back straw used for bedding, (3) speak politely, (4) return borrowed articles, (5) replace damaged articles, (6) be honest in transactions with the peasantry, (7) pay for articles purchased, and (8) be sanitary. The eight points are summarized from *Red Star*, in which Mao notes that the last two points were added by Lin Biao. After Lin Biao's fall from grace, these were reduced to "Six Points."

64. Liang Qin, "Jinggangshan douzheng jingyan" (The Jinggang Mountains struggle experience), in Zhu Chengjia, *Zhonggong dangshi yanjiu lunwenxuan*, 2:121–22.
65. *Zhejiang Collection*, 2:69.
66 The same point is included in the Party Central's December 21, 1927, letter to Zhu De contained in Kuo, *Analytical History*, 1:478–79.
67. *Zhejiang Collection*, 2:72.

Chapter 10

1. A student at Sun Yat-sen University attending the congress identified the village as Zvenigorod. See Yüeh Sheng, *Sun Yat-sen University in Moscow and the Chinese Revolution: A Personal Account* (Lawrence: The University Press of Kansas, 1971), 193.
2. Ibid., 188; James P. Harrison, *The Long March to Power* (New York: Praeger Publishers, 1972), 156; Tian Fu and Wang Zhixin, "A Brief Review of the Chinese Communist Party's National Congresses," *Renmin Ribao* (August 30, 1982), in FBIS *Daily Report* (September 2, 1982), K14. Zhou Enlai who attended reported that there were seventy-five delegates who with staff members serving as observers totaled 112; see *Selected Works of Zhou Enlai* (Beijing: Foreign Languages Press, 1981), 1:207.
3. Two routes have been reported for the delegates traveling from China to the congress. Zhang Guotao reported journeying through the port city of Dairen and then moving on, presumably by rail, to Harbin, where he must have transferred to the trans-Manchurian section of the Chinese Eastern Railway. He noted entering Soviet Siberia through the border town of Manzhouli, which was the connecting point for the Soviet Siberian Railway system and the Chinese Eastern Railroad. Zhang related that the entire journey, from Shanghai to Moscow, took "about two weeks" to complete. See Chang Kuo-t'ao, *The Rise of the Chinese Communist Party, 1921–1927: An Autobiography of Chang Kuo-t'ao* (Lawrence: The University Press of Kansas, 1971), 2:68. Another account noted similar rail arrangements across Manchuria and the Soviet Union, but entailed initial sailing aboard unscheduled Russian commercial vessels between Shanghai and Vladivostok. See Yüeh Sheng, *Sun Yat-sen University*, 188.
4. Zhou Enlai, *Selected Works*, 1:208. Zhou claimed that Liu Shaoqi also did not attend. This is supported by Zhang Guotao's statement that after February 1928 he did not see Liu again until 1937 at Yan'an. Chang Kuo-t'ao, *Autobiography*, 2:58.
5. Zhang Guotao's dramatic but self-serving account details the quarreling and factionalism that he maintained permeated the proceedings. See Chang Kuo-t'ao, *Autobiography*, 2:68–84. Zhou Enlai's essay, delivered as a report to the Central Party School in Yan'an in March 1944, identifies key mistakes made at the congress while praising Mao Zedong for pursuing "correct" policies at the time of the congress. Zhou Enlai, *Selected Works*, 1:177–210.
6. Pavel Mif received administrative support from his protégé Chen Shaoyu (Wang Ming), who made some brief appearances at the congress and later in 1931 came to dominate the CCP along with the "Russian-returned students," or twenty-eight Bolsheviks (Internationalists).
7. This university was established in Moscow in April 1921. Sun Yat-sen University,

established in 1925, focused exclusively on training cadres for the Chinese revolution. See Yüeh Sheng, *Sun Yat-sen University*, 154–55.

8. Zhou Enlai, *Selected Works*, 1:208.

9. No definitive listing of Central Committee members and alternates yet exists. Wang Chien-min provided a partial listing that includes Xiang Zhongfa, Li Lisan, Zhou Enlai, Xiang Ying, Zhang Guotao, Qu Qiubai, Chen Yu, He Zhang, Yun Daiying, Mao Zedong, Luo Yiyuan, Quan Xiangying, Xu Xiken, Luo Zhanglong, Peng Pai, Xia Xi, Yang Pao'an, Zhang Kundi, Yu Fei, Shi Wenbing, Wang Kequan, Zhang Jinbao, Gu Shunzhang, Su Zhaozheng, Deng Zhongxia, Liu Changqun, Li Qi, and Shen Cemin. See Wang Chien-min, *Draft History of the Chinese Communist Party* (Taipei: 1965), 2:3. For another listing that adds Cai Hesen but excludes the last four names in the above list, see Warren Kuo, *Analytical History of the Chinese Communist Party* (Taipei: Institute of International Relations, 1966), 2:51. For still another listing, see Chang Kuo-t'ao, *Autobiography*, 2:81–82.

10. A brief account of the Sixth Congress in *Renmin Ribao* (August 30, 1982) noted that seven alternate Politburo members were elected but did not identify them. See FBIS *Daily Report* (September 2, 1982), K15.

11. Chen reportedly increased his isolation within Party circles by refusing the Comintern's invitation to attend the Sixth Congress. See Chang Kuo-t'ao, *Autobiography*, 2:65–67.

12. Li was criticized at the congress for alleged cowardly behavior during the Hunan Autumn Harvest Uprisings and elected only to alternate membership on the Central Committee. However, reportedly with Qu Qiubai's support, he soon took over Party organizational work. See Donald W. Klein and Anne B. Clark, *Biographic Dictionary of Chinese Communism, 1921–1965* (Cambridge, Mass.: Harvard University Press, 1971), 1:536.

13. Harrison, *The Long March to Power*, 157.

14. Chang Kuo-t'ao, *Autobiography*, 2:77–78; Klein and Clark, *Biographic Dictionary*, 1:319. Zhou Enlai claimed Mif used Xiang "as a mouthpiece," *Selected Works*, 1:207.

15. Chang Kuo-t'ao, *Autobiography*, 2:77.

16. Ibid.; Zhou Enlai, *Selected Works*, 1:207.

17. Li Yu-ning, "A Biography of Ch'ü Ch'iu-pai: From Youth to Party Leadership (1899–1928)" (Ph.D. dissertation, Columbia University, 1967), 193–94.

18. This key document used throughout this book is found in *Chinese Studies in History* (Fall 1971), 4–72.

19. Bukharin's speech was published in Chinese in book form in April 1929 (publication place unknown). It was translated in two parts: "The Chinese Revolution and the Tasks of the Chinese Communists—An International Delegate's Political Report to the Sixth Congress of the Chinese [Communist] Party," part 1, in *Chinese Studies in History* 3, no. 4 (Summer 1970), 261–324, and part 2, in ibid. 4, no. 1 (Fall 1970), 4–28. Journal Editor Li Yuning explained that the Chinese book omitted authorship, but, through corroborative materials and interviews, she was persuaded that Bukharin was the author.

20. Ibid., 3:324.

21. Ibid.

22. Ibid., 4:8.

23. Zhou Enlai, *Selected Works*, 1:206.

24. *Chinese Studies in History* 4 (Fall 1970), 20.

25. Ibid., 26.

26. Ibid., 27.

27. A Central Notice entitled "On the Current Situation," dated June 21, 1928, stressed developing the anti-imperialist movement and using it both to revive the urban movement and to direct it against the KMT. It included instructions and a set of demands for carrying out this urban program, noting that four notices had been issued previously on this area of Communist work. See Hyobom Pak, ed. and trans., *Documents of the Chinese Communist Party, 1927–30* (Hong Kong: Union Research Institute, 1971), 447–58.

28. The English language text of the "Political Resolution [of the Sixth National Congress of the CCP]" is contained in Conrad Brandt, Benjamin Schwartz, and John K. Fairbank, eds., *A Documentary History of Chinese Communism*) Cambridge, Mass.: Harvard University Press, 1952), 127–55. An original handwritten text, with introductory notations in Russian, is contained in *Zhongguo gongchandang di liuci daibiao dahui jueyian* (Resolutions of the Sixth Party Congress of the CCP), Moscow, 1928, in the Library of Congress, Washington, D.C. This collection includes nine resolutions produced at this congress. See *Zhengzhi jueyian* (The Political Resolution), resolution no. 1.

29. Zhou Enlai, *Selected Works*, 1:207. Zhou claimed that Pavel Mif's role in preparing the resolutions "was not very significant."

30. Chang Kuo-t'ao, *Autobiography*, 2:78.

31. This "Resolution on the Matter of Organizing Soviet Political Power" (Suweiai zhengzhide zuzhi wenti jueyian) is resolution no. 8, contained in *Zhongguo gongchandang di liuci daibiao dahui jueyian*, 102–26.

32. Zhou Enlai, *Selected Works*, 1:205.

33. Resolution no. 8, *Zhongguo gongchandang di liuci daibiao dahui jueyian*, 13.

34. Ibid., 16.

35. Ibid., 19.

36. Ibid., 21–22.

37. Chang Kuo-t'ao, *Autobiography*, 2:80.

38. Zhou Enlai, *Selected Works*, 1:201–2.

39. The text of this resolution is found in *Chinese Studies in History* 4, no. 4 (Summer 1971), 204–12.

40. The resolution states that the Central Military Department of the CCP Central Committee provides policy guidance to Military Affairs Committees attached to each level of the Party structure. At the same time, and in seeming contradiction to the above, the Red Army was directed to "obey in everything, the order, and direction of the highest level soviet regime in its region." With a soviet in one region and a Party's provincial headquarters in another, this was bound to breed future tension and confusion. See ibid., 212.

41. Ibid., 211.

42. The English text of this "Resolution of the Sixth National Congress (of the CCP) on the

Peasant Movement" is contained in Brandt, Schwartz, Fairbank, *Documentary History*, 156–65; see also resolution no. 2, *Zhongguo gongchandang di liuci daibiao dahui jueyian*.

43. Brandt, Schwartz, Fairbank, *Documentary History*, 163; *Zhejiang Collection*, 2:70.

44. Qu Qiubai, "The Question of Armed Insurrection," *Bu-er-se-wei-ke* (Bolshevik), no. 10 (December 19, 1927), 294–97.

45. "Resolution on the Land Question" (Tudi wenti jueyian), resolution no. 3, *Zhongguo gongchandang di liuci daibiao dahui jueyian*.

46. Ibid., resolution no. 3, 14.

47. "Draft Resolution on CCP Organization" (Guanyu gongchandang zuzhi jueyian caoyi), ibid., resolution no. 9.

48. Ibid., 2.

49. This constitution is contained as an appendix to Paul Linebarger, *The China of Chiang K'ai-shek: A Political Study* (Boston: World Peace Foundation, 1943), 359–70. See also Wang Chien-min, *Draft History*, 2:28–37.

50. *Zhejiang Collection*, 1:1–12.

51. "Current Propaganda Work" (Suanchuan gongcuo muqian renwu), resolution no. 7, *Zhongguo gongchandang di liuci daibiao jueyian*.

52. "Resolution on the Trade Union Movement" (Zhigong yundong jueyian), resolution no. 4, ibid. Also resolutions were produced to guide the women's movement and the Communist Youth Movement, resolutions no. 5 and 6, ibid.

53. Chang Kuo-t'ao, *Autobiography*, 2:83.

54. At the Comintern Congress Qu participated in the discussions concerning the colonial question and during the next two years published several contributions on this subject under his Russian pseudonym, Strakhov, in the international Communist press. In one key speech he emphasized the predominant role to be played by the peasantry in carrying the struggle forward in the peasant-populated "colonies" of the world's "rural districts." See "Concluding Speech by Comrade Strakhov," *International Press Correspondence* (Vienna) 8, no. 78, "Special Issue on the Sixth Congress of the Communist International" (November 8, 1928), 1476.

55. Liang Qin, "Jinggang shan douzheng jingyan yu Xiang-E-Xi suqude jianli," in Zhu Chengjia, ed., *Zhonggong dangshi yanjiu lunwenxuan* (Changsha: Hunan renmin chubanshe, 1983), 2:120.

56. Harrison, *The Long March to Power*, 174; Ilpyong J. Kim, *The Politics of Chinese Communism: Kiangsi Under the Soviets* (Berkeley: University of California Press, 1973), 188.

57. Kim, *The Politics of Chinese Communism*, 116–17.

58. Ibid., 106.

59. Benjamin Yang, "The Zunyi Conference as One Step in Mao's Rise to Power: A Survey of Historical Studies of the Chinese Communist Party," *The China Quarterly*, no. 106 (June 1986), 239.

Bibliography

Akimova, Vera Vladimirovna (Vishnyakova). *Two Years in Revolutionary China, 1925–1927*. Translated by Steven I. Levine. Cambridge, Mass.: East Asian Research Center, Harvard University Press, 1971.

Ash, R. "Land Tenure in Pre-Revolutionary China: Kiangsu Province in the 1920s and 1930s." *Research Notes and Studies* (School of Oriental and African Studies, University of London), no. 1 (1976).

Barret, David P., ed. "Post-Mao Reevaluations of the Early CCP Leadership." *Chinese Law and Government* 17, no. 1–2 (Spring–Summer 1984).

Baruch Knei-paz. *The Social and Political Thought of Leon Trotsky*. Oxford: Oxford University Press, 1978.

Belden, Jack. *China Shakes the World*. New York: Harper, 1949.

Bianco, Lucien. *Origins of the Chinese Revolution*. Translated by Muriel Bell. Stanford: Stanford University Press, 1971.

Bing, Dov. "Sneevliet and the Early Years of the CCP." *The China Quarterly*, no. 48 (October–December 1971).

Boorman, Howard L., and Richard C. Howard, eds. *Biographical Dictionary of Republican China*. 4 vols. Vol. 5, *A Personal Name Index*. Compiled by Janet Krompart. New York: Columbia University Press, 1967.

Brandt, Conrad. *Stalin's Failure in China, 1924–1927*. Cambridge, Mass.: Harvard University Press, 1958.

Brandt, Conrad, Benjamin Schwartz, and John K. Fairbank, eds. *A Documentary History of Chinese Communism*. Cambridge, Mass.: Harvard University Press, 1952.

Braun, Otto. *A Comintern Agent in China, 1932–1939*. Translated by Jeanne Moore. Stanford: Stanford University Press, 1982.

Bu-er-se-wei-ke (Bolshevik) (Shanghai) (October 1927–February 1928). Library of Congress, Washington, D.C.

"Bu-er-se-wei-ke zhuyi wansui" (Long live Bolshevism!). *Bolshevik*, no. 6 (November 28, 1927).

Bukharin, Nikolai. "An Abrupt Turn in the Chinese Revolution," *International Press Correspondence* 7, nos. 41–42 (July 14–21, 1927).

———. "Reply to Ch'u." *International Press Correspondence* (Vienna) 8, no. 50 (August 16, 1928).

————. "The Revolution in Colonial and Semicolonial Countries." *International Press Correspondence* (Vienna) 8, no. 41 (July 30, 1928).

Cai Hesen. "Jihui zhuyishi" (History of opportunism). *Gongfei huoguo shiliao huibian* (Documents on the Communists' destruction of the nation). Vol. 1. Taipei, 1961, 578–608.

Cai Kangzhi and Zhao Qingqu. "E-Yu-Wan suqu gongnong wuzhuang geju wenti chutan" (Preliminary exploration of the question of the E-Yu-Wan soviet district armed independent regime of workers and peasants). Reprinted from *Zhongzhou xuekan*, no. 2 (1981), in *Zhonggong dangshi yanjiu lunwenxuan*, edited by Zhu Chengjia. 3 vols. Changsha: Hunan renmin chubanshe, 1983–84.

Cai Luo and Liu Linsong. "Comrade Peng Pai's Contribution to the Theory of the Peasant Movement." *Renmin Ribao* (20 October 1981). Translated in JPRS 79635, *China Report*, no. 245 (10 December 1981).

Caute, David, ed. *Essential Writings of Karl Marx*. New York: Collier Books, 1967.

Chan, F. Gilbert, and Thomas Etzold, eds. *China in the 1920s: Nationalism and Revolution*. New York: New Viewpoints, 1976.

Chan, Ming K. *Historiography of the Chinese Labor Movement, 1895–1949*. Stanford: Hoover Institution Press, 1981.

Chang Kuo-t'ao. *The Rise of the Chinese Communist Party, 1921–1927: An Autobiography of Chang Kuo-t'ao*. 2 vols. Lawrence: The University Press of Kansas, 1971.

Chao Kuo-chun. *Agrarian Policy of the Chinese Communist Party, 1921–1959*. Bombay: Asia Publications House, 1960.

Chapman, Herbert O. *The Chinese Revolution, 1926–1927*. Westport, Conn.: Hyperion Press, 1977.

Chen Gongbo (Ch'en Kung-po). *Ku xiao lu* (Bitter smile: memoirs of Chen Gongbo, 1925–1936), translated by N. Lee et al. University of Hong Kong Center of Asian Studies. Occasional Papers and Monographs, no. 36, 1979.

Ch'en, Jerome. *Mao and The Chinese Revolution*. London: Oxford University Press, 1965.

Ch'en Kung-po. *The Communist Movement in China*, edited by C. Martin Wilbur. Reproduced for private distribution by the East Asian Institute of Columbia University, September 1960.

Ch'en Po-ta. *Notes on Ten Years of Civil War (1927–1936)*. Westport, Conn.: Hyperion Press, 1977.

Ch'en Shao-yu. *Lenin, Leninism and the Chinese Revolution*. Moscow: Novosti Press Agency Publishing House, 1970.

Ch'en Tu-hsiu. "Letter to All Comrades of the Party." *Chinese Studies in History* 3, no. 3 (Spring 1970).

Cherepanov, A. I. *As Military Advisor to China*. Moscow: Progress Publishers, 1982.

Chesneaux, Jean. *Le mouvement ouvrier Chinois de 1919 à 1927*. Paris: Mouton, 1962.

Chesneaux, Jean. *Le movement paysan Chinois*. Paris: Editions du Seuil, 1976.

China Year Book, 1925. Edited by H. G. W. Woodhead. Tientsin: Tientsin Press, n.d.

Chinese Workers' Correspondence, no. 3 (October 1933).

Chow Tse-tsung. *The May Fourth Movement: Intellectual Revolution in Modern China*. Stanford: Stanford University Press, 1967.

Cohen, Steven F. *Bukharin and the Bolshevik Revolution: A Political Biography, 1888–1938*. New York: Alfred A. Knopf, 1973.

Day, M. Henri. *Mao Zedong 1917–1927: Documents*. Orientaliska Studier, no. 14, Stockholm, 1975.

Degras, Jane. *Communist International, 1919–1943: Documents*. 3 vols. London: Frank Cass, 1956–1971.

Deliusin, L. P. "From the August Conference to the Kwangchow Uprising (August–December 1927)." *Chinese Studies in History* (Summer 1974).

————. "The Sixth Congress of the Chinese Communist Party and Its Agrarian-Peasant Program." *Chinese Studies in History* (Spring 1975).

d'Encausse, Hélène Carrère, and Stuart R. Schram. *Marxism and Asia: An Introduction with Readings*. London: Allen Lane, The Penguin Press, 1969.

Deutscher, Isaac. *The Prophet Unarmed: Trotsky: 1921–1929*. London: Oxford University Press, 1959.

Ding Ling. "Wo suo renshide Qu Qiubai tongzhi" (The Qu Qiubai that I remember). *Xinhua yuebao*, no. 5 (1980).

Dirlik, Arif. "The Predicament of Marxist Revolutionary Consciousness: Mao Zedong, Antonio Gramsci and the Reformulation of Marxist Revolutionary Theory." *Modern China* 9, no. 2 (April 1983).

————. *Revolution and History: Origins of Marxist Historiography in China, 1919–1937*. Berkeley: University of California Press, 1978.

Donovan, Peter, Carl E. Dorris, and Lawrence R. Sullivan. *Chinese Communist Materials at the Bureau of Investigation Archives, Taiwan*. Michigan Papers in Chinese Studies, no. 24, 1976.

Dorris, Carl E. "Peasant Mobilization in North China and the Origins of Yenan Communism." *The China Quarterly*, no. 68 (October–December 1976).

Drachkovitch, Milorad M., and Branko Lazitch, eds. *The Comintern: Historical Highlights, Essays, Recollections, Documents*. Stanford: Hoover Institution Press, 1966.

Eastman, Lloyd E. *The Abortive Revolution: China Under Nationalist Rule, 1927–1937*. Cambridge, Mass.: Harvard University Press, 1974.

Easton, Loyd D., and Kurt H. Guddat, eds. and trans. *Writings of the Young Marx on Philosophy and Society*. Garden City, N.Y.: Doubleday, 1967.

Emerson, Rupert. *From Empire to Nation*. Cambridge, Mass.: Harvard University Press, 1960.

Esherick, Joseph W. *Reform and Revolution in China: The 1911 Revolution in Hunan and Hubei*. Berkeley: University of California Press, 1975.

Eto Shinkichi. "Hai-lu-feng—The First Chinese Soviet Government." Parts 1, 2. *The China Quarterly*, no. 8 (October–December 1961); no. 9 (January–March 1962).

Eudin, Xenia J., and Robert C. North. *Soviet Russia and the East, 1920–1927: A Documentary Survey*. Stanford: Stanford University Press, 1957.

Eudin, Xenia J., and Robert Slusser, eds. *Soviet Foreign Policy, 1928–1934: Documents and Materials*. University Park: Pennsylvania State University Press, 1966.

Evans, Les, and Russell Block, eds. *Leon Trotsky on China: Introduction by P'eng Shu-tse*. New York: Monad Press, 1976.

Feng Jianhui. "Wo dang kaichuang nongcun baowei chengshi daolude lishi kaocha (A historical review of how our party initiated the path of encircling the cities from the countryside). *Zhongguo shehui kexue*, no. 2 (1980).

Feng Jianhui and Sun Xiangzhu. "Congci fengleibian jiugai—jinian Nanchang qiyi wushizhounian" (From here on, wind and thunder spread to all parts of the world—in commemoration of the 50th anniversary of the Nanchang Uprising). Reprinted from *Lishi yanjiu*, no. 4 (1977), in *Zhonggong dangshi yanjiu lunwenxuan*, edited by Zhu Chengjia. 3 vols. Changsha: Hunan renmin chubanshe, 1983–84.

Fogel, Joshua, and William Rowe, eds. *Perspectives on a Changing China: Essays in Honor of C. Martin Wilbur*. Boulder, Colo.: Westview Press, 1979.

Fokin, N. "In Memory of the Organizer of the Canton Rising—Comrade Chang T'ai-lei." *Communist International* (March 15, 1929).

Fountain, Kevin, ed. "Ch'en Tu-hsiu: Lifetime Oppositionist." *Chinese Law and Government* 12:3 (Fall 1979).

Funnell, Victor. "The Chinese Communist Youth Movement, 1949–1966." *The China Quarterly*, no. 42 (April–June 1970).

Galbiati, Fernando. *P'eng P'ai and the Hai-lu-feng Soviet*. Stanford: Stanford University Press, 1985.

Gillin, Donald G. *Warlord: Yen Hsi-shan in Shansi Province, 1911–1949*. Princeton: Princeton University Press, 1967.

Gittings, John. *The Role of the Chinese Army*. New York: Oxford University Press, 1967.

Gong Chu. "Canjia Zhonggong wuzhuang douzheng zhishi" (A record of my participation in the Chinese Communist armed struggles). *Mingbao* (Hong Kong) (March 1971–February 1974).

———. *Wo yu hongjun* (I and the Red Army). Hong Kong, 1954.

"A Great Historical Undertaking—In Commemoration of the 50th Anniversary of the Nanchang Uprising." *Selections from PRC Magazines*, nos. 940–41, (September 7–16, 1977).

Griffin, Patricia E. *The Chinese Communist Treatment of Counterrevolutionaries: 1924–1949*. Princeton: Princeton University Press, 1976.

Griffith, Samuel B. *The Chinese People's Liberation Army*. New York: McGraw-Hill, 1967.

Grigoriev, A. M. "An Important Landmark in the History of the Chinese Communist Party." *Chinese Studies in History* 5, no. 3 (Spring 1975).

Guillermaz, Jacques. *A History of the Chinese Communist Party, 1921–1949*. Translated by Anne Destenay. New York: Random House, 1972.

———. "The Nanchang Uprising." *The China Quarterly*, no. 11 (July–September 1962).

Guo Dehong. "The Development of the Land Policy of the Chinese Communist Party During the Second Revolutionary Civil War Period (1927–1937)." *Social Sciences in China*, no. 1 (1981).

Han Taihua. "Guanyu dageming shibaihou wo dang fangqi Guomindang qizhi wenti" (Concerning the question of our Party's abandoning the KMT banner after the failure of the Great Revolution). Reprinted from *Qiluxuekan*, no. 5 (1981), in *Zhonggong dangshi yanjiu lunwenxuan*, edited by Zhu Chengjia. 3 vols. Changsha: Hunan renmin chubanshe, 1983–84.

Harrison, James P. *The Communist and Chinese Peasant Rebellions*. New York: Atheneum Press, 1969.

––––––. "The Li Li-san Line and the CCP in 1930." Parts 1, 2. *The China Quarterly*, no. 14 (April–June 1963); no. 15 (July–September 1963).

––––––. *The Long March to Power*. New York: Praeger Publishers, 1972.

He Ganzhi. *Zhongguo xiandai gemingshi* (A history of the modern Chinese revolution). Beijing, 1959.

Hinton, William. *Fanshen: A Documentary of Revolution in a Chinese Village*. New York: Vintage Books, 1968.

Hofheinz, Roy M., Jr. "The Autumn Harvest Insurrection." *The China Quarterly*, no. 32 (October–December 1967).

––––––. *The Broken Wave: The Chinese Communist Peasant Movement, 1922–28*. Cambridge, Mass.: Harvard University Press, 1977.

––––––. "The Ecology of Chinese Communist Success: Rural Influence Patterns, 1923–1945." *Chinese Communist Politics in Action*. Edited by A. Doak Barnett. Seattle: University of Washington Press, 1969.

Holubnychy, Lydia. *Michael Borodin and the Chinese Revolution, 1923–25*. Ann Arbor: Published for East Asian Institute, Columbia University, by University Microfilms International, 1979.

Hongqi piaopiao. 16 vols. Beijing: Zhongguo qingnian chubanshe, 1957 and following.

Hoover Institution Archives. Jay Calvin Huston Collection. "The Chinese Communist Party and Its Activities in Shanghai"; "The Shanghai Youths Anti-Imperialistic League of the Chinese Communist Party." Shanghai, 1929.

Hsia, T. A. "Ch'ü Ch'iu-pai's Autobiographical Writings: The Making and Destruction of a 'Tender-hearted' Communist." *The China Quarterly*, no. 25 (January–March 1966).

––––––. *The Gate of Darkness: Studies on the Leftist Literary Movement in China*. Seattle: University of Washington Press, 1968.

Hsiao Tso-liang. "Chinese Communism and the Canton Soviet of 1927." *The China Quarterly*, no. 30 (April–June 1967).

––––––. *Chinese Communism in 1927: City vs. Countryside*. Hong Kong: Chinese University of Hong Kong, 1970.

––––––. "The Dispute over a Wuhan Insurrection in 1927." *The China Quarterly*, no. 33 (January–March 1968).

––––––. *Power Relations Within the Chinese Communist Movement, 1930–1934*. Seattle: University of Washington Press, 1961.

Hsu Kai-yu. *Chou En-lai: China's Gray Eminence*. Garden City, N.Y.: Doubleday, 1968.

Hsüeh Chün-tu and Robert C. North, trans. "The Founding of the Chinese Red Army." In *Contemporary China*, edited by E. S. Kirby. Vol. 4. Hong Kong, 1962–64.

Hu Chi-hsi. *Bibliographie annotée des principaux articles et documents parus dans les périodiques de la République Soviétique Chinoise du Jiangxi, 1931–1934*. The Hague: Mouton, 1971–72.

Hu Chiao-mu. *Thirty Years of the Communist Party of China*. Peking: Foreign Languages Press, 1952.

Hu Hua, ed. *Zhonggong dangshi renwu zhuan* (Biographies of leading figures in Chinese

Communist Party history). 10 vols. Xi'an: Shaanxi renmin chubanshe, 1980.

Hua Ying-shen, ed. *Zhongguo gongchandang lieshizhuan* (Biographies of Chinese Communist Party martyrs). Hong Kong, 1949.

Huang, Dao. *Zhongguo renmin jiefangjun di sanshi nian* (Thirty years of the Chinese People's Liberation Army). Vol. 2. Beijing: Renmin chubanshe, 1958.

Huang, Philip C. "Mao Tse-tung and the Middle Peasants, 1925–1928." *Modern China* 1, no. 3 (July 1975).

Huang, Philip C. C., Lynda Schaeffer Bell, and Kathy Lemons Walker. *Chinese Communist and Rural Society, 1927–34.* Chinese Research Monograph no. 13. Berkeley: University of California, 1978.

Hunansheng zhexue shehui kexue yanjiu suo xiandai shizu (Modern history group of the Hunan Provincial Philosophy and Social Sciences Research Institute). "Qiushou qiyi he Jinggang shan jinjun" (The Autumn Harvest Uprising and the march toward the Jinggang Mountains). Reprinted from *Lishi yanjiu*, no. 4 (1977), in *Zhonggong dangshi yanjiu lunwenxuan*, edited by Zhu Chengjia. 3 vols. Changsha: Hunan renmin chubanshe, 1983–84.

Hung Mao-tien. *Government and Politics in KMT China, 1927–1937.* Stanford: Stanford University Press, 1972.

Huston Report. In Jay Calvin Huston Collection, Hoover Institution Archives, Stanford University.

"Important Excerpts from Communist Evidence." 3 vols. Procurator's Office of the Zhejiang High Court, comp., n.p., n.d. In the *Zhejiang Collection*, Shanghai Municipal Police Files. Record Group 263. Shanghai Municipal Police Document no. 4772. National Archives, Washington, D.C.

Isaacs, Harold R. "Five Years of Kuomintang Reaction." *China Forum*. Shanghai, May 1932.

————. *The Tragedy of the Chinese Revolution.* Stanford: Stanford University Press, 1961.

Israel, John. *Student Nationalism in China, 1927–1937.* Stanford: Stanford University Press, 1966.

Israel, John, and Donald Klein. *Rebels and Bureaucrats: China's December Niners.* Berkeley: University of California Press, 1976.

Jacobs, Daniel N. *Borodin: Stalin's Man in China.* Cambridge, Mass.: Harvard University Press, 1981.

Jin Zaiji. "Shilun baqi huiyi dao 'liuda' de gongzuo zhuanbian" (My view of the changes in work from the August Seventh Meeting in 1927 to the Sixth Chinese Communist Party Congress in 1928). *Lishi yanjiu* (Historical research), no. 1, 1983.

Johnson, Chalmers. *Peasant Nationalism and Communist Power.* Stanford: Stanford University Press, 1962.

Jordan, Donald A. *The Northern Expedition: China's National Revolution of 1926–1928.* Honolulu: The University Press of Hawaii, 1976.

Kau Ying-mao. "Urban and Rural Strategies in the Chinese Communist Revolution." In *Peasant Rebellion and Communist Revolution in Asia*, edited by John Wilson Lewis. Stanford: Stanford University Press, 1974.

Kiang Wen-han. *The Chinese Student Movement.* New York: King's Crown Press, 1948.

Kim, Ilpyong J. "Mass Mobilization Policies and Techniques Developed in the Period of the Chinese Soviet Republic." In *Chinese Communist Politics in Action*, edited by A. Doak Barnett. Seattle: University of Washington Press, 1969.

———. "The Origins of Communist and Soviet Movements in China." In *China at the Crossroads: Nationalists and Communists, 1927–1949*, edited by F. Gilbert Chan. Boulder, Colo.: Westview Press, 1980.

———. *The Politics of Chinese Communism: Kiangsi Under the Soviets*. Berkeley: University of California Press, 1973.

Klein, Donald W., and Anne B. Clark. *Biographic Dictionary of Chinese Communism, 1921–1965*. Cambridge, Mass.: Harvard University Press, 1971.

Kuo, Thomas. *Ch'en Tu-hsiu (1879–1942) and the Chinese Communist Movement*. South Orange, N.J.: Seton Hall University Press, 1975.

Kuo, Warren. *Analytical History of the Chinese Communist Party*. 4 vols. Taipei: Institute of International Relations, 1966.

Lary, Diana. *Region and Nation: The Kwangsi Clique in Chinese Politics, 1925–1937*. London: Cambridge University Press, 1974.

Lazitch, Branko, and Milorad M. Drachkovitch. *Biographical Dictionary of the Comintern*. Stanford: Hoover Institution Press, 1973.

———. *Lenin and the Comintern*. Vol. 1. Stanford: Hoover Institution Press, 1972.

Lee Feigon. *Chen Duxiu: Founder of the Chinese Communist Party*. Princeton: Princeton University Press, 1983.

Lenin, V. I. *The Young Generation*. New York: International Publishers, 1940.

Li Ch'ang. "Recollections of the National Liberation Vanguard of China." Parts 1, 2. *Survey of China Mainland Magazines*, no. 296 (15 January 1962); no. 297 (22 January 1962).

Li Chien-nung. *The Political History of China 1840–1928*. Translated and edited by Ssu-yu Teng and Jeremy Ingalls. New York: Van Nostrand, 1956.

Li Jui. *The Early Revolutionary Activities of Comrade Mao Tse-tung*. White Plains, N.Y.: M. E. Sharpe, 1977.

Li Peicheng and Liu Menghua. "Pingjiang qiyi" (Pingjiang Uprising). Reprinted from *Lishi yanjiu*, no. 2 (1979), in *Zhonggong dangshi yanjiu lunwenxuan*, edited by Zhu Chengjia. 3 vols. Changsha: Hunan renmin chubanshe, 1983.

Li Qun. "Cong Yiheng baodong kan Fang Zhiminshi gongnong wuzhuang geju daolude xingcheng" (Based on the Yiheng Uprising, examination of the emergence of the process of establishing an armed independent regime of workers and peasants in the style of Fang Zhimin). Reprinted from *Dangshi yanjiu*, no. 3 (1980), in *Zhonggong dangshi yanjiu lunwenxuan*, edited by Zhu Chengjia. 3 vols. Changsha: Hunan renmin chubanshe, 1983.

Li T'ien-min. *Chou En-lai*. Taipei: Institute of International Relations, 1970.

Li Wei-han. "A Retrospective Study of Qu Qiubai's 'Left' Adventurism." *Social Sciences in China*, no. 3 (September 1983).

Li Yu-ning (Bernadette). "A Biography of Ch'ü Ch'iu-pai: From Youth to Party Leadership (1899–1928)." Ph.D. dissertation, Columbia University, 1967.

———. *The Introduction of Socialism into China*. Occasional Papers of the East Asian Institute. Columbia University Press, 1971.

262 China's Art of Revolution

Li Yu-ning and Gasster, Michael. "Ch'ü Ch'iu-pai's Journey to Russia, 1920–1922." *Monumenta Serica*, no. 29 (1970–71).

Liang Qin. "Jinggang shan douzheng jingyan yu Xiang-E-Xi suqude jianli" (The Jinggang Mountains struggle experience and the establishment of the Xiang-E-Xi Soviet District). Reprinted from *Huazhong shifan xueyuan xuebao*, no. 3 (1980), in *Zhonggong dangshi yanjiu lunwenxuan*, edited by Zhu Chengjia. 3 vols. Changsha: Hunan renmin chubanshe, 1983–84.

Liao Gailong. "The Chinese People Will Always Remember Him—in Commemoration of Cai Hesen, Brilliant Leader in the Early Period of Our Party." *Renmin Ribao* (December 3, 1981). Translated in JPRS 79777, *China Report*, no. 254 (January 4, 1982).

Lin Yu-sheng. *The Crisis of Chinese Consciousness: Radical Antitraditionalism in the May Fourth Era*. Madison: University of Wisconsin Press, 1979.

Linebarger, Paul. *The China of Chiang Kai-shek: A Political Study*. Boston: World Peace Foundation, 1943.

Liu, F. F. *A Military History of Modern China 1924–1949*. Princeton: Princeton University Press, 1956.

Liu Yitao. "Mao Zedong tongzhi yu Xiang-Gan bian qiushou qiyi" (Comrade Mao Zedong and the Autumn Harvest Uprising on the Hunan-Jiangxi Border). Reprinted from *Dangshi yanjiu*, no. 5 (1981), in *Zhonggong dangshi yanjiu lunwenxuan*, edited by Zhu Chengjia. 3 vols. Changsha: Hunan renmin chubanshe, 1983–84.

Lominadze, B. "Historical Significance of the Canton Rising." *Communist International* (15 January 1928).

———. "Speech to the Congress" (Sixth Comintern Congress). *Chinese Studies in History* 4, no. 4 (Summer 1971).

Lotveit, Trygve. *Chinese Communism 1931–1934: Experience in Civil Government*. Lund: Studentlitteratur, 1973.

McColl, Robert C. "The Oyüwan Soviet Area, 1927–1932." *The Journal of Asian Studies* 27, no. 1 (November 1967).

McDonald, Angus W. *The Urban Origins of Rural Revolution: Elites and the Masses in Hunan Province, China, 1911–1927*. Berkeley: University of California Press, 1978.

McLane, Charles. *Soviet Policy and the Chinese Communists, 1931–1946*. New York: Columbia University Press, 1958.

Mao Dun. "Huiyi Qu Qiubai." Transcribed from *Hongqi*, no. 6 (1980), in *Dongxi fang* (East and west), no. 17 (May 10, 1980).

Mao Zedong. *Selected Works*. Peking: Foreign Languages Press, 1975.

Marks, Robert B. *Rural Revolution in South China*. Madison: University of Wisconsin Press, 1984.

Marx, Karl. *The German Ideology*. London: Lawrence and Wishart, 1970.

Marx, Karl, and Frederick Engels. *Selected Works*. 3 vols. Moscow: Progress Publishers, 1970.

Meisner, Maurice. "Leninism and Maoism: Some Perspectives on Marxism-Leninism in China." *The China Quarterly*, no. 45 (January–March 1971).

———. *Li Ta-chao and the Origins of Chinese Marxism*. Cambridge, Mass.: Harvard University Press, 1967.

Miao Min. *Fang Chih-min: Revolutionary Fighter*. Peking: Foreign Languages Press, 1962.

Mif, Pavel. *Heroic China: Fifteen Years of the Communist Party of China*. New York: Workers Library Publishers, 1937.

Myers, Ramon H. *The Chinese Peasant Economy*. Cambridge, Mass.: Harvard University Press, 1970.

Nie Rongzhen. "The Nanchang Uprising: Memoirs." *Renmin Ribao* (July 27, 1983). Translated in JPRS 84202, *China Report*, no. 451 (August 25, 1983).

North, Robert C. *Kuomintang and Chinese Communist Elites*. Stanford: Stanford University Press, 1952.

———. *Moscow and Chinese Communists*. Stanford: Stanford University Press, 1953.

North, Robert C., and Xenia J. Eudin. *M. N. Roy's Mission to China*. Berkeley: University of California Press, 1963.

Pak, Hyobom, ed. and trans. *Documents of the Chinese Communist Party, 1927–30*. Hong Kong: Union Research Institute, 1971.

Pang Yong-pil. "Peng Pai: From Landlord to Revolutionary." *Modern China*, no. 1 (1975).

Peng Dehuai zishu (Peng Dehuai's memoirs). Beijing: Renmin chubanshe, 1981.

Peng Pai. *Seeds of Peasant Revolt: Report on the Haifeng County Peasant Movement*. Translated by D. Holoch. East Asia Papers no. 1. Ithaca, N.Y.: Cornell University Press, 1973.

Peng Pai zhuanlue (Short biography of Peng Pai). Guangzhou, 1980.

P'eng Shu-tse. *The Chinese Communist Party in Power*. New York: Monad Press, 1980.

Perry, Elizabeth. *Rebels and Revolutionaries in North China, 1845–1945*. Stanford: Stanford University Press, 1980.

Pi Mingxiu. "Guanyu 'baqi' huiyide jige wenti" (Several questions concerning the August 7 meeting). Reprinted from *Jindaishi yanjiu*, no. 4 (1980), in *Zhonggong dangshi yanjiu lunwenxuan*, edited by Zhu Chengjia. 3 vols. Changsha: Hunan renmin chubanshe, 1983–84.

Pickowicz, Paul G. "Ch'ü Ch'iu-pai's Critique of the May Fourth Generation: Early Chinese Marxist Literary Criticism." In *Modern Chinese Literature in the May Fourth Era*, edited by Merle Goldman. Cambridge, Mass.: Harvard University Press, 1977.

Pringsheim, Klaus H. "The Functions of the Chinese Communist Youth Leagues, 1920–1949." *The China Quarterly*, no. 12 (October–December 1962).

Protokoll des II Weltkongresses. Reprint. 8 vols. Milano: Fetrinelli, 1967.

Qian Feng and Liu Qifa. "The Problem of Leadership in the Chinese Revolution in the Period 1924–27." *Social Sciences in China*, no. 4 (1980).

Qu Qiubai (Ch'ü Ch'iu-pai). "An Appraisal of the Past and Strategy for the Present." *International Press Correspondence* (Vienna) 8, no. 68 (October 4, 1928).

———. "Comment on the Comintern Theses." *International Press Correspondence* (Vienna) 8, no. 49 (August 13, 1928).

———. "Concluding Speech by Comrade Strakhov (Ch'ü Ch'iu-pai)." *International Press Correspondence* (Vienna) 8, no. 78, "Special Issue on the Sixth Congress of the Communist International" (November 8, 1928).

———. *Minquan zhuyi yu suweiai zhidu* (Democracy and the soviet system). *Bolshevik*, no. 15, 1928.

————. "The Past and Future of the Chinese Communist Party." *Chinese Studies in History* 5, no. 1 (Fall 1971).

————. "Wuzhuang baodong de wenti" (The question of armed insurrection). *Bolshevik*, no. 10 (December 19, 1927).

————. "Zhongguo geming shi shenmeyang de geming" (What kind of revolution is the Chinese revolution?). *Bolshevik*, no. 5 (November 21, 1927).

————. "Zhongguo geming yu gongchandang" (The Chinese revolution and the Communist Party). Moscow, 1928.

"Resolution of the ECCI on the Present Situation of the Chinese Revolution." *International Press Correspondence* (Vienna) (July 28, 1927).

Rigby, Richard W. *The May 30 Movement: Events and Themes*. Folkestone, Kent: Dawson Publishing, 1980.

Rosenberg, William G., and Marilyn B. Young. *Transforming Russia and China: Revolutionary Struggle in the Twentieth Century*. New York: Oxford University Press, 1982.

Roy, M. N. *My Experiences in China*. Bombay: Renaissance Publishing Co., 1938.

————. *Revolution and Counter-Revolution in China*. Westport, Conn.: Hyperion Press, 1973.

Rue, John. *Mao Tse-tung in Opposition 1927–35*. Stanford: Stanford University Press, 1966.

Schram, Stuart R. *Mao Tse-tung: A Political Biography*. New York: Simon and Schuster, 1966.

————. "Mao Tse-tung and the Theory of the Permanent Revolution, 1958–69." *The China Quarterly*, no. 46 (April–June 1971).

————. "On the Nature of Mao Tse-tung's 'Deviation' in 1927." *The China Quarterly*, no. 18 (April–June 1964).

————. *The Political Thought of Mao Tse-tung*. New York: Frederick A. Praeger, 1969.

Schwartz, Benjamin. *Chinese Communism and the Rise of Mao*. New York: Harper and Row, 1967.

————. "The Legend of the 'Legend of "Maoism." ' " *The China Quarterly*, no. 2 (April–June 1960).

————, ed. *Reflections on the May Fourth Movement: A Symposium*. Cambridge, Mass.: Harvard University Press, 1968.

Selden, Mark. *The Yenan Way in Revolutionary China*. Cambridge, Mass.: Harvard University Press, 1971.

Serge, Victor. *1927–1929: la revolution chinoise*. Paris: Savelli, 1977.

Shang Mingxuan and Wang Xuezhuang. "Liao Zhongkai and the First KMT–CCP Cooperation." FBIS *Daily Report: China* (August 26, 1982).

Shewmaker, Kenneth. *Americans and Chinese Communists, 1927–1945: A Persuading Encounter*. Ithaca, N.Y.: Cornell University Press, 1971.

Sixth CCP Congress. "Funu yundong jueyian" (Resolution on the women's movement). Moscow, 1928.

————. "Guanyu gongchan qingnian yundongde jueyian" (Resolution concerning the Communist youth movement). Moscow, 1928.

————. "Guanyu gongchandang zuzhi jueyian caoyi" (Draft resolution on CCP organization). Moscow, 1928.

————. "Nongmin yundong jueyian" (Resolution on the peasant movement). Moscow, 1928.

————. "Political Resolution." In *A Documentary History of Chinese Communism*, edited by Conrad Brandt, Benjamin Schwartz, and John K. Fairbank. Cambridge, Mass.: Harvard University Press, 1952.

————. "Resolution of the Sixth National Congress on the Peasant Movement." In *A Documentary History of Chinese Communism*, edited by Conrad Brandt, Benjamin Schwartz, and John K. Fairbank. Cambridge, Mass.: Harvard University Press, 1952.

————. "Resolution on Work in Military Affairs (Draft)." *Chinese Studies in History* 4, no. 4 (Summer 1971).

————. "Suanchuan gongcuo muqian renwu" (Current propaganda work). Moscow, 1928.

————. "Suweiai zhengzhide zuzhi wenti jueyian" (Resolution on the matter of organizing soviet political power). Moscow, 1928.

————. "Tudi wenti jueyian" (Resolution on the land question). Moscow, 1928.

————. "Various Minor Resolutions Passed by the Congress." *Chinese Studies in History* 4, no. 4 (Summer 1971).

————. "Zhengzhi jueyian" (The political resolution). Moscow, 1928.

————. "Zhigong yondong jueyian" (Resolution on the trade union movement). Moscow, 1928.

Smedley, Agnes. *The Great Road: The Life and Times of Chu Teh*. New York: Monthly Review Press, 1956.

Snow, Edgar. *Random Notes on China, 1936–45*. Cambridge, Mass.: Harvard University Press, 1957.

————. *Red Star Over China*. New York: Random House, 1938.

Solomon, Richard H. *Mao's Revolution and the Chinese Political Culture*. Berkeley: University of California Press, 1971.

Sullivan, Lawrence R. "Reconstruction and Rectification of the Communist Party in the Shanghai Underground: 1931–34." *The China Quarterly*, no. 101 (March 1985).

"Suweiai zhengquan wansui" (Long live the soviet system). *Bolshevik*, no. 11 (December 26, 1927).

Su Yu. "Memories of Zhu De and Chen Yi." Parts 1, 2. *China Reconstructs* (August 1979; September 1979).

Swarup, Shanti. *A Study of the Chinese Communist Movement, 1927–34*. London: Oxford University Press, 1966.

T'ang Leang-li. *The Inner History of the Chinese Revolution*. London: George Routledge, 1930.

————. *Suppressing Chinese Banditry in China*. Shanghai: China United Press, 1934.

Teng Ssu-yü. *The Nien Army and Their Guerrilla Warfare, 1851–1868*. Paris, 1961.

Thaxton, Ralph. "On Peasant Revolution and National Resistance: Toward a Theory of Peasant Mobilization and Revolutionary War with Special Reference to Modern China." *World Politics*, no. 30 (October 1977).

Thomas, Bernard S. *Labor and the Chinese Revolution: Class Strategies and Contradictions of Chinese Communism, 1928–48*. Ann Arbor: Center for Chinese Studies, the University of Michigan, 1983.

————. *Proletarian Hegemony in the Chinese Revolution and the Canton Commune of 1927*. Michigan Papers in Chinese Studies, no. 23, 1975.

Thornton, Richard C. *The Comintern and the Chinese Communists, 1928–1931*. Seattle: University of Washington Press, 1969.

————. "The Emergence of a New Comintern Strategy for China, 1928." *The Comintern: Historical Highlights, Essays, Recollections and Documents*. Edited by M. Drackhovitch and B. Lazitch. Stanford: Hoover Institution Press, 1966.

Tian Fu and Wang Zhixin. "A Brief Review of CPC National Congresses." *Renmin Ribao* (August 20, 1982). Translated in FBIS *Daily Report: China* (September 2, 1982).

Townsend, James R. *Political Participation in Communist China*. Berkeley: University of California Press, 1967.

Trotsky, Leon. *Problems of the China Revolution*. Translated by Max Shachtman. Ann Arbor: University of Michigan Press, 1967.

Union Research Institute (URI), ed. *The Collected Works of Liu Shao-ch'i*. 3 vols. Hong Kong, 1968–69.

Van Slyke, Lyman P. *Enemies and Friends: The United Front in Chinese Communist History*. Stanford: Stanford University Press, 1967.

Vladimirov, O., and V. Ryazantsev. *Mao Tse-tung. A Political Portrait*. Moscow: Progress Publishers, 1976.

Wakeman, Frederick, Jr. *History and Will: Philosophical Perspectives of Mao Tse-tung's Thought*. Berkeley: University of California Press, 1973.

————. "Rebellion and Revolution: The Study of Popular Movements in Chinese History." *Journal of Asian Studies* 36, no. 2 (February 1977).

Wales, Nym (Helen Snow). *The Chinese Labor Movement*. Freeport, N.Y.: Books for Libraries Press, 1945.

————. *Inside Red China*. New York: Doubleday, Doran, 1939.

————. "My Yenan Notebooks." Madison, Conn., 1961. Mimeograph.

————. "Notes on the Chinese Student Movement." Madison, Conn., 1959. Mimeograph.

————. *Red Dust: Autobiographies of Chinese Communists*. Stanford: Stanford University Press, 1952.

Waller, Derek. *The Kiangsi Soviet Republic: Mao and the National Congresses of 1931 and 1934*. Berkeley: University of California Press, 1973.

Wang Chang-ling. *Zhongguo gongchandang qingniantuan lishi* (Analytical history of the Chinese Communist Youth League, 1920–27). Taipei: National Cheng Chi University, 1973.

Wang Fan-hsi. *Chinese Revolutionary: Memoirs, 1919–1949*. Translated by Gregor Benton. London: Oxford University Press, 1980.

Wang Jianmin (Wang Chien-min). *Zhongguo gongchandang shigao* (Draft history of the Chinese Communist Party). 3 vols. Taipei, 1965.

Wang Jianying. "Kangri zhanzheng yiqian zhongguo gongchandang lingdao jigou di bianhua gaikuang" (General survey of the changes in the organizational structure of Chinese Communist Party leadership before the anti-Japanese war). *Jindaishi yanjiu* (Modern history research), no. 1 (1983).

Whiting, Allen S. *Soviet Policies in China, 1917–1924*. Stanford: Stanford University Press, 1968.

Wilbur, Martin C. "The Ashes of Defeat." *The China Quarterly*, no. 18 (April–June 1964).

Wilbur, Martin C. "The Influence of the Past: How the Early Years Helped Shape the Future of the Chinese Communist Party." *The China Quarterly*, no. 36 (October–December 1968).

Wilbur, Martin C. *Sun Yat-sen: Frustrated Patriot*. New York: Columbia University Press, 1976.

Wilbur, C. Martin, and Julie Lien-ying How, eds. *Documents on Communism, Nationalism, and Soviet Advisers in China, 1918–1927*. New York: Columbia University Press, 1956; reprint ed., New York: Octagon Books, 1976.

Wittfogel, Karl A. "The Legend of 'Maoism.'" Parts 1, 2. *The China Quarterly*, no. 1 (January–March 1960); no. 2 (April–June 1960).

———. "The Marxist View of China." Parts 1, 2. *The China Quarterly*, no. 11 (July–September 1962); no. 12 (October–December 1962).

Womack, Brantly. *The Foundations of Mao Zedong's Political Thought*. Honolulu: University of Hawaii Press, 1982.

Wu T'ien-wei. "Chiang Kai-shek's March Twentieth Coup d'etat of 1926." *Journal of Asian Studies* 27, no. 3 (May 1968).

———. "The Kiangsi Soviet Period." *The Journal of Asian Studies*, no. 29 (February 1970).

Wylie, Raymond F. *The Emergence of Maoism: Mao Tse-tung, Ch'en Po-ta and the Search for Chinese Theory, 1935–1945*. Stanford: Stanford University Press, 1980.

Xia Yirong. "Yetan Guangzhou qiyide lishi diwei—jianji gongnong wuzhuang gejude youlai" (Also discussing the historical position of the Guangzhou Uprising and the origins of the armed independent regime of workers and peasants). Reprinted from *Xinan minzu xueyuan xuebao*, no. 2 (1980), in *Zhonggong dangshi yanjiu lunwenxuan*, edited by Zhu Chengjia. 3 vols. Changsha: Hunan renmin chubanshe, 1983–84.

Xiao Ke. "Real Gold Stands the Test of Strong Fire—Reading Comrade Zhu De's 'From the Nanchang Uprising to Going Up Jinggang Mountain.'" *Renmin Ribao* (August 2, 1982). Translated in JPRS 81560, *China Report*, no. 326 (August 17, 1982).

Xin qingnian (New youth), nos. 92–94 (1926).

Xinghuo liaoyuan (A single spark can light a prairie fire). Vols. 1, 2. Beijing: Zhongguo renmin jiefangjun zhanshi chubanshe, 1979–80.

Yakhontoff, Victor A. *The Chinese Soviets*. New York: Coward-McCann, 1934.

Yang, Benjamin. "The Zunyi Conference as One Step in Mao's Rise to Power: A Survey of Historical Studies of the Chinese Communist Party." *The China Quarterly*, no. 106 (June 1986).

Yüeh Sheng. *Sun Yat-sen University in Moscow and the Chinese Revolution: A Personal Account*. Lawrence: The University Press of Kansas, 1971.

Zhang Zetao. "Shanghai shi dangan guan" (Shanghai Municipal Archives). *Lishi dangan* (Historical archives), no. 4 (1981).

Zhongguo gongchandang diliuci daibiao dahui jueyian (Resolutions of the Sixth Party Congress of the Chinese Communist Party). Moscow, 1928. Library of Congress.

"Zhongguo suweiai zhengguan yu shehuizhuyi" (The Chinese soviet regime and socialism). *Bolshevik*, no. 14 (January 16, 1928).

"Zhongguo xianzhuang yu gongchandang de renwu jueyian" (Resolution on the present situation and tasks of the Communist Party). *Bolshevik*, no. 6 (November 28, 1927).

Zhongyang geming genjudi shiliao xuanbian (Selected historical materials on the central revolutionary base area). 3 vols. Nanchang: Jiangxi renmin chubanshe, 1982.

Zhou Enlai. *Selected Works of Zhou Enlai*. Vol. 1. Beijing: Foreign Languages Press, 1981.

Zhou Yongxiang, ed. *Qu Qiubai nianpu* (A Chronicle of Qu Qiubai's life). Guangdong renmin chubanshe, 1983.

Zhu Chengjia, ed. *Zhonggong dangshi yanjiu lunwenxuan* (Anthology of research papers on Chinese Communist Party history). 3 vols. Changsha: Hunan renmin chubanshe, 1983–84.

Zhu De. "From the Nanchang Uprising to Going Up the Jinggang Mountain." (June 1962). FBIS *Daily Report: China* (August 3, 1982).

Zhu De. *Xuanji* (Selected works of Zhu De). Beijing: Renmin chubanshe, 1983.

Index

About the Author

Marcia R. Ristaino has been a research analyst with the Library of Congress since 1981. In the 1970s she was a political analyst on Chinese affairs serving as a consultant to the State Department and other government agencies. She has taught courses on Chinese and Asian history and the Chinese communist movement at colleges and universities in the Washington, D.C., area. She is the author of several articles on the Chinese communist revolution.

Library of Congress Cataloging-in-Publication Data
Ristaino, Marcia R., 1939–
China's art of revolution.
Bibliography: p.
Includes index.
1. Communism—China—History. 2. China—Politics and government—1912–1949. I. Title.
HX418.R57 1987   324.51'075'09042   87-470
ISBN 0-8223-0718-9